PREFACE

The *Aviation Instructor's Handbook* is designed for ground instructors, flight instructors, and aviation maintenance instructors. It is developed by the Flight Standards Service, Airman Testing Standards Branch in cooperation with aviation educators and industry. This handbook provides the foundation for beginning instructors to understand and apply the fundamentals of instructing. This handbook also provides aviation instructors with up-to-date information on learning and teaching, and how to relate this information to the task of conveying aeronautical knowledge and skills to students. Experienced aviation instructors also may find the new and updated information useful for improving their effectiveness in training activities.

Chapters 1 through 5 concentrate on learning theory and the teaching process, emphasizing the characteristics of human behavior and the importance of communication. Chapters 6 and 7 provide valuable tools for critiquing and evaluating student performance and enhancing instructional presentations with teaching aids and new training technologies. Chapter 8 defines instructor responsibilities and emphasizes ways that instructors can develop and portray a professional image to their students. Chapter 9 contains useful information that can be applied when teaching in the aircraft, and also provides comprehensive treatment for teaching aeronautical decision making (ADM) and judgment. Chapters 10 and 11 provide valuable information for planning instructional activity and continuing professional development. Occasionally, the word "must" or similar language is used where the desired action is deemed critical. The use of such language is not intended to add to, interpret, or relieve a duty imposed by Title 14 of the Code of Federal Regulations (14 CFR).

This handbook supersedes AC 60-14, *Aviation Instructor's Handbook*, dated 1977; AC 61-101, *Presolo Written Test*, dated 1989; and AC 61-115, *Positive Exchange of Flight Controls*, dated 1995. It can be purchased from the Superintendent of Documents, U.S. Government Printing Office (GPO), Washington, DC 20402-9325, or from U.S. Government Bookstores located in major cities throughout the United States.

The current Flight Standards Service airman training and testing material and subject matter knowledge codes for all instructor certificates and ratings can be obtained from the Regulatory Support Division, AFS-600, home page on the Internet.

The Regulatory Support Division's Internet address is: http://www.mmac.jccbi.gov/afs/afs600

Comments regarding this handbook should be sent to U.S. Department of Transportation, Federal Aviation Administration, Airman Testing Standards Branch, AFS-630, P.O. Box 25082, Oklahoma City, OK 73125.

AC 00-2, *Advisory Circular Checklist*, transmits the current status of FAA advisory circulars and other flight information and publications. This checklist is free of charge and may be obtained by sending a request to U.S. Department of Transportation, Subsequent Distribution Office, SVC-121.23, Ardmore East Business Center, 3341 Q 75th Avenue, Landover, MD 20785. The checklist is also available on the Internet at http://www.faa.gov/abc/ac-chklst/actoc.htm

D0795866

AVIATION INSTRUCTOR'S HANDBOOK

1999

U.S. DEPARTMENT OF TRANSPORTATION
FEDERAL AVIATION ADMINISTRATION
Flight Standards Service

CONTENTS

Chapter 1

The Learning Process

To learn is to acquire knowledge or skill. Learning also may involve a change in attitude or behavior. Children learn to identify objects at an early age; teenagers may learn to improve study habits; and adults can learn to solve complex problems. Pilots and aviation maintenance technicians (AMTs) need to acquire the higher levels of knowledge and skill, including the ability to exercise judgment and solve problems. The challenge for the aviation instructor is to understand how people learn, and more importantly, to be able to apply that knowledge to the learning environment. This handbook is designed as a basic guide to educational psychology. This chapter addresses that branch of psychology directly concerned with how people learn.

LEARNING THEORY

Learning theory may be described as a body of principles advocated by psychologists and educators to explain how people acquire skills, knowledge, and attitudes. Various branches of learning theory are used in formal training programs to improve and accelerate the learning process. Key concepts such as desired learning outcomes, objectives of the training, and depth of training also apply. When properly integrated, learning principles, derived from theories, can be useful to aviation instructors and developers of instructional programs for both pilots and maintenance technicians.

Over the years, many theories have attempted to explain how people learn. Even though psychologists and educators are not in complete agreement, most do agree that learning may be explained by a combination of two basic approaches—behaviorism and the cognitive theories.

BEHAVIORISM

Behaviorists believe that animals, including humans, learn in about the same way. **Behaviorism** stresses the importance of having a particular form of behavior reinforced by someone, other than the student, to shape or control what is learned. In aviation training, the instructor provides the reinforcement. Frequent, positive reinforcement and rewards accelerate learning. This theory provides the instructor with ways to manipulate students with stimuli, induce the desired behavior or response, and reinforce the behavior with appropriate rewards. In general, the behaviorist theory emphasizes positive reinforcement rather than no reinforcement or punishment.

Other features of behaviorism are considerably more complex than this simple explanation. Instructors who need more details should refer to psychology texts for a better understanding of behaviorism. As an instructor, it is important to keep in mind that behaviorism is still widely used today, because controlling learning experiences helps direct students toward specific learning outcomes.

COGNITIVE THEORY

Much of the recent psychological thinking and experimentation in education includes some facets of the cognitive theory. This is true in basic as well as more advanced training programs. Unlike behaviorism, the cognitive theory focuses on what is going on inside the student's mind. Learning is not just a change in behavior; it is a change in the way a student thinks, understands, or feels.

There are several branches of cognitive theory. Two of the major theories may broadly be classified as the information processing model and the social interaction model. The first says that the student's brain has internal structures which select and process incoming material, store and retrieve it, use it to produce behavior, and receive and process feedback on the results. This involves a number of cognitive processes, including executive functions of recognizing expectancies, planning and monitoring performance, encoding and chunking information, and producing internal and external responses.

The social interaction theories gained prominence in the 1980s. They stress that learning and subsequent changes in behavior take place as a result of interaction between the student and the environment. Behavior is modeled either by people or symbolically. Cultural influences, peer pressure, group dynamics, and film and television are some of the significant factors. Thus, the social environment to which the student is exposed demonstrates or models behaviors, and the student cognitively processes the observed behaviors and consequences. The cognitive processes include attention, retention, motor responses, and motivation. Techniques for learning include direct modeling and verbal instruction. Behavior, personal factors, and environmental events all work together to produce learning.

Both models of the cognitive theory have common principles. For example, they both acknowledge the importance of reinforcing behavior and measuring changes. Positive reinforcement is important, particularly with cognitive concepts such as knowledge and understanding. The need to evaluate and measure behavior remains because it is the only way to get a clue about what the student understands. Evaluation is often limited to the kinds of knowledge or behavior that can be measured by a paper-and-pencil exam or a performance test. Although psychologists agree that there often are errors in evaluation, some means of measuring student knowledge, performance, and behavior is necessary.

COMBINED APPROACH

Both the behavioristic and the cognitive approaches are useful learning theories. A reasonable way to plan, manage, and conduct aviation training is to include the best features of each major theory. This provides a way to measure behavioral outcomes and promote cognitive learning. The combined approach is not simple, but neither is learning.

DEFINITION OF LEARNING

The ability to learn is one of the most outstanding human characteristics. Learning occurs continuously throughout a person's lifetime. To define learning, it is necessary to analyze what happens to the individual. For example, an individual's way of perceiving, thinking, feeling, and doing may change as a result of a learning experience. Thus, **learning** can be defined as a change in behavior as a result of experience. This can be physical and overt, or it may involve complex intellectual or attitudinal changes which affect behavior in more subtle ways. In spite of numerous theories and contrasting views, psychologists generally agree on many common characteristics of learning.

CHARACTERISTICS OF LEARNING

Aviation instructors need a good understanding of the general characteristics of learning in order to apply them in a learning situation. If learning is a change in behavior as a result of experience, then instruction must include a careful and systematic creation of those experiences that promote learning. This process can be quite complex because, among other things, an individual's background strongly influences the way that person learns. To be effective, the learning situation also should be purposeful, based on experience, multifaceted, and involve an active process. [Figure 1-1]

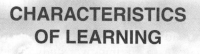

CHARACTERISTICS OF LEARNING

- **Purposeful**
- **Result of Experience**
- **Multifaceted**
- **Active Process**

Figure 1-1. Effective learning shares several common characteristics.

LEARNING IS PURPOSEFUL

Each student sees a learning situation from a different viewpoint. Each student is a unique individual whose past experiences affect readiness to learn and understanding of the requirements involved. For example, an instructor may give two aviation maintenance students the assignment of learning certain inspection procedures. One student may learn quickly and be able to competently present the assigned material. The combination of an aviation background and future goals may enable that student to realize the need and value of learning the procedures. A second student's goal may only be to comply with the instructor's assignment, and may result in only minimum preparation. The responses differ because each student acts in accordance with what he or she sees in the situation.

Most people have fairly definite ideas about what they want to do and achieve. Their goals sometimes are short term, involving a matter of days or weeks. On the other hand, their goals may be carefully planned for a career or a lifetime. Each student has specific intentions and goals. Some may be shared by other students. Students learn from any activity that tends to further their goals. Their individual needs and attitudes may determine what they learn as much as what the instructor is trying to get them to learn. In the process of learning, the student's goals are of paramount significance. To be effective, aviation instructors need to find ways to relate new learning to the student's goals.

LEARNING IS A RESULT OF EXPERIENCE

Since learning is an individual process, the instructor cannot do it for the student. The student can learn only from personal experiences; therefore, learning and knowledge cannot exist apart from a person. A person's knowledge is a result of experience, and no two people have had identical experiences. Even when observing the same event, two people react differently; they learn different things from it, according to the manner in which the situation affects their individual needs. Previous experience conditions a person to respond to some things and to ignore others.

All learning is by experience, but learning takes place in different forms and in varying degrees of richness and depth. For instance, some experiences involve the whole person while others may be based only on hearing and memory. Aviation instructors are faced with the problem of providing learning experiences that are meaningful, varied, and appropriate. As an example, students can learn to say a list of words through repeated drill, or they can learn to recite certain principles of flight by rote. However, they can make them meaningful only if they understand them well enough to apply them correctly to real situations. If an experience challenges the students, requires involvement with feelings, thoughts, memory of past experiences, and physical activity, it is more effective than a learning experience in which all the students have to do is commit something to memory.

It seems clear enough that the learning of a physical skill requires actual experience in performing that skill. Student pilots learn to fly aircraft only if their experiences include flying them; student aviation maintenance technicians learn to overhaul powerplants only by actually performing that task. Mental habits are also learned through practice. If students are to use sound judgment and develop decision-making skills, they need learning experiences that involve knowledge of general principles and require the use of judgment in solving realistic problems.

LEARNING IS MULTIFACETED

If instructors see their objective as being only to train their students' memory and muscles, they are underestimating the potential of the teaching situation. Students may learn much more than expected if they fully exercise their minds and feelings. The fact that these items were not included in the instructor's plan does not prevent them from influencing the learning situation.

Psychologists sometimes classify learning by types, such as verbal, conceptual, perceptual, motor, problem solving, and emotional. Other classifications refer to intellectual skills, cognitive strategies, and attitudinal changes, along with descriptive terms like surface or deep learning. However useful these divisions may be, they are somewhat artificial. For example, a class learning to apply the scientific method of problem solving may learn the method by trying to solve real problems. But in doing so, the class also engages in verbal learning and sensory perception at the same time. Each student approaches the task with preconceived ideas and feelings, and for many students, these ideas change as a result of experience. Therefore, the learning process may include verbal elements, conceptual elements, perceptual elements, emotional elements, and problem solving elements all taking place at once. This aspect of learning will become more evident later in this handbook when lesson planning is discussed.

Learning is multifaceted in still another way. While learning the subject at hand, students may be learning other things as well. They may be developing attitudes about aviation—good or bad—depending on what they experience. Under a skillful instructor, they may learn self-reliance. The list is seemingly endless. This type of learning is sometimes referred to as incidental, but it may have a great impact on the total development of the student.

LEARNING IS AN ACTIVE PROCESS

Students do not soak up knowledge like a sponge absorbs water. The instructor cannot assume that students remember something just because they were in the classroom, shop, or airplane when the instructor presented the material. Neither can the instructor assume that the students can apply what they know because they can quote the correct answer verbatim. For students to learn, they need to react and respond, perhaps outwardly, perhaps only inwardly, emotionally, or intellectually. But if learning is a process of changing behavior, clearly that process must be an active one.

LEARNING STYLES

Although characteristics of learning and learning styles are related, there are distinctions between the two. **Learning style** is a concept that can play an important role in improving instruction and student success. It is concerned with student preferences and orientation at several levels. For example, a student's information processing technique, **personality**, social interaction tendencies, and the instructional methods used are all significant factors which apply to how individual students learn. In addition, today's culturally diverse society, including international students, must be considered. The key point is that all students are different, and training programs should be sensitive to the differences.

Some students are fast learners and others have difficulties; and, as already mentioned, motivation, experience, and previous training affect learning style. Any number of adjectives may be used to describe learning styles. Some common examples include:

- Right/left brain
- Holistic/serialist
- Dependent/independent
- Reflective/impulsive

Theories abound concerning right- or left-brain dominance. In general, those with right-brain dominance are characterized as being spatially oriented, creative, intuitive, and emotional. Those with left-brain dominance are more verbal, analytical, and objective. However, the separate hemispheres of the brain do not function independently. For example, the right hemisphere may recognize a face, while the left associates a name to go with the face. The term dominance is probably misleading when applied to brain hemispheres; specialization would be a more appropriate word.

Learning style differences certainly depend on how students process information. Some rely heavily on visual references while others depend more on auditory presentations. For example, visual students learn readily through reading and graphic displays, and auditory students have more success if they hear the subject matter described. Another difference is that some learn more easily when an idea is presented in a mathematical equation, while others may prefer a verbal explanation of the same idea. In addition, where hands-on activities are involved, students also learn by feel. This is sometimes called kinesthetic learning.

Information processing theories contain several other useful classifications. As an example, in the holistic/serialist theory, the holist strategy is a top-down concept where students have a big picture, global perspective. These students seek overall comprehension, especially through the use of analogies. In contrast, the serialist student focuses more narrowly and needs well-defined, sequential steps where the overall picture is developed slowly, thoroughly, and logically. This is a bottom-up strategy.

Two additional information processing classifications describe deep-elaborative and the shallow-reiterative learners. Testing practices which demand comprehension, rather than a regurgitation of facts, obviously encourage students to adopt a deep-elaborative learn-ing style. Detailed information on testing procedures, as well as curriculum design and instructor techniques, is included later in this handbook.

As indicated, personality also affects how students learn. Dependent students require a lot of guidance, direction, and external stimulation. These students tend to focus on the instructor. The more independent students require only a minimum amount of guidance and external stimulation. They are not overly concerned with how the lesson is presented.

Students with a reflective-type personality may be described as tentative. They tend to be uncertain in problem-solving exercises. The opposite applies to impulsive students. Typically, they dive right in with enthusiasm and are prone to make quick, and sometimes faulty, decisions.

The social interaction concept contains further classifications of student learning styles. Like most of the other information on learning styles, these classifications are derived from research on tendencies of undergraduate students.

Some generalizations about these classifications indicate that compliant students are typically task oriented, and anxious-dependent students usually score lower than others on standardized tests. Discouraged students often have depressed feelings about the future, and independent students tend to be older, intelligent, secure, and comfortable with the academic environment. Attention seekers have a strong social orientation and are frequently involved in joking, showing off, and bragging. In contrast, silent students usually are characterized by helplessness, vulnerability, and other disconcerting behaviorisms.

Other studies identify more categories that are easily recognized. Among these are collaborative, sharing students who enjoy working with others, and competitive students who are grade conscious and feel they must do better than their peers. Participant students normally have a desire to learn and enjoy attending class, and avoidant students do not take part in class activities and have little interest in learning.

The existing learning environment also influences learning style. In real life, most students find it necessary to adapt to a traditional style learning environment provided by a school, university, or other educational/training establishment. Thus, the student's learning style may or may not be compatible.

Instructors who can recognize student learning style differences and associated problems will be much more effective than those who do not understand this concept. Also, these instructors will be prepared to develop appropriate lesson plans and provide guidance, counseling, or other advisory services, as required.

PRINCIPLES OF LEARNING

Over the years, educational psychologists have identified several principles which seem generally applicable to the learning process. They provide additional insight into what makes people learn most effectively.

READINESS

Individuals learn best when they are ready to learn, and they do not learn well if they see no reason for learning. Getting students ready to learn is usually the instructor's responsibility. If students have a strong purpose, a clear objective, and a definite reason for learning something, they make more progress than if they lack motivation. **Readiness** implies a degree of single-mindedness and eagerness. When students are ready to learn, they meet the instructor at least halfway, and this simplifies the instructor's job.

Under certain circumstances, the instructor can do little, if anything, to inspire in students a readiness to learn. If outside responsibilities, interests, or worries weigh too heavily on their minds, if their schedules are overcrowded, or if their personal problems seem insoluble, students may have little interest in learning.

EXERCISE

The principle of **exercise** states that those things most often repeated are best remembered. It is the basis of drill and practice. The human memory is fallible. The mind can rarely retain, evaluate, and apply new concepts or practices after a single exposure. Students do not learn to weld during one shop period or to perform crosswind landings during one instructional flight. They learn by applying what they have been told and shown. Every time practice occurs, learning continues. The instructor must provide opportunities for students to practice and, at the same time, make sure that this process is directed toward a goal.

EFFECT

The principle of **effect** is based on the emotional reaction of the student. It states that learning is strengthened when accompanied by a pleasant or satisfying feeling, and that learning is weakened when associated with an unpleasant feeling. Experiences that produce feelings of defeat, frustration, anger, confusion, or futility are unpleasant for the student. If, for example, an instructor attempts to teach landings during the first flight, the student is likely to feel inferior and be frustrated.

Instructors should be cautious. Impressing students with the difficulty of an aircraft maintenance problem, flight maneuver, or flight crew duty can make the teaching task difficult. Usually it is better to tell students that a problem or maneuver, although difficult, is within their capability to understand or perform.

Whatever the learning situation, it should contain elements that affect the students positively and give them a feeling of satisfaction.

PRIMACY

Primacy, the state of being first, often creates a strong, almost unshakable, impression. For the instructor, this means that what is taught must be right the first time. For the student, it means that learning must be right. Unteaching is more difficult than teaching. If, for example, a maintenance student learns a faulty riveting technique, the instructor will have a difficult task correcting bad habits and reteaching correct ones. Every student should be started right. The first experience should be positive, functional, and lay the foundation for all that is to follow.

INTENSITY

A vivid, dramatic, or exciting learning experience teaches more than a routine or boring experience. A student is likely to gain greater understanding of slow flight and stalls by performing them rather than merely reading about them. The principle of **intensity** implies that a student will learn more from the real thing than from a substitute. In contrast to flight instruction and shop instruction, the classroom imposes limitations on the amount of realism that can be brought into teaching. The aviation instructor should use imagination in approaching reality as closely as possible. Today, classroom instruction can benefit from a wide variety of instructional aids to improve realism, motivate learning, and challenge students. Chapter 7, Instructional Aids and Training Technologies, explores the wide range of teaching tools available for classroom use.

RECENCY

The principle of **recency** states that things most recently learned are best remembered. Conversely, the further a student is removed time-wise from a new fact or understanding, the more difficult it is to remember. It is easy, for example, for a student to recall a torque value used a few minutes earlier, but it is usually impossible to remember an unfamiliar one used a week earlier. Instructors recognize the principle of recency when they carefully plan a summary for a ground school lesson, a shop period, or a postflight critique. The instructor repeats, restates, or reemphasizes important points at the end of a lesson to help the student remember them. The principle of recency often determines the sequence of lectures within a course of instruction.

HOW PEOPLE LEARN

Initially, all learning comes from perceptions which are directed to the brain by one or more of the five senses:

sight, hearing, touch, smell, and taste. Psychologists have also found that learning occurs most rapidly when information is received through more than one sense. [Figure 1-2]

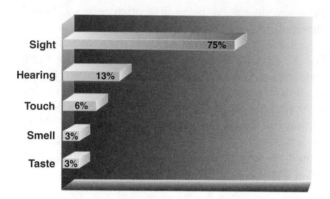

Figure 1-2. Most learning occurs through sight, but the combination of sight and hearing accounts for about 88 percent of all perceptions.

PERCEPTIONS

Perceiving involves more than the reception of stimuli from the five senses. Perceptions result when a person gives meaning to sensations. People base their actions on the way they believe things to be. The experienced aviation maintenance technician, for example, perceives an engine malfunction quite differently than does an inexperienced student.

Real meaning comes only from within a person, even though the perceptions which evoke these meanings result from external stimuli. The meanings which are derived from perceptions are influenced not only by the individual's experience, but also by many other factors. Knowledge of the factors which affect the perceptual process is very important to the aviation instructor because **perceptions** are the basis of all learning.

FACTORS WHICH AFFECT PERCEPTION

There are several factors that affect an individual's ability to perceive. Some are internal to each person and some are external.

- Physical organism
- Basic need
- Goals and values
- Self-concept
- Time and opportunity
- Element of threat

Physical Organism

The **physical organism** provides individuals with the perceptual apparatus for sensing the world around

them. Pilots, for example, must be able to see, hear, feel, and respond adequately while they are in the air. A person whose perceptual apparatus distorts reality is denied the right to fly at the time of the first medical examination.

Basic Need

A person's **basic need** is to maintain and enhance the organized self. The self is a person's past, present, and future combined; it is both physical and psychological. A person's most fundamental, pressing need is to preserve and perpetuate the self. All perceptions are affected by this need.

Just as the food one eats and the air one breathes become part of the physical self, so do the sights one sees and the sounds one hears become part of the psychological self. Psychologically, we are what we perceive. A person has physical barriers which keep out those things that would be damaging to the physical being, such as blinking at an arc weld or flinching from a hot iron. Likewise, a person has perceptual barriers that block those sights, sounds, and feelings which pose a psychological threat.

Helping people learn requires finding ways to aid them in developing better perceptions in spite of their defense mechanisms. Since a person's basic need is to maintain and enhance the self, the instructor must recognize that anything that is asked of the student which may be interpreted by the student as imperiling the self will be resisted or denied. To teach effectively, it is necessary to work with this life force.

Goals and Values

Perceptions depend on one's **goals and values**. Every experience and sensation which is funneled into one's central nervous system is colored by the individual's own beliefs and value structures. Spectators at a ball game may see an infraction or foul differently depending on which team they support. The precise kinds of commitments and philosophical outlooks which the student holds are important for the instructor to know, since this knowledge will assist in predicting how the student will interpret experiences and instructions.

Goals are also a product of one's value structure. Those things which are more highly valued and cherished are pursued; those which are accorded less value and importance are not sought after.

Self-Concept

Self-concept is a powerful determinant in learning. A student's self-image, described in such terms as confident and insecure, has a great influence on the total perceptual process. If a student's experiences tend to support a favorable self-image, the student tends to remain receptive to subsequent experiences. If a student has negative experiences which tend to contradict self-concept, there is a tendency to reject additional training.

A negative self-concept inhibits the perceptual processes by introducing psychological barriers which tend to keep the student from perceiving. They may also inhibit the ability to properly implement that which is perceived. That is, self-concept affects the ability to actually perform or do things unfavorable. Students who view themselves positively, on the other hand, are less defensive and more receptive to new experiences, instructions, and demonstrations.

Time and Opportunity

It takes **time and opportunity** to perceive. Learning some things depends on other perceptions which have preceded these learnings, and on the availability of time to sense and relate these new things to the earlier perceptions. Thus, sequence and time are necessary.

A student could probably stall an airplane on the first attempt, regardless of previous experience. Stalls cannot really be learned, however, unless some experience in normal flight has been acquired. Even with such experience, time and practice are needed to relate the new sensations and experiences associated with stalls in order to develop a perception of the stall. In general, lengthening an experience and increasing its frequency are the most obvious ways to speed up learning, although this is not always effective. Many factors, in addition to the length and frequency of training periods, affect the rate of learning. The effectiveness of the use of a properly planned training syllabus is proportional to the consideration it gives to the time and opportunity factor in perception.

Element of Threat

The **element of threat** does not promote effective learning. In fact, fear adversely affects perception by narrowing the perceptual field. Confronted with threat, students tend to limit their attention to the threatening object or condition. The field of vision is reduced, for example, when an individual is frightened and all the perceptual faculties are focused on the thing that has generated fear.

Flight instruction provides many clear examples of this. During the initial practice of steep turns, a student pilot may focus attention on the altimeter and completely disregard outside visual references. Anything an instructor does that is interpreted as threatening makes the student less able to accept the experience the instructor is trying to provide. It adversely affects all the student's physical, emotional, and mental faculties.

Learning is a psychological process, not necessarily a logical one. Trying to frighten a student through threats of unsatisfactory reports or reprisals may seem logical, but is not effective psychologically. The effective instructor can organize teaching to fit the psychological needs of the student. If a situation seems overwhelming, the student feels unable to handle all of the factors involved, and a threat exists. So long as the student feels capable of coping with a situation, each new experience is viewed as a challenge.

A good instructor realizes that behavior is directly influenced by the way a student perceives, and perception is affected by all of these factors. Therefore, it is important for the instructor to facilitate the learning process by avoiding any actions which may inhibit or prevent the attainment of teaching goals. Teaching is consistently effective only when those factors which influence perceptions are recognized and taken into account.

INSIGHT

Insight involves the grouping of perceptions into meaningful wholes. Creating insight is one of the instructor's major responsibilities. To ensure that this does occur, it is essential to keep each student constantly receptive to new experiences and to help the student realize the way each piece relates to all other pieces of the total pattern of the task to be learned.

As an example, during straight-and-level flight in an airplane with a fixed-pitch propeller, the RPM will increase when the throttle is opened and decrease when it is closed. On the other hand, RPM changes can also result from changes in airplane pitch attitude without changes in power setting. Obviously, engine speed, power setting, airspeed, and airplane attitude are all related.

True learning requires an understanding of how each of these factors may affect all of the others and, at the same time, knowledge of how a change in any one of them may affect all of the others. This mental relating and grouping of associated perceptions is called insight.

Insight will almost always occur eventually, whether or not instruction is provided. For this reason, it is possible for a person to become an electrician by trial and error, just as one may become a lawyer by reading law. Instruction, however, speeds this learning process by teaching the relationship of perceptions as they occur, thus promoting the development of the student's insight.

As perceptions increase in number and are assembled by the student into larger blocks of learning, they develop insight. As a result, learning becomes more meaningful and more permanent. Forgetting is less of a problem when there are more anchor points for tying insights together. It is a major responsibility of the instructor to organize demonstrations and explanations, and to direct practice, so that the student has better opportunities to understand the interrelationship of the many kinds of experiences that have been perceived. Pointing out the relationships as they occur, providing a secure and nonthreatening environment in which to learn, and helping the student acquire and maintain a favorable self-concept are key steps in fostering the development of insight.

MOTIVATION

Motivation is probably the dominant force which governs the student's progress and ability to learn. Motivation may be negative or positive, tangible or intangible, subtle and difficult to identify, or it may be obvious.

Negative motivation may engender fear, and be perceived by the student as a threat. While negative motivation may be useful in certain situations, characteristically it is not as effective in promoting efficient learning as positive motivation.

Positive motivation is provided by the promise or achievement of rewards. These rewards may be personal or social; they may involve financial gain, satisfaction of the self-concept, or public recognition. Motivation which can be used to advantage by the instructor includes the desire for personal gain, the desire for personal comfort or security, the desire for group approval, and the achievement of a favorable self-image.

The desire for personal gain, either the acquisition of possessions or status, is a basic motivational factor for all human endeavor. An individual may be motivated to dig a ditch or to design a supersonic airplane solely by the desire for financial gain.

Students are like typical employees in wanting a tangible return for their efforts. For motivation to be effective, students must believe that their efforts will be suitably rewarded. These rewards must be constantly apparent to the student during instruction, whether they are to be financial, self-esteem, or public recognition.

Lessons often have objectives which are not obvious at first. Although these lessons will pay dividends during later instruction, the student may not appreciate this fact. It is important for the instructor to make the student aware of those applications which are not immediately apparent. Likewise, the devotion of too much time and effort to drill and practice on operations which do not directly contribute to competent performance should be avoided.

The desire for personal comfort and security is a form of motivation which instructors often forget. All students want secure, pleasant conditions and a safe environment. If they recognize that what they are learning may promote these objectives, their attention is easier to attract and hold. Insecure and unpleasant training situations inhibit learning.

Everyone wants to avoid pain and injury. Students normally are eager to learn operations or procedures which help prevent injury or loss of life. This is especially true when the student knows that the ability to make timely decisions, or to act correctly in an emergency, is based on sound principles.

The attractive features of the activity to be learned also can be a strong motivational factor. Students are anxious to learn skills which may be used to their advantage. If they understand that each task will be useful in preparing for future activities, they will be more willing to pursue it.

Another strong motivating force is group approval. Every person wants the approval of peers and superiors. Interest can be stimulated and maintained by building on this natural desire. Most students enjoy the feeling of belonging to a group and are interested in accomplishment which will give them prestige among their fellow students.

Every person seeks to establish a favorable self-image. In certain instances, this self-image may be submerged in feelings of insecurity or despondency. Fortunately, most people engaged in a task believe that success is possible under the right combination of circumstances and good fortune. This belief can be a powerful motivating force for students. An instructor can effectively foster this motivation by the introduction of perceptions which are solidly based on previously learned factual information that is easily recognized by the student. Each additional block of learning should help formulate insight which contributes to the ultimate training goals. This promotes student confidence in the overall training program and, at the same time, helps the student develop a favorable self-image. As this confirmation progresses and confidence increases, advances will be more rapid and motivation will be strengthened.

Positive motivation is essential to true learning. Negative motivation in the form of reproofs or threats should be avoided with all but the most overconfident and impulsive students. Slumps in learning are often due to declining motivation. Motivation does not remain at a uniformly high level. It may be affected by outside influences, such as physical or mental disturbances or inadequate instruction. The instructor should strive to maintain motivation at the highest possible level. In addition, the instructor should be alert to detect and counter any lapses in motivation.

LEVELS OF LEARNING

Levels of learning may be classified in any number of ways. Four basic levels have traditionally been included in aviation instructor training. The lowest level is the ability to repeat something which one has been taught, without understanding or being able to apply what has been learned. This is referred to as **rote learning**. Progressively higher levels of learning are **understanding** what has been taught, achieving the skill for **application** of what has been learned, and **correlation** of what has been learned with other things previously learned or subsequently encountered. [Figure 1-3]

For example, a flight instructor may explain to a beginning student the procedure for entering a level, left turn. The procedure may include several steps such as: (1) visually clear the area, (2) add a slight amount of power to maintain airspeed, (3) apply aileron control pressure to the left, (4) add sufficient rudder pressure in the direction of the turn to avoid slipping and skidding, and (5) increase back pressure to maintain altitude. A student who can verbally repeat this instruction has learned the procedure by rote. This will not be very useful to the student if there is never an opportunity to make a turn in flight, or if the student has no knowledge of the function of airplane controls.

With proper instruction on the effect and use of the flight controls, and experience in controlling the airplane during straight-and-level flight, the student can consolidate these old and new perceptions into an insight on how to make a turn. At this point, the student has developed an understanding of the procedure for turning the airplane in flight. This understanding is basic to effective learning, but may not necessarily enable the student to make a correct turn on the first attempt.

When the student understands the procedure for entering a turn, has had turns demonstrated, and has practiced turn entries until consistency has been achieved, the student has developed the skill to apply what has been learned. This is a major level of learning, and one at which the instructor is too often willing to stop. Discontinuing instruction on turn entries at this point and directing subsequent instruction exclusively to other elements of piloting performance is characteristic of piecemeal instruction, which is usually inefficient. It violates the building block concept of instruction by failing to apply what has been learned to future learning tasks. The building block concept will be covered later in more detail.

The correlation level of learning, which should be the objective of aviation instruction, is that level at which the student becomes able to associate an element which has been learned with other segments or blocks of learning. The other segments may be items or skills previously learned, or new learning tasks to be undertaken in the future. The student who has achieved this level of

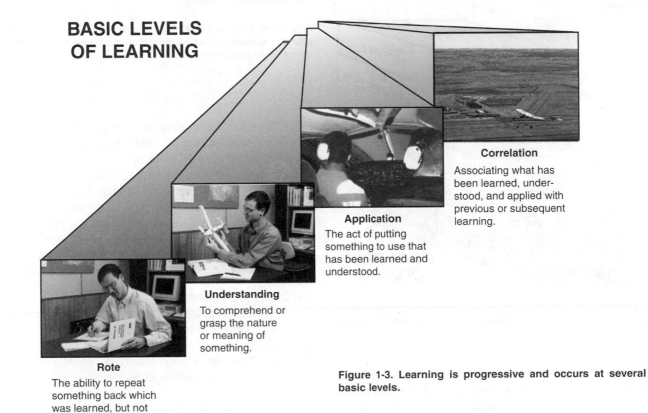

BASIC LEVELS OF LEARNING

Rote
The ability to repeat something back which was learned, but not understood.

Understanding
To comprehend or grasp the nature or meaning of something.

Application
The act of putting something to use that has been learned and understood.

Correlation
Associating what has been learned, understood, and applied with previous or subsequent learning.

Figure 1-3. Learning is progressive and occurs at several basic levels.

learning in turn entries, for example, has developed the ability to correlate the elements of turn entries with the performance of chandelles and lazy eights.

DOMAINS OF LEARNING

Besides the four basic levels of learning, educational psychologists have developed several additional levels. These classifications consider what is to be learned. Is it knowledge only, a change in attitude, a physical skill, or a combination of knowledge and skill? One of the more useful categorizations of learning objectives includes three domains: **cognitive domain** (knowledge), **affective domain** (attitudes, beliefs, and values), and **psychomotor domain** (physical skills). Each of the domains has a hierarchy of educational objectives.

The listing of the hierarchy of objectives is often called a taxonomy. A **taxonomy of educational objectives** is a systematic classification scheme for sorting learning outcomes into the three broad categories (cognitive, affective, and psychomotor) and ranking the desired outcomes in a developmental hierarchy from least complex to most complex.

COGNITIVE DOMAIN

The cognitive domain, described by Dr. Benjamin Bloom, is one of the best known educational domains. It contains additional levels of knowledge and understanding and is commonly referred to as Bloom's taxonomy of educational objectives. [Figure 1-4]

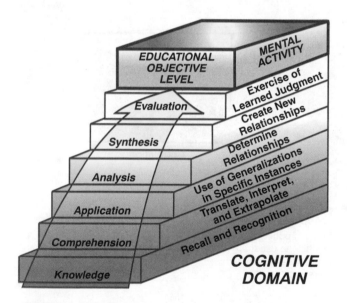

Figure 1-4. Dr. Bloom's hierarchical taxonomy for the cognitive domain (knowledge) includes six educational objective levels.

In aviation, educational objectives in the cognitive domain refer to knowledge which might be gained as the result of attending a ground school, reading about aircraft systems, listening to a preflight briefing,

reviewing meteorological reports, or taking part in computer-based training. The highest educational objective level in this domain may also be illustrated by learning to correctly evaluate a flight maneuver, repair an airplane engine, or review a training syllabus for depth and completeness of training.

AFFECTIVE DOMAIN

The affective domain may be the least understood, and in many ways, the most important of the learning domains. A similar system for specifying attitudinal objectives has been developed by D.R. Krathwohl. Like the Bloom taxonomy, Krathwohl's hierarchy attempts to arrange these objectives in an order of difficulty. [Figure 1-5]

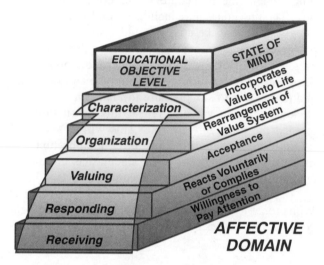

Figure 1-5. D. R. Krathwohl's hierarchical taxonomy for the affective domain (attitudes, beliefs, and values) contains five educational objective levels.

Since the affective domain is concerned with a student's attitudes, personal beliefs, and values, measuring educational objectives in this domain is not easy. For example, how is a positive attitude toward safety evaluated? Observable safety-related behavior indicates a positive attitude, but this is not like a simple pass/fail test that can be used to evaluate cognitive educational objective levels. Although a number of techniques are available for evaluation of achievement in the affective domain, most rely on indirect inferences.

PSYCHOMOTOR DOMAIN

There are several taxonomies which deal with the psychomotor domain (physical skills), but none are as popularly recognized as the Bloom and Krathwohl taxonomies. However, the taxonomy developed by E.J. Simpson also is generally acceptable. [Figure 1-6]

Psychomotor or physical skills always have been important in aviation. Typical activities involving these

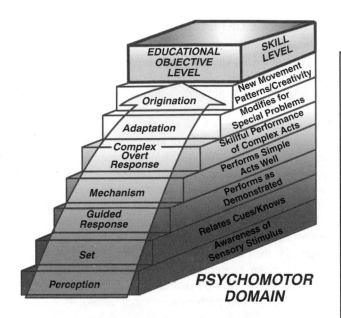

Figure1-6. E.J. Simpson's hierarchical taxonomy for the psychomotor domain (physical skills) consists of seven educational objective levels.

skills include learning to fly a precision instrument approach procedure, programming a GPS receiver, or using sophisticated maintenance equipment. As physical tasks and equipment become more complex, the requirement for integration of cognitive and physical skills increases.

PRACTICAL APPLICATION OF LEARNING OBJECTIVES

The additional levels of learning definitely apply to aviation flight and maintenance training. A comparatively high level of knowledge and skill is required. The student also needs to have a well-developed, positive attitude. Thus, all three domains of learning, cognitive, affective, and psychomotor, are pertinent.

These additional levels of learning are the basis of the knowledge, attitude, and skill learning objectives commonly used in advanced qualification programs for airline training. They also can be tied to the practical test standards to show the level of knowledge or skill required for a particular task. A list of action verbs for the three domains shows appropriate behavioral objectives at each level. [Figure 1-7]

Instructors who are familiar with curricula development will recognize that the action verbs are examples of performance-based objectives. Expanded coverage of the concept of performance-based objectives is included in Chapter 4 of this handbook.

LEARNING PHYSICAL SKILLS

Even though the process of learning is profound, the main objective or purpose of most instruction typically is teaching a concept, a generalization, an attitude,

OBJECTIVE LEVEL		ACTION VERBS FOR EACH LEVEL
COGNITIVE DOMAIN	Evaluation	assess, evaluate, interpret, judge, rate, score, or write
	Synthesis	compile, compose, design, reconstruct, or formulate
	Analysis	compare, discriminate, distinguish, or separate
	Application	compute, demonstrate, employ, operate, or solve
	Comprehension	convert, explain, locate, report, restate, or select
	Knowledge	describe, identify, name, point to, recognize, or recall
AFFECTIVE DOMAIN	Characterization	assess, delegate, practice, influence, revise, and maintain
	Organization	accept responsibility, adhere, defend, and formulate
	Valuing	appreciate, follow, join, justify, show concern, or share
	Responding	conform, greet, help, perform, recite, or write
	Receiving	ask, choose, give, locate, select, rely, or use
PSYCHOMOTOR DOMAIN	Origination	combine, compose, construct, design, or originate
	Adaptation	adapt, alter, change, rearrange, reorganize, or revise
	Complex Overt Response	same as below except more highly coordinated
	Mechanism	same as below except with greater proficiency
	Guided Response	assemble, build, calibrate, fix, grind, or mend
	Set	begin, move, react, respond, start, or select
	Perception	choose, detect, identify, isolate, or compare

Figure 1-7. A listing such as the one shown here is useful for development of almost any training program.

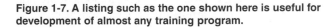

or a skill. The process of learning a psychomotor or physical skill is much the same, in many ways, as cognitive learning. To provide a real illustration of physical skill learning, try the following exercise:

On a separate sheet of paper, write the word "learning" 15 times with your left hand or with your right hand, if you are left handed. Try to improve the speed and quality of your writing as you go along.

PHYSICAL SKILLS INVOLVE MORE THAN MUSCLES

The above exercise contains a practical example of the multifaceted character of learning. It should be obvious that, while a muscular sequence was being learned, other things were happening as well. The perception changed as the sequence became easier. Concepts of how to perform the skill were developed and attitudes were changed.

DESIRE TO LEARN

Thinking back over their past experiences in learning to perform certain skills, students might be surprised at how much more readily they learned those skills that appealed to their own needs (principle of readiness). Shorter initial learning time and more rapid progress in improving the skill normally occurred. Conversely, where the desire to learn or improve was missing, little progress was made. A person may read dozens of books a year, but the reading rate will not increase unless there is a deliberate intent to increase it. In the preceding learning exercise, it is unlikely that any improvement occurred unless there was a clear intention to improve. To improve, one must not only recognize mistakes, but also make an effort to correct them. The person who lacks the desire to improve is not likely to make the effort and consequently will continue to practice errors. The skillful instructor relates the lesson objective to the student's intentions and needs and, in so doing, builds on the student's natural enthusiasm.

PATTERNS TO FOLLOW

Logically, the point has been emphasized that the best way to prepare the student to perform a task is to provide a clear, step-by-step example. Having a model to follow permits students to get a clear picture of each step in the sequence so they understand what is required and how to do it. In flight or maintenance training, the instructor provides the demonstration, emphasizing the steps and techniques. During classroom instruction, an outside expert may be used, either in person or in a video presentation. In any case, students need to have a clear impression of what they are to do.

PERFORM THE SKILL

After experiencing writing a word with the wrong hand, consider how difficult it would be to tell someone else how to do it. Even demonstrating how to do it would not result in that person learning the skill. Obviously, practice is necessary. The student needs coordination between muscles and visual and tactile senses. Learning to perform various aircraft maintenance skills or flight maneuvers requires this sort of practice. There is another benefit of practice. As the student gains proficiency in a skill, verbal instructions mean more. Whereas a long, detailed explanation is confusing before the student begins performing, specific comments are more meaningful and useful after the skill has been partially mastered.

KNOWLEDGE OF RESULTS

In learning some simple skills, students can discover their own errors quite easily. In other cases, such as learning complex aircraft maintenance skills, flight maneuvers, or flight crew duties, mistakes are not always apparent. A student may know that something is wrong, but not know how to correct it. In any case, the instructor provides a helpful and often critical function in making certain that the students are aware of their progress. It is perhaps as important for students to know when they are right as when they are wrong. They should be told as soon after the performance as possible, and should not be allowed to practice mistakes. It is more difficult to unlearn a mistake, and then learn it correctly, than to learn correctly in the first place. One way to make students aware of their progress is to repeat a demonstration or example and to show them the standards their performance must ultimately meet.

PROGRESS FOLLOWS A PATTERN

The experience of learning to write a word with the wrong hand probably confirmed what has been consistently demonstrated in laboratory experiments on skill learning. The first trials are slow, and coordination is lacking. Mistakes are frequent, but each trial provides clues for improvement in subsequent trials. The student modifies different aspects of the skill such as how to hold the pencil, or how to execute finger and hand movement.

Graphs of the progress of skill learning, such as the one shown below, usually follow the same pattern. There is rapid improvement in the early stages, then the curve levels off and may stay level for a significant period of time. Further improvement may seem unlikely. This is a typical **learning plateau**. [Figure 1-8]

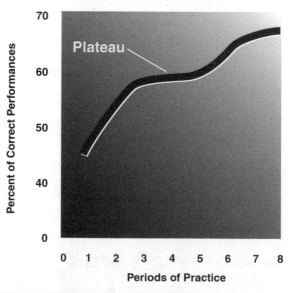

Figure 1-8. Students will more than likely experience a learning plateau at some point in their training.

A learning plateau may signify any number of conditions. For example, the student may have reached capability limits, may be consolidating levels of skill, interest may have waned, or the student may need a more efficient method for increasing progress. Keep in mind that the apparent lack of increasing proficiency does not necessarily mean that learning has ceased. The point is that, in learning motor skills, a leveling off process, or a plateau, is normal and should be expected after an initial period of rapid improvement. The instructor should prepare the student for this situation to avert discouragement. If the student is aware of this learning plateau, frustration may be minimized.

DURATION AND ORGANIZATION OF LESSON

In planning for student performance, a primary consideration is the length of time devoted to practice. A beginning student reaches a point where additional practice is not only unproductive, but may even be harmful. When this point is reached, errors increase, and motivation declines. As a student gains experience, longer periods of practice are profitable.

Another consideration is the problem of whether to divide the practice period. Perhaps even the related instruction should be broken down into segments, or it may be advantageous to plan one continuous, integrated sequence. The answer depends on the nature of the skill. Some skills are composed of closely related steps, each dependent on the preceding one. Learning to pack a parachute is a good example. Other skills are composed of related subgroups of skills. Learning to overhaul an aircraft engine is a good example.

EVALUATION VERSUS CRITIQUE

If an instructor were to evaluate the fifteenth writing of the word "learning," only limited help could be given toward further improvement. The instructor could judge whether the written word was legible and evaluate it against some criterion or standard, or perhaps even assign it a grade of some sort. None of these actions would be particularly useful to the beginning student. However, the student could profit by having someone watch the performance and critique constructively to help eliminate errors.

In the initial stages, practical suggestions are more valuable to the student than a grade. Early evaluation is usually teacher oriented. It provides a check on teaching effectiveness, can be used to predict eventual student learning proficiency, and can help the teacher locate special problem areas. The observations on which the evaluations are based also can identify the student's strengths and weaknesses, a prerequisite for making constructive criticism.

APPLICATION OF SKILL

The final and critical question is, Can the student use what has been learned? It is not uncommon to find that students devote weeks and months in school learning new abilities, and then fail to apply these abilities on the job. To solve this problem, two conditions must be present. First, the student must learn the skill so well that it becomes easy, even habitual; and second, the student must recognize the types of situations where it is appropriate to use the skill. This second condition involves the question of transfer of learning, which is briefly discussed later in this chapter.

MEMORY

Memory is an integral part of the learning process. Although there are several theories on how the memory works, a widely accepted view is the multi-stage concept which states that memory includes three parts: sensory, working or short-term, and long-term systems. As shown in figure 1-9 on the following page, the total system operates somewhat like an advanced computer that accepts input (stimuli) from an external source, contains a processing apparatus, a storage capability, and an output function.

SENSORY REGISTER

The **sensory register** receives input from the environment and quickly processes it according to the individual's preconceived concept of what is important. However, other factors can influence the reception of information by the sensory system. For example, if the input is dramatic and impacts more than one of the five senses, that information is more likely to make an impression. The sensory register processes inputs or stimuli from the environment within seconds, discards what is considered extraneous, and processes what is determined by the individual to be relevant. This is a selective process where the sensory register is set to recognize certain stimuli and immediately transmit them to the working memory for action. The process is called precoding. An example is sensory precoding to recognize a fire alarm. No matter what is happening at the time, when the sensory register detects a fire alarm, the working memory is immediately made aware of the alarm and preset responses begin to take place.

WORKING OR SHORT-TERM MEMORY

Within seconds the relevant information is passed to the **working or short-term memory** where it may temporarily remain or rapidly fade, depending on the individual's priorities. Several common steps help retention in the short-term memory. These include rehearsal or repetition of the information and sorting or categorization into systematic chunks. The sorting process is usually called coding or chunking. A key limitation of the working memory is that it takes 5–10 seconds to properly code information. If the coding process is interrupted, that information is lost after about 20 seconds.

MEMORY SYSTEMS

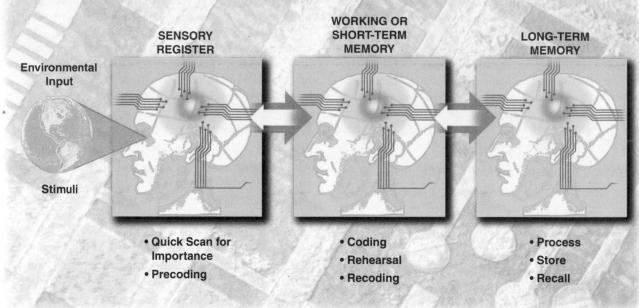

Figure 1-9. Information processing within the sensory register, working or short-term memory, and long-term memory includes complex coding, sorting, storing, and recall functions.

The working or short-term memory is not only time limited, it also has limited capacity, usually about seven bits or chunks of information. A seven-digit telephone number is an example. As indicated, the time limitation may be overcome by rehearsal. This means learning the information by a rote memorization process. Of course, rote memorization is subject to imperfections in both the duration of recall and in its accuracy. The coding process is more useful in a learning situation. In addition, the coding process may involve recoding to adjust the information to individual experiences. This is when actual learning begins to take place. Therefore, recoding may be described as a process of relating incoming information to concepts or knowledge already in memory.

Methods of coding vary with subject matter, but typically they include some type of association. Use of rhymes or mnemonics is common. An example of a useful mnemonic is the memory aid for one of the magnetic compass errors. The letters "ANDS" indicate:

> **A**ccelerate
> **N**orth
> **D**ecelerate
> **S**outh

Variations of the coding process are practically endless. They may consist of the use of acronyms, the chronology of events, images, semantics, or an individually developed structure based on past experiences.

Developing a logical strategy for coding information is a significant step in the learning process.

In this brief discussion of memory, it may appear that sensory memory is distinct and separate from working or short-term memory. This is not the case. In fact, all of the memory systems are intimately related. Many of the functions of working or short-term memory are nearly identical to long-term memory functions.

LONG-TERM MEMORY

What then is distinctive about the **long-term memory**? This is where information is stored for future use. For the stored information to be useful, some special effort must have been expended during the coding process in working or short-term memory. The coding should have provided meaning and connections between old and new information. If initial coding is not properly accomplished, recall will be distorted and it may be impossible. The more effective the coding process, the easier the recall. However, it should be noted that the long-term memory is a reconstruction, not a pure recall of information or events. It also is subject to limitations, such as time, biases, and, in many cases, personal inaccuracies. This is why two people who view the same event will often have totally different recollections.

Memory also applies to psychomotor skills. For example, with practice, a tennis player may be able to serve a tennis ball at a high rate of speed and with accuracy.

This may be accomplished with very little thought. For a pilot, the ability to instinctively perform certain maneuvers or other tasks which require manual dexterity and precision provides obvious benefits. For example, it allows the pilot more time to concentrate on other essential duties such as navigation, communications with air traffic control facilities, and visual scanning for other aircraft.

As implied, one of the major responsibilities of the instructor is to help students use their memories effectively. Strategies designed to aid students in retention and recall of information from the long-term memory are included later in this chapter. At the same time, an associated phenomenon, forgetting, cannot be ignored.

THEORIES OF FORGETTING

A consideration of why people forget may point the way to help them remember. Several theories account for forgetting, including disuse, interference, and repression.

DISUSE

The theory of **disuse** suggests that a person forgets those things which are not used. The high school or college graduate is saddened by the lack of factual data retained several years after graduation. Since the things which are remembered are those used on the job, a person concludes that forgetting is the result of disuse. But the explanation is not quite so simple. Experimental studies show, for example, that a hypnotized person can describe specific details of an event which normally is beyond recall. Apparently the memory is there, locked in the recesses of the mind. The difficulty is summoning it up to consciousness.

INTERFERENCE

The basis of the **interference** theory is that people forget something because a certain experience has overshadowed it, or that the learning of similar things has intervened. This theory might explain how the range of experiences after graduation from school causes a person to forget or to lose knowledge. In other words, new events displace many things that had been learned. From experiments, at least two conclusions about interference may be drawn. First, similar material seems to interfere with memory more than dissimilar material; and second, material not well learned suffers most from interference.

REPRESSION

Freudian psychology advances the view that some forgetting is **repression** due to the submersion of ideas into the subconscious mind. Material that is unpleasant or produces anxiety may be treated this way by the individual, but not intentionally. It is subconscious and protective. The repression theory does not appear to account for much forgetfulness of the kind discussed in this chapter, but it does tend to explain some cases.

RETENTION OF LEARNING

Each of the theories implies that when a person forgets something, it is not actually lost. Rather, it is simply unavailable for recall. The instructor's problem is how to make certain that the student's learning is readily available for recall. The following suggestions can help.

Teach thoroughly and with meaning. Material thoroughly learned is highly resistant to forgetting. This is suggested by experimental studies and it also was pointed out in the sections on skill learning. Meaningful learning builds patterns of relationship in the student's consciousness. In contrast, rote learning is superficial and is not easily retained. Meaningful learning goes deep because it involves principles and concepts anchored in the student's own experiences. The following discussion emphasizes five principles which are generally accepted as having a direct application to remembering.

PRAISE STIMULATES REMEMBERING

Responses which give a pleasurable return tend to be repeated. Absence of praise or recognition tends to discourage, and any form of negativism in the acceptance of a response tends to make its recall less likely.

RECALL IS PROMOTED BY ASSOCIATION

As discussed earlier, each bit of information or action which is associated with something to be learned tends to facilitate its later recall by the student. Unique or disassociated facts tend to be forgotten unless they are of special interest or application.

FAVORABLE ATTITUDES AID RETENTION

People learn and remember only what they wish to know. Without motivation there is little chance for recall. The most effective motivation is based on positive or rewarding objectives.

LEARNING WITH ALL OUR SENSES IS MOST EFFECTIVE

Although we generally receive what we learn through the eyes and ears, other senses also contribute to most perceptions. When several senses respond together, a fuller understanding and greater chance of recall is achieved.

MEANINGFUL REPETITION AIDS RECALL

Each repetition gives the student an opportunity to gain a clearer and more accurate perception of the subject to be learned, but mere repetition does not guarantee retention. Practice provides an opportunity for learning, but does not cause it. Further, some research indicates that three or four repetitions provide the maximum effect, after which the rate of learning and probability of retention fall off rapidly.

Along with these five principles, there is a considerable amount of additional literature on retention of learning during a typical academic lesson. After the first 10–15 minutes, the rate of retention drops significantly until about the last 5–10 minutes when students wake up again. Students passively listening to a lecture have roughly a five percent retention rate over a 24–hour period, but students actively engaged in the learning process have a much higher retention. This clearly reiterates the point that active learning is superior to just listening.

TRANSFER OF LEARNING

During a learning experience, the student may be aided by things learned previously. On the other hand, it is sometimes apparent that previous learning interferes with the current learning task. Consider the learning of two skills. If the learning of skill A helps to learn skill B, positive transfer occurs. If learning skill A hinders the learning of skill B, negative transfer occurs. For example, the practice of slow flight (skill A) helps the student learn short-field landings (skill B). However, practice in making a landing approach in an airplane (skill A) may hinder learning to make an approach in a helicopter (skill B). It should be noted that the learning of skill B may affect the retention or proficiency of skill A, either positively or negatively. While these processes may help substantiate the interference theory of forgetting, they are still concerned with the transfer of learning.

It seems clear that some degree of transfer is involved in all learning. This is true because, except for certain inherent responses, all new learning is based upon previously learned experience. People interpret new things in terms of what they already know.

Many aspects of teaching profit by this type of transfer. It may explain why students of apparently equal ability have differing success in certain areas. Negative transfer may hinder the learning of some; positive transfer may help others. This points to a need to know a student's past experience and what has already been learned. In lesson and syllabus development, instructors should plan for transfer by organizing course materials and individual lesson materials in a meaningful sequence. Each phase should help the student learn what is to follow.

The cause of transfer and exactly how it occurs is difficult to determine, but no one disputes the fact that transfer does occur. The significance of this ability for the instructor is that the students can be helped to achieve it. The following suggestions are representative of what educational psychologists believe should be done.

- Plan for transfer as a primary objective. As in all areas of teaching, the chance for success is increased if the teacher deliberately plans to achieve it.

- Make certain that the students understand that what is learned can be applied to other situations. Prepare them to seek other applications.

- Maintain high-order learning standards. Overlearning may even be appropriate. The more thoroughly the students understand the material, the more likely they are to see its relationship to new situations. Avoid unnecessary rote learning, since it does not foster transfer.

- Provide meaningful learning experiences that build students' confidence in their ability to transfer learning. This suggests activities that challenge them to exercise their imagination and ingenuity in applying their knowledge and skills.

- Use instructional material that helps form valid concepts and generalizations. Use materials that make relationships clear.

HABIT FORMATION

The formation of correct habit patterns from the beginning of any learning process is essential to further learning and for correct performance after the completion of training. Remember, primacy is one of the fundamental principles of learning. Therefore, it is the instructor's responsibility to insist on correct techniques and procedures from the outset of training to provide proper habit patterns. It is much easier to foster proper habits from the beginning of training than to correct faulty ones later.

Due to the high level of knowledge and skill required in aviation for both pilots and maintenance technicians, training traditionally has followed a **building block concept**. This means new learning and habit patterns are based on a solid foundation of experience and/or old learning. Everything from intricate cognitive processes to simple motor skills depends on what the student already knows and how that knowledge can be applied in the present. As knowledge and skill increase, there is an expanding base upon which to build for the future.

Chapter 2

Human Behavior

As indicated in Chapter 1, learning is a change of behavior resulting from experience. To successfully accomplish the task of helping to bring about this change, the instructor must know why people act the way they do. A knowledge of basic human needs and defense mechanisms is essential for organizing student activities and promoting a productive learning experience.

CONTROL OF HUMAN BEHAVIOR

The relationship between the instructor and the students has a profound impact on how much the students learn. To students, the instructor usually is a symbol of authority. Students expect the instructor to exercise certain controls, and they tend to recognize and submit to authority as a valid means of control. The instructor's challenge is to know what controls are best for the existing circumstances. The instructor should create an atmosphere that enables and encourages students to help themselves.

Every student works toward a goal of some kind. It may be success itself; it may simply be a grade or other form of personal recognition. The successful instructor directs and controls the behavior of the students and guides them toward a goal. This is a part of the process of directing the students' actions to modify their behavior. Without the instructor's active intervention, the students may become passive and perhaps resistant to learning. The controls the instructor exercises—how much, how far, to what degree—should be based on more than trial and error.

Some interesting generalizations have been made about motivation and human nature. While these assumptions are typically applied to industrial management, they have implications for the aviation instructor as well.

- The expenditure of physical and mental effort in work is as natural as play and rest. The average person does not inherently dislike work. Depending on conditions, work may be a source of satisfaction and, if so, it will be performed voluntarily. On the other hand, when work is a form of punishment, it will be avoided, if possible.

- Most people will exercise self-direction and self-control in the pursuit of goals to which they are committed.

- Commitment to goals relates directly to the reward associated with their achievement, the most significant of which is probably the satisfaction of ego.

- Under proper conditions, the average person learns, not only to accept, but also to seek responsibility. Shirking responsibility and lack of ambition are not inherent in human nature. They are usually the consequences of experience.

- The capacity to exercise a relatively high degree of imagination, ingenuity, and creativity in the solution of common problems is widely, not narrowly, distributed in the population.

- Under the conditions of modern life, the intellectual potentialities of the average person are only partially used.

An instructor who accepts these assumptions should recognize the student's vast, untapped potential. At the same time, ingenuity must be used in discovering how to realize the potentialities of the student. The responsibility rests squarely on the instructor's shoulders. If the student is perceived as lazy, indifferent, unresponsive, uncooperative, and antagonistic, these basic assumptions imply that the instructor's methods of control are at fault. The raw material is there, in most cases, and the shaping and directing of it lie in the hands of those who have the responsibility of controlling it.

How to mold a solid, healthy, productive relationship with students depends, of course, on the instructor's knowledge of students as human beings and of the needs, drives, and desires they continually try to satisfy in one way or another. Some of their needs and drives are discussed in the following paragraphs.

HUMAN NEEDS

The instructor should always be aware of the fact that students are human beings. The needs of students, and of all mankind, have been studied by psychologists and categorized in a number of ways. In 1938, a U.S. psychologist, Henry A. Murray, published a catalog of human motives, which he called needs. These needs were described as being either primary (biological, innate) or secondary (learned, acquired); they were seen as a force related to behavior and goals. Among the motives that Murray discussed were what he identified as needs for achievement, affiliation, power, dependence, and succor (the need to be taken care of), as well as many others. During the 1950s, Abraham Maslow organized human needs into levels of importance. They originally were called a hierarchy of human motives, but are now commonly referred to as a **hierarchy of human needs**. [Figure 2-1]

Figure 2-1. Maslow's hierarchy of human needs is frequently depicted as a pyramid with the lower-level needs at the bottom and progressively higher-level needs above each other in ascending order.

In the intervening years since the 1950s, several other theories on human needs have been published, but psychologists have not adopted any particular one. Meanwhile, Maslow's hierarchical categorization remains a popular and acceptable concept.

PHYSICAL

At the bottom of the pyramid is the broadest, most basic category, the physical needs. Each person is first concerned with a need for food, rest, and protection from the elements. Until these needs are satisfied, a person cannot concentrate fully on learning, self-expression, or any other tasks. Instructors should monitor their students to make sure that their basic physical needs have been met. A hungry or tired student may not be able to perform as expected. Once a need is satisfied, it no longer provides motivation. Thus, the person strives to satisfy the needs of the next higher level.

SAFETY

The safety needs are protection against danger, threats, deprivation, and are labeled by some as the security needs. Regardless of the label, however, they are real, and student behavior is influenced by them. This is especially true in flight training and aviation maintenance where safety is a major concern.

SOCIAL

When individuals are physically comfortable and do not feel threatened, they seek to satisfy their social needs. These are to belong, to associate, and to give and receive friendship and love. An example of the social need might apply to the spouse of a professional pilot. In this case, the need to be included in conversation and other pilot-related activities could induce the spouse to learn how to fly. Since students are usually out of their normal surroundings during flight training, their need for association and belonging will be more pronounced. Instructors should make every effort to help new students feel at ease and to reinforce their decision to pursue aviation.

EGO

The egoistic needs usually have a strong influence on the instructor-student relationship. These needs consist of at least two types: those that relate to one's self-esteem, such as self-confidence, independence, achievement, competence, and knowledge; and the needs that relate to one's reputation, such as status, recognition, appreciation, and respect of associates. The egoistic need may be the main reason for a student's interest in aviation training.

SELF–FULFILLMENT

At the apex of the hierarchy of human needs is self-fulfillment. This includes realizing one's own potential for continued development, and for being creative in the broadest sense of that term. Maslow included various cognitive and aesthetic goals in this highest level. Self-fulfillment for a student should offer the greatest challenge to the instructor. Aiding another in realizing self-fulfillment is perhaps the most rewarding accomplishment for an instructor.

In summary, instructors should strive to help students satisfy their human needs in a manner that will create a healthy learning environment. In this type of environment, students experience fewer frustrations and, therefore, can devote more attention to their studies. Fulfillment of needs can be a powerful motivation in complex learning situations.

DEFENSE MECHANISMS

The concept of defense mechanisms was introduced by Freud in the 1890s. In general, **defense mechanisms** are subconscious, almost automatic, ego-protecting reactions to unpleasant situations. People use these defenses to soften feelings of failure, to alleviate feelings of guilt, and to protect their sense of personal worth or adequacy. Originally, Freud described a mechanism which is now commonly called repression. Since then, other defense mechanisms have gradually been added. In some cases, more than one name has been attached to a particular type of defense mechanism. In addition, it is not always easy to differentiate between defenses which are closely related. Thus, some confusion often occurs in identifying the different types. [Figure 2-2]

DEFENSE MECHANISMS

- Compensation
- Projection
- Rationalization
- Denial of Reality
- Reaction Formation
- Flight
- Aggression
- Resignation

Figure 2-2. Several common defense mechanisms may apply to aviation students.

COMPENSATION

With compensation, students often attempt to disguise the presence of a weak or undesirable quality by emphasizing a more positive one. They also may try to reduce tension by accepting and developing a less preferred but more attainable objective instead of a more preferred but less attainable objective. Students who regard themselves as unattractive may develop exceptionally winning personalities to compensate. Students may say they would rather spend their evenings studying aircraft systems than anything else, but, in fact, they would rather be doing almost anything except aircraft systems study.

PROJECTION

With projection, students relegate the blame for their own shortcomings, mistakes, and transgressions to others or attribute their motives, desires, characteristics, and impulses to others. The athlete who fails to make the team may feel sure the coach was unfair, or the tennis player who examines the racket after a missed shot is projecting blame. When students say, "Everybody will cheat on an exam if given the chance," they are projecting.

RATIONALIZATION

If students cannot accept the real reasons for their behavior, they may rationalize. This device permits them to substitute excuses for reasons; moreover, they can make those excuses plausible and acceptable to themselves. Rationalization is a subconscious technique for justifying actions that otherwise would be unacceptable. When true rationalization takes place, individuals sincerely believe in their excuses. The excuses seem real and justifiable to the individual.

DENIAL OF REALITY

Occasionally students may ignore or refuse to acknowledge disagreeable realities. They may turn away from unpleasant sights, refuse to discuss unpopular topics, or reject criticism.

REACTION FORMATION

Sometimes individuals protect themselves from dangerous desires by not only repressing them, but actually developing conscious attitudes and behavior patterns that are just the opposite. A student may develop a who-cares-how-other-people-feel attitude to cover up feelings of loneliness and a hunger for acceptance.

FLIGHT

Students often escape from frustrating situations by taking flight, physical or mental. To take flight physically, students may develop symptoms or ailments that give them satisfactory excuses for removing themselves from frustration. More frequent than physical flights are mental flights, or daydreaming. Mental flight provides a simple and satisfying escape from problems. If students get sufficient satisfaction from daydreaming, they may stop trying to achieve their goals altogether. When carried to extremes, the world of fantasy and the world of reality can become so confused that the dreamer cannot distinguish one from the other. This mechanism, when carried to the extreme, is referred to as fantasy.

AGGRESSION

Everyone gets angry occasionally. Anger is a normal, universal human emotion. Angry people may shout, swear, slam a door, or give in to the heat of emotions in a number of ways. They become aggressive against something or somebody. After a cooling-off period, they may see their actions as childish. In a classroom, shop, or airplane, such extreme behavior is relatively infrequent, partly because students are taught to repress their emotions in the interest of safety. Because of safety concerns or social strictures, student aggressiveness may be expressed in subtle ways. They may ask irrelevant questions, refuse to participate in the activities of the class, or disrupt activities within their own group. If students cannot deal directly with the cause of their frustration, they may vent their aggressiveness on a neutral object or person not related to the problem.

RESIGNATION

Students also may become so frustrated that they lose interest and give up. They may no longer believe it profitable or even possible to go on, and as a result, they accept defeat. The most obvious and apparent cause for this form of resignation takes place when, after completing an early phase of a course without grasping the fundamentals, a student becomes bewildered and lost in the more advanced phases. From that point on, learning is negligible although the student may go through the motions of participating.

More information on these and other defense mechanisms, such as fantasy, repression, displacement, emotional insulation, regression, and introjection, can be obtained from a good psychology text. Instructors should recognize that most defense mechanisms fall within the realm of normal behavior and serve a useful purpose. However, in some cases, they may be associated with a potentially serious mental health problem. Since defense mechanisms involve some degree of self-deception and distortion of reality, they do not solve problems; they alleviate symptoms, not causes. Moreover, because defense mechanisms operate on a

subconscious level, they are not subject to normal conscious checks and controls. Once an individual realizes there is a conscious reliance on one of these devices, behavior ceases to be a subconscious adjustment mechanism and becomes, instead, an ineffective way of satisfying a need.

It may be difficult for an instructor to identify excessive reliance on defense mechanisms by a student, but a personal crisis or other stressful event is usually the cause. For example, a death in the family, a divorce, or even a failing grade on an important test may trigger harmful defensive reactions. Physical symptoms such as a change in personality, angry outbursts, depression, or a general lack of interest may point to a problem. Drug or alcohol abuse also may become apparent. Less obvious indications may include social withdrawal, preoccupation with certain ideas, or an inability to concentrate.

Some people seem to have the proper attitude and skills necessary to cope with a crisis while others do not. An instructor needs to be familiar with typical defense mechanisms and have some knowledge of related behavioral problems. A perceptive instructor can help by using common sense and talking over the problem with the student. The main objective should be to restore motivation and self-confidence. It should be noted that the human psyche is fragile and could be damaged by inept measures. Therefore, in severe cases involving the possibility of deep psychological problems, timely and skillful help is needed. In this event, the instructor should recommend that the student use the services of a professional counselor.

THE FLIGHT INSTRUCTOR AS A PRACTICAL PSYCHOLOGIST

While it is obviously impossible for every flight instructor to be an accomplished psychologist, there are a number of additional considerations which will assist in learning to analyze students before and during each lesson. As already implied, flight instructors must also be able to evaluate student personality to effectively develop and use techniques appropriate for instruction.

ANXIETY

Anxiety is probably the most significant psychological factor affecting flight instruction. This is true because flying is a potentially threatening experience for persons who are not accustomed to being off the ground. The fear of falling is universal in human beings. Anxiety also is a factor in maintenance training because lives may depend on consistently doing it right the first time. The following paragraphs are primarily concerned with flight instruction and student reactions.

Anxiety is described by Webster as "a state of mental uneasiness arising from fear . . ." It results from the fear of anything, real or imagined, which threatens the person who experiences it, and may have a potent effect on actions and the ability to learn from perceptions.

The responses to anxiety vary extensively. They range from a hesitancy to act to the impulse to do something even if it's wrong. Some people affected by anxiety will react appropriately, adequately, and more rapidly than they would in the absence of threat. Many, on the other hand, may freeze and be incapable of doing anything to correct the situation which has caused their anxiety. Others may do things without rational thought or reason.

Both normal and abnormal reactions to anxiety are of concern to the flight instructor. The normal reactions are significant because they indicate a need for special instruction to relieve the anxiety. The abnormal reactions are even more important because they may signify a deep-seated problem.

Anxiety can be countered by reinforcing students' enjoyment of flying, and by teaching them to cope with their fears. An effective technique is to treat fears as a normal reaction, rather than ignoring them. Keep in mind that anxiety for student pilots usually is associated with certain types of flight operations and maneuvers. Instructors should introduce these maneuvers with care, so that students know what to expect, and what their reactions should be. When introducing stalls, for example, instructors should first review the aerodynamic principles and explain how stalls affect flight characteristics. Then, carefully describe the sensations to be expected, as well as the recovery procedures.

Student anxieties can be minimized throughout training by emphasizing the benefits and pleasurable experiences which can be derived from flying, rather than by continuously citing the unhappy consequences of faulty performances. Safe flying practices should be presented as conducive to satisfying, efficient, uninterrupted operations, rather than as necessary only to prevent catastrophe.

NORMAL REACTIONS TO STRESS

When a threat is recognized or imagined, the brain alerts the body. The adrenal gland activates hormones which prepare the body to meet the threat, or to retreat from it. This often is called the fight or flight syndrome. The heart rate quickens, certain blood vessels constrict to divert blood to the organs which will need it, and numerous other physiological changes take place.

Normal individuals begin to respond rapidly and exactly, within the limits of their experience and training. Many responses are automatic, which points out the need for proper training in emergency operations prior to an actual emergency. The affected individual thinks rationally, acts rapidly, and is extremely sensitive to all aspects of the surroundings.

ABNORMAL REACTIONS TO STRESS

Reactions to stress may produce abnormal responses in some people. With them, response to anxiety or stress may be completely absent or at least inadequate. Their responses may be random or illogical, or they may do more than is called for by the situation.

During flight instruction, instructors normally are the only ones who can observe students when they are under pressure. Instructors, therefore, are in a position to differentiate between safe and unsafe piloting actions. Instructors also may be able to detect potential psychological problems. The following student reactions are indicative of abnormal reactions to stress. None of them provides an absolute indication, but the presence of any of them under conditions of stress is reason for careful instructor evaluation.

- Inappropriate reactions, such as extreme over-cooperation, painstaking self-control, inappropriate laughter or singing, and very rapid changes in emotions.

- Marked changes in mood on different lessons, such as excellent morale followed by deep depression.

- Severe anger directed toward the flight instructor, service personnel, and others.

In difficult situations, flight instructors must carefully examine student responses and their own responses to the students. These responses may be the normal products of a complex learning situation, but they also can be indicative of psychological abnormalities which will inhibit learning, or potentially be very hazardous to future piloting operations.

FLIGHT INSTRUCTOR ACTIONS
REGARDING SERIOUSLY ABNORMAL STUDENTS

A flight instructor who believes a student may be suffering from a serious psychological abnormality has a responsibility to refrain from certifying that student. In addition, a flight instructor has the personal responsibility of assuring that such a person does not continue flight training or become certificated as a pilot. To accomplish this, the following steps are available:

- If an instructor believes that a student may have a disqualifying psychological defect, arrangements should be made for another instructor, who is not acquainted with the student, to conduct an evaluation flight. After the flight, the two instructors should confer to determine whether they agree that further investigation or action is justified.

- An informal discussion should be initiated with the local Flight Standards District Office (FSDO), suggesting that the student may be able to meet the skill standards, but may be unsafe psychologically. This action should be taken as soon as a question arises regarding the student's fitness. It should not be delayed until the student feels competent to solo.

- A discussion should be held with a local aviation medical examiner (AME), preferably the one who issued the student's medical certificate, to obtain advice and to decide on the possibility of further examination of the student.

The flight instructor's primary legal responsibility concerns the decision whether to certify the student to be competent for solo flight operations, or to make a recommendation for the practical test leading to certification as a pilot. If, after consultation with an unbiased instructor, the FSDO, and the AME, the instructor believes that the student suffers a serious psychological deficiency, such authorizations and recommendations must be withheld.

Chapter 3

Effective Communication

The ability to communicate effectively is essential for all aviation instructors. However, communication does not occur automatically even though the instructor has a high level of technical knowledge in a particular subject area. The beginning instructor must understand the complex process involved in communication, and become aware of the common barriers to effective communication. Mere awareness of these factors is not enough. The new instructor must also develop a comfortable style of communication that meets the goal of conveying information to students.

BASIC ELEMENTS

Communication takes place when one person transmits ideas or feelings to another person or group of people. Its effectiveness is measured by the similarity between the idea transmitted and the idea received.

The process of communication is composed of three elements: the source (sender, speaker, transmitter, or instructor), the symbols used in composing and transmitting the message (words or signs), and the receiver (listener, reader, or student). The three elements are dynamically interrelated since each element is dependent on the others for effective communication to take place. The relationship between instructor and student also is dynamic and depends on the two-way flow of symbols between the instructor and student. The instructor depends on feedback from the student to properly tailor the communication to the situation. The instructor also provides feedback to the student to reinforce the desired student responses.

SOURCE

As indicated, the **source** in communication is the sender, speaker, transmitter, or instructor. The instructor's effectiveness as a communicator is related to at least three basic factors. First, an ability to select and

use language is essential for transmitting symbols which are meaningful to listeners and readers. Second, an instructor consciously or unconsciously reveals his or her attitudes toward themselves as a communicator, toward the ideas being communicated, and toward the students. Third, an instructor is more likely to communicate effectively if material is accurate, up-to-date, and stimulating.

An instructor should exercise great care that ideas and feelings are meaningful to the students. A speaker or a writer may depend on a highly technical or professional background with its associated vocabulary that is meaningful only to others with a similar background. It is the responsibility of the instructor, as the source of communication, to realize that the effectiveness of the communication is dependent on the student's understanding of the symbols or words being used. For instance, if an instructor were to use any of the many aviation acronyms, slang, and abbreviations with a new student, effective communication would be difficult if not impossible. Terms like SIGMET, taildragger, FBO, IO-540 do not carry the same meaning to a beginning student. Use of technical language will always be necessary, but the student must be taught the language first.

In addition to using the correct symbols to communicate effectively, the instructor must reveal a positive attitude while delivering a message. The presentation should show that the instructor is confident in the information. It should also show that the message is important and that the student has a need to know the information.

An instructor must constantly strive to have the most current and interesting information possible. In this way, the student's interest can be held. Out-of-date information causes the instructor to lose credibility in the eyes of the student. Use of boring or uninteresting information runs the risk of losing the student's attention.

SYMBOLS

At its basic level, communication is achieved through **symbols** which are simple oral and visual codes. The words in the vocabulary constitute a basic code. Common gestures and facial expressions form another, but words and gestures alone do not communicate ideas. They should be combined into units (sentences, paragraphs, lectures, or chapters) that mean something to the student. When symbols are combined into these units, each portion becomes important to effective communication.

The parts of the total idea should be analyzed to determine which are most suited to starting or ending the communication, and which are best for the purpose of explaining, clarifying, or emphasizing. All of these functions are required for effective transmission of ideas. The process finally culminates in the determination of the medium best suited for their transmission. Most frequently, communicators select the channels of hearing and seeing. For motor skills, the sense of touch, or kinesthetic learning, is added as the student practices the skill.

The instructor will be more successful in gaining and retaining the student's attention by using a variety of channels. As an example, instead of telling students to adjust the trim, the instructor can move the trim wheel while the student tries to maintain a given aircraft attitude. The student will experience, by feel, that the trim wheel affects the amount of control wheel pressure needed to maintain the attitude. At the same time, the instructor can explain to the student that what is felt is forward or back pressure on the control wheel. After

that, the student will begin to understand the correct meaning of control pressure and trim, and when told to adjust the trim to relieve control pressure, the student will respond in the manner desired by the instructor.

The feedback an instructor is getting from a student needs to be constantly monitored in order to modify the symbols, as required, to optimize communication. In figure 3-1, the instructor realizes from the response of the student that stall has been interpreted by the student to have something to do with the engine quitting. Recognizing that the student has misunderstood, the instructor is able to clarify the information and help the student to obtain the desired outcome.

In addition to feedback received by the instructor from the students, students need feedback from the instructor on how they are doing. The feedback not only informs the students of their performance, but also can serve as a valuable source of motivation. An instructor's praise builds the student's ego and reinforces favorable behavior. On the other hand, negative feedback must be used carefully. To avoid embarrassing a student, use negative feedback only in private. This information should be delivered as a description of actual performance and given in a non-judgmental manner. For example, it would be appropriate to tell a maintenance student that a safety wire installation is not satisfactory. But to refer to the work as careless would not be good and could do harm to the student's feeling of self-worth.

RECEIVER

Remember, the **receiver** is the listener, reader, or student. Instructors should always keep in mind that communication succeeds only in relation to the reaction of their students. When students react with understanding and change their behavior according to the intent of the instructor, effective communication has taken place.

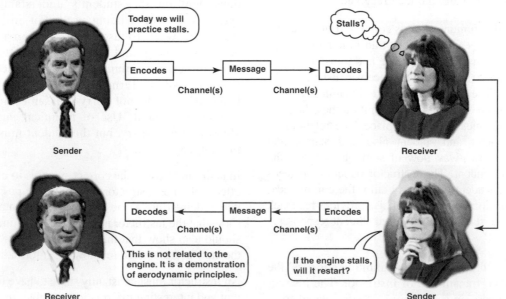

Figure 3-1. The instructor must constantly monitor student feedback.

In order for an instructor to change the behavior of students, some of the students' abilities, attitudes, and experiences need to be understood. First, students come to aviation training with a wide variety of abilities. Some may be familiar with aviation in some form while others barely know what an airplane looks like. Some students arrive with highly developed motor skills, and others have not had opportunities to develop these skills. The instructor needs to determine the abilities of the students and to understand the students in order to properly communicate. The process is complicated by differences in gender, age, cultural background, and level of education. For instance, the instructor would want to tailor a presentation differently for a teenage student than for an older student. Likewise, a student with a strong technical background would require a different level of communication than one with no such background.

The instructor also must understand that the viewpoint and background of people may differ significantly because of cultural differences. However, this consciousness of the differences between people should not be overdone. The instructor should be aware of possible differences, but not overreact or assume certain values because of these differences. For example, just because a student is a college graduate does not guarantee rapid advancement in aviation training. A student's education will certainly affect the instructor's style of presentation, but that style should be based on the evaluation of the student's knowledge of the aviation subject being taught.

Second, the attitudes students exhibit may indicate resistance, willingness, or passive neutrality. To gain and hold the students' attention, attitudes should be molded into forms that promote reception of information. A varied communicative approach will succeed best in reaching most students since they all have different attitudes.

Third, the student's experience, background, and educational level will determine the approach an instructor will take. What the student knows, along with the student's abilities and attitudes, will guide the instructor in communicating. It is essential to understand the dynamics of communication, but the instructor also needs to be aware of several barriers to communication that can inhibit learning.

BARRIERS TO EFFECTIVE COMMUNICATION

The nature of language and the way it is used often lead to misunderstandings. An example might be a maintenance instructor telling a student to time the magnetos. A student new to the maintenance field might think a stopwatch or clock would be necessary to do the requested task. Instruction would be necessary for the student to understand that the procedure has nothing to do with the usual concept of time. This is an example of a lack of common experience, one of four barriers to effective communication. [Figure 3-2]

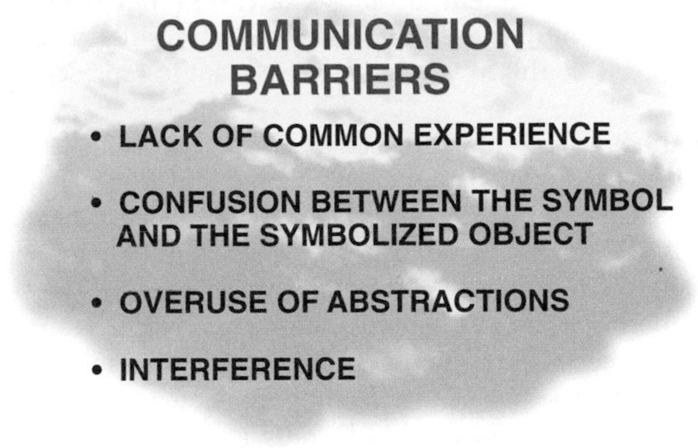

COMMUNICATION BARRIERS

- **LACK OF COMMON EXPERIENCE**

- **CONFUSION BETWEEN THE SYMBOL AND THE SYMBOLIZED OBJECT**

- **OVERUSE OF ABSTRACTIONS**

- **INTERFERENCE**

Figure 3-2. Misunderstandings stem primarily from four barriers to effective communication.

LACK OF COMMON EXPERIENCE

Lack of common experience between instructor and student is probably the greatest single barrier to effective communication. Many people seem to believe that words transport meanings from speaker to listener in the same way that a truck carries bricks from one location to another. Words, however, rarely carry precisely the same meaning from the mind of the instructor to the mind of the student. In fact, words, in themselves, do not transfer meanings at all. Whether spoken or written, they are merely stimuli used to arouse a response in the student. The student's past experience with the words and the things to which they refer determines how the student responds to what the instructor says. A communicator's words cannot communicate the desired meaning to another person unless the listener or reader has had some experience with the objects or concepts to which these words refer. Since it is the students' experience that forms vocabulary, it is also essential that instructors speak the same language as the students. If the instructor's terminology is necessary to convey the idea, some time needs to be spent making certain the students understand that terminology.

The English language abounds in words that mean different things to different people. To a farmer, the word tractor means the machine that pulls the implements to cultivate the soil; to a trucker, it is the vehicle used to pull a semitrailer; in aviation, a tractor propeller is the opposite of a pusher propeller. Each technical field has its own vocabulary. Technical words might mean something entirely different to a person outside that field, or perhaps, mean nothing at all. In order for communication to be effective, the students' understanding of the meaning of the words needs to be the same as the instructor's understanding.

CONFUSION BETWEEN THE SYMBOL AND THE SYMBOLIZED OBJECT

Languages abound with words that mean different things to different people. **Confusion between the symbol and the symbolized object** results when a word is confused with what it is meant to represent.

Although it is obvious that words and the connotations they carry can be different, people sometimes fail to make the distinction. An aviation maintenance technician (AMT) might be introduced as a mechanic. To many people, the term mechanic conjures up images of a person laboring over an automobile. Being referred to as an aircraft mechanic might be an improvement in some people's minds, but neither really portrays the training and skill of the trained AMT. Words and symbols do not always represent the same thing to every person. To communicate effectively, speakers and writers should be aware of these differences. Words and symbols can then be carefully chosen to represent exactly what the speaker or writer intends.

OVERUSE OF ABSTRACTIONS

Abstractions are words that are general rather than specific. Concrete words or terms refer to objects that people can relate directly to their experiences. They specify an idea that can be perceived or a thing that can be visualized. Abstract words, on the other hand, stand for ideas that cannot be directly experienced, things that do not call forth mental images in the minds of the students. The word aircraft is an abstract word. It does not call to mind a specific aircraft in the imaginations of various students. One student may visualize an airplane, another student might visualize a helicopter, and still another student might visualize an airship. Although the word airplane is more specific, various students might envision anything from a Boeing 777 to a Piper Cub. [Figure 3-3]

Another example of abstractions would be if an instructor referred to aircraft engines. Some students might think of jet engines, while others would think of reciprocating engines. Even reciprocating engine is too abstract since it could be a radial engine, an inline engine, a V-type engine, or an opposed type engine. Use of the technical language of engines, as in Lycoming IO-360, would narrow the engine type, but would only be understood by students who have learned the terminology particular to aircraft engines.

Abstractions should be avoided in most cases, but there are times when abstractions are necessary and useful. Aerodynamics is applicable to all aircraft and is an example of an abstraction that can lead to understanding aircraft flight characteristics. The danger of abstractions is that they will not evoke the same specific items of experience in the minds of the students that the instructor intends. When such terms are used, they should be linked with specific experiences through examples and illustrations. For instance, when an approach to landing is going badly, telling a student to take appropriate measures might not result in the desired action. It would be better to tell the student to conduct a go-around since this is an action that has the

Figure 3-3. Overuse of abstract terms can interfere with effective communication.

same meaning to both student and instructor. When maintenance students are being taught to torque the bolts on an engine, it would be better to tell them to torque the bolts in accordance with the maintenance manual for that engine rather than simply to torque the bolts to the proper values. Whenever possible, the level of abstraction should be reduced by using concrete, specific terms. This better defines and gains control of images produced in the minds of the students.

INTERFERENCE

Barriers to effective communication are usually under the direct control of the instructor. However, **interference** is made up of factors that are outside the direct control of the instructor: physiological, environmental, and psychological interference. To communicate effectively, the instructor should consider the effects of these factors.

Physiological interference is any biological problem that may inhibit symbol reception, such as hearing loss, injury, or physical illness. These, and other physiological factors, can inhibit communication because the student is not comfortable. The instructor must adapt the presentation to allow the student to feel better about the situation and be more receptive to new ideas. Adaptation could be as simple as putting off a lesson until the student is over an illness. Another accommodation could be the use of a seat cushion to allow a student to sit properly in the airplane.

Environmental interference is caused by external physical conditions. One example of this is the noise level found in many light aircraft. Noise not only impairs the communication process, but also can result in long-term damage to hearing. One solution to this problem is the use of headphones and an intercom system. If an intercom system is not available, a good solution is the use of earplugs. It has been shown that in addition to protecting hearing, use of earplugs actually clarifies speaker output.

Psychological interference is a product of how the instructor and student feel at the time the communication process is occurring. If either instructor or student is not committed to the communication process, communication is impaired. Fear of the situation or mistrust between the instructor and student could severely inhibit the flow of information.

DEVELOPING COMMUNICATION SKILLS

Communication skills must be developed; they do not occur automatically. The ability to effectively communicate stems from experience. The experience of instructional communication begins with role playing during the training to be an instructor, continues during the actual instruction, and is enhanced by additional training.

ROLE PLAYING

Experience in instructional communication comes from actually doing it. This is learned in the beginning by way of role playing during the instructor's initial training. A new instructor can try out different instructional techniques with an assigned instructor in the case of a flight instructor applicant, or with a mentor or supervisor in the case of a maintenance instructor. A new instructor is more likely to find a comfortable style of communication in an environment that is not threatening. For a prospective flight instructor, this might take the form of conducting a practice ground training session. The new instructor is naturally most concerned about developing flight instruction skills. But it also is essential that he or she develop good ground instructional skills to prepare students for what is to transpire in the air. Likewise, the maintenance instructor must develop skills in the classroom to prepare the maintenance student for the practical, hands-on tasks. In both cases, effective communication will be necessary to reinforce the skills that have been attempted and to assess or critique the results. This development continues as an instructor progresses; nothing remains static. What worked early on might be refined or replaced by some other technique as the instructor gains more experience.

INSTRUCTIONAL COMMUNICATION

Instruction has taken place when the instructor has explained a particular procedure and subsequently determined that the desired student response has occurred. The instructor can improve communication by adhering to several techniques of good communication. One of the basic principles used in public speaking courses is to encourage students to talk about something they understand. It would not be good if an instructor without a maintenance background tried to teach a course for aviation maintenance. Instructors will perform better when speaking of something that they know very well and for which they have a high level of confidence.

The instructor should not be afraid to use examples of past experiences to illustrate particular points. When teaching the procedures to be used for transitioning from instrument meteorological conditions to visual cues during an approach, it would be helpful to be able to tell the student about encountering these same conditions. An instructor's personal experiences make instruction more valuable than reading the same information in a textbook.

Communication has not occurred unless desired results of the communication have taken place. The instructor needs some way of determining results, and the method used should be related to the expected outcome. In the case of flight training, the instructor can judge the actual

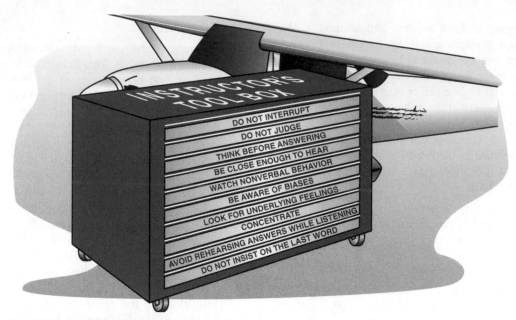

Figure 3-4. Instructors can use a number of tools to become better at listening.

performance of a maneuver. For a maintenance student, the instructor can judge the level of accomplishment of a maintenance procedure. In both cases, the instructor must determine whether the student has actually received and retained the knowledge or if acceptable performance was a one-time event.

The aviation student should know how and why something should be done. For example, a maintenance student may know how to tighten a particular fastener to a specified torque, but it is more important for the student to know that the security and integrity of any fastener depends on proper torque. In this way, the student would be more likely to torque all fasteners properly in the future. For a flight student, simply knowing the different airspeeds for takeoffs and landings is not enough. It is essential to know the reasons for different airspeeds in specific situations to fully understand the importance of proper airspeed control. Normally, the instructor must determine the level of understanding by use of some sort of evaluation.

Written examinations are sometimes appropriate. Well constructed written exams can indicate whether the student has absorbed the desired information or not. Since written examinations also provide a permanent record, training programs usually require them. Another testing technique is to have the student explain a procedure. This works well because it allows the student to put the information in his or her own words. The instructor can then judge whether or not the information received by the student matches with what the instructor intended.

LISTENING

Instructors must know something about their students in order to communicate effectively. As discussed ear-

lier, an instructor needs to determine the abilities of the students and understand the students to properly communicate. One way of becoming better acquainted with students is to be a good listener. Instructors can use a number of techniques to become better at listening. It is important to realize that in order to master the art of listening, an attitude of wanting to listen must be developed. [Figure 3-4]

Just as it is important for instructors to want to listen in order to be effective listeners, it is necessary for students to want to listen. Wanting to listen is just one of several techniques which allow a student to listen effectively. Instructors can improve the percentage of information transfer by teaching students how to listen. [Figure 3-5]

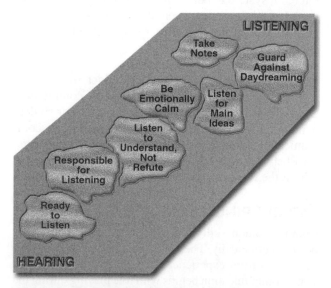

Figure 3-5. Students can improve their listening skills by applying the steps to effective listening.

Listening is more than hearing. As mentioned earlier, it is important for students to be able to hear the radio and the instructor. But simply hearing is not enough. An example of hearing that is not listening would be a pilot acknowledging instructions from the tower, but then having no idea what the tower operator said. When calling back to the tower to get the information, the pilot will want to hear what is being said and will be more inclined to do a better job of listening. This time the pilot must be ready to listen and be responsible for listening. Otherwise, communication will fail again.

Students also need to be reminded that emotions play a large part in determining how much information is retained. One emotional area to concentrate on is listening to understand rather than refute. An example is the instrument student pilot who anticipates drastic changes in requested routing and is already upset. With this frame of mind, it will be very difficult for the student to listen to the routing instructions and then retain very much. In addition, instructors must ensure that students are aware of their emotions concerning certain subjects. If certain areas arouse emotion in a student, the student should be aware of this and take extra measures to listen carefully. For example, if a student who is terrified of the prospect of spins is listening to a lesson on spins, the emotions felt by the student might overwhelm the attempt to listen. If the student, aware of this possibility, made a conscious effort to put that fear aside, listening would probably be more successful.

Another listening technique that can be taught to students is that of listening for the main ideas. This is primarily a technique for listening to a lecture or formal lesson presentation, but is sometimes applicable to hands-on situations as well. People who concentrate on remembering or recording facts might very well miss the message because they have not picked up on the big picture. A listener must always ask, what is the purpose of what I am listening to? By doing this, the listener can relate the words to the overall concept.

The instructor must ensure that the student is aware of the danger of daydreaming. Most people can listen much faster than even the fastest talker can speak. This leaves room for the mind to get off onto some other subject. The listener who is aware of this problem can concentrate on repeating, paraphrasing, or summarizing the speaker's words. Doing so will use the extra time to reinforce the speaker's words, allowing the student to retain more of the information.

Nobody can remember everything. Teaching a student to take notes allows the student to use an organized system to reconstruct what was said during the lesson. Every student will have a slightly different system, but no attempt to record the lecture verbatim should be made.

In most cases a shorthand or abbreviated system of the student's choosing should be encouraged. Note taking is merely a method of allowing the student to recreate the lecture so that it can be studied. The same note taking skills can be used outside the classroom any time information needs to be retained. An example of this would be copying an instrument clearance. It is very difficult to copy an instrument clearance word for word. By knowing the format of a typical clearance, student instrument pilots can develop their own system of abbreviations. This allows them to copy the clearance in a useful form for readback and for flying of the clearance. By incorporating all or some of these techniques, students will retain more information. Instructors can vastly improve their students' retention of information by making certain their students have the best possible listening skills.

QUESTIONING

Good questioning can determine how well the student understands. It also shows the student that the instructor is paying attention. And it shows that the instructor is interested in the student's response. An instructor should ask both open-ended and focused questions. Open-ended questions allow the student to explain more fully. Focused questions allow the instructor to concentrate on desired areas. An instructor may ask for additional details, examples, and impressions from the student. This allows the instructor to ask further questions if necessary. The presentation can then be modified to fit the understanding of the student.

Two ways of confirming that the student and instructor understand things in the same way are the use of paraphrasing and perception checking. The instructor can use paraphrasing to show what the student's statement meant to the instructor. In this way, the student can then make any corrections or expansions on the statement in order to clarify. Perception checking gets to the feelings of the student, again by stating what perceptions the instructor has of the student's behavior and the student can then clarify as necessary.

Since it is important that the instructor understand as much as possible about the students, instructors can be much more effective by using improved listening skills and effective questions to help in putting themselves in the place of the students.

Knowledge of the subject material and skill at instructional communication are necessary to be an instructor. Increasing the depth of knowledge in either area will make the instructor more effective.

INSTRUCTIONAL ENHANCEMENT

The deeper the knowledge of a particular area, the better the instructor is at conveying that information.

For example, a maintenance instructor teaching basic electricity might be able to teach at a minimally satisfactory level if the instructor had only the same training level as that being taught. If asked a question that exceeded the instructor's knowledge, the instructor could research the answer and get back to the student. It would be much better if the instructor, through experience or additional training, was prepared to answer the question initially. Additional knowledge and training would also bolster the instructor's confidence and give the instructional presentation more depth. Advanced courses in the instructional area and on instructional techniques are widely available. These are discussed in Chapter 11. The instructor must be careful to put adequate information into the presentation without providing excessive information.

Otherwise, the essential elements could get lost in a depth of presentation more suited to an advanced course on the subject.

An awareness of the three basic elements of the communicative process (the source, the symbols, and the receiver) indicates the beginning of the understanding required for the successful communicator. Recognizing the various barriers to communication further enhances the flow of ideas between an instructor and the student. The instructor must develop communication skills in order to convey desired information to the students and must recognize that communication is a two-way process. In the end, the true test of whether successful communication has taken place is to determine if the desired results have been achieved.

Chapter 4

The Teaching Process

Effective teaching is based on principles of learning which have been discussed in some detail in Chapter 1. The learning process is not easily separated into a definite number of steps. Sometimes, learning occurs almost instantaneously, and other times it is acquired only through long, patient study and diligent practice. The teaching process, on the other hand, can be divided into steps. Although there is disagreement as to the number of steps, examination of the various lists of steps in the teaching process reveals that different authors are saying essentially the same thing: the teaching of new material can be reduced to preparation, presentation, application, and review and evaluation. Discussions in this handbook focus on these four basic steps. [Figure 4-1]

- PREPARATION
- PRESENTATION
- APPLICATION
- REVIEW AND EVALUATION

Figure 4-1. The teaching process consists of four basic steps.

PREPARATION

For each lesson or instructional period, the instructor must prepare a lesson plan. Traditionally, this plan includes a statement of lesson objectives, the procedures and facilities to be used during the lesson, the specific goals to be attained, and the means to be used for review and evaluation. The lesson plan should also include home study or other special preparation to be done by the student. The instructor should make certain that all necessary supplies, materials, and equipment needed for the lesson are readily available and that the equipment is operating properly. **Preparation** of the lesson plan may be accomplished after reference to the syllabus or practical test standards (PTS), or it may be in pre-printed form as prepared by a publisher of training materials. These documents will list general objectives that are to be accomplished. Objectives are needed to bring the unit of instruction into focus. The instructor can organize the overall instructional plan by writing down the objectives and making certain that they flow in a logical sequence from beginning to end. The objectives allow the instructor to structure the training and permit the student to clearly see what is required along the way. It also allows persons outside the process to see and evaluate what is supposed to take place.

PERFORMANCE-BASED OBJECTIVES

One good way to write lesson plans is to begin by formulating performance-based objectives. The instructor uses the objectives as listed in the syllabus or the appropriate PTS as the beginning point for establishing performance-based objectives. These objectives are very helpful in delineating exactly what needs to be done and how it will be done during each lesson. Once the performance-based objectives are written, most of the work of writing a final lesson plan is completed. Chapter 10 discusses lesson plans in depth and provides examples of a variety of acceptable formats.

Performance-based objectives are used to set measurable, reasonable standards that describe the desired performance of the student. This usually involves the term behavioral objective, although it may be referred to as a performance, instructional, or educational objective. All refer to the same thing, the behavior of the student.

These objectives provide a way of stating what performance level is desired of a student before the student is allowed to progress to the next stage of instruction. Again, objectives must be clear, measurable, and repeatable. In other words, they must mean the same thing to any knowledgeable reader. The objectives must be written. If they are not written, they become subject to the fallibility of recall, interpretation, or loss of specificity with time.

Performance-based objectives consist of three parts: description of the skill or behavior, conditions, and criteria. Each part is required and must be stated in a way that will leave every reader with the same picture of the objective, how it will be performed, and to what level of performance. [Figure 4-2]

ELEMENTS OF PERFORMANCE-BASED OBJECTIVES

- **Description of the Skill or Behavior**—Desired outcome of training stated in concrete terms that can be measured.

- **Conditions**—The framework under which the skill or behavior will be demonstrated.

- **Criteria**—The standard which will be used to measure the accomplishment of the objective.

Figure 4-2. Performance-based objectives are made up of a description of the skill or behavior, conditions, and criteria.

DESCRIPTION OF THE SKILL OR BEHAVIOR

The **description of the skill or behavior** explains the desired outcome of the instruction. It actually is a learned capability, which may be defined as knowledge, a skill, or an attitude. The description should be in concrete terms that can be measured. Terms such as "knowledge of..." and "awareness of..." cannot be measured very well and are examples of the types of verbiage which should be avoided. Phrases like "able to select from a list of..." or "able to repeat the steps to..." are better because they can be measured. Furthermore, the skill or behavior described should be logical and within the overall instructional plan.

CONDITIONS

Conditions are necessary to specifically explain the rules under which the skill or behavior is demonstrated. If a desired capability is to navigate from point A to point B, the objective as stated is not specific enough for all students to do it in the same way. Information such as equipment, tools, reference material, and limiting parameters should be included. For example, inserting conditions narrows the objective as follows: "Using sectional charts, a flight computer, and a Cessna 172, navigate from point A to point B while maintaining standard hemispheric altitudes." Sometimes, in the process of writing the objective, a difficulty is encountered. This might be someone saying, "But, what if...?" This is a good indication that the original version was confusing to that person. If it is confusing to one person, it will be confusing to others and should be corrected.

CRITERIA

Criteria is a list of standards which measure the accomplishment of the objective. The criteria should be stated so that there is no question whether the objective has been met. In the previous example, the criteria may include that navigation from A to B be accomplished within five minutes of the preplanned flight time and that en route altitude be maintained within 200 feet. The revised performance-based objective may now read, "Using a sectional chart and a flight computer, plan a flight and fly from point A to point B in a Cessna 172. Arrival at point B should be within five minutes of planned arrival time and cruise altitude should be maintained within 200 feet during the en route phase of the flight." The alert reader has already noted that the conditions and criteria have changed slightly during the development of these objectives, and that is exactly the way it will occur. Conditions and criteria should be refined as necessary.

As noted earlier, the practical test standards already have many of the elements needed to formulate performance-based objectives. In most cases, the objective is listed along with sufficient conditions to describe the scope of the objective. The PTS also has specific criteria or standards upon which to grade performance; however, the criteria may not always be specific enough for a particular lesson. The instructor should feel free to write performance-based objectives to fit the desired outcome of the lesson. The objective formulated in the last few paragraphs, for instance, is a well-defined lesson objective from the task, Pilotage and Dead Reckoning, in the *Private Pilot Practical Test Standards*.

OTHER USES OF PERFORMANCE-BASED OBJECTIVES

The use of performance-based objectives expands the conventional idea of an objective to include conditions and criteria. This expansion opens the way for the performance-based objective to be used to fill in many of the blanks on the lesson plan. For example, having formulated the conditions under which the student will accomplish the objective, the instructor has already done most of the work toward determining the elements of the lesson and the schedule of events. The equipment necessary, and the instructor and student actions anticipated during the lesson have also been specified. By listing the criteria for the performance-based objectives, the instructor has already established the completion standards normally included as part of the lesson plan.

Use of performance-based objectives also provides the student with a better understanding of the big picture, as well as knowledge of exactly what is expected. This overview can alleviate a significant source of frustration on the part of the student.

As indicated in Chapter 1, performance-based objectives apply to all three domains of learning — cognitive (knowledge), affective (attitudes, beliefs, values), and psychomotor (physical skills). In addition, since each domain includes several educational or skill levels, performance-based objectives may easily be adapted to a specific performance level of knowledge or skill.

PRESENTATION

Instructors have several methods of **presentation** from which to choose. In this handbook, the discussion is limited to the lecture method, the demonstration-performance method, and the guided discussion. The nature of the subject matter and the objective in teaching it normally determine the method of presentation. The **lecture method** is suitable for presenting new material, for summarizing ideas, and for showing relationships between theory and practice. For example, it is suitable for the presentation of a ground school lesson on aircraft weight and balance. This method is most effective when accompanied by instructional aids and training devices. In the case of a lecture on weight and balance, a chalkboard, a marker board, or flip chart could be used effectively.

The **demonstration-performance method** is desirable for teaching a skill, such as a ground school lesson on the flight computer, or during instruction on most flight maneuvers. Showing a student pilot how to recognize stalls, for example, would be appropriate for this method. The instructor would first demonstrate the common indications of a stall, and then have the student attempt to identify the same stall indications.

Combining the lecture and the demonstration-performance methods would be useful for teaching students to overhaul an engine. The initial information on overhaul procedures would be taught in the classroom using the lecture method, and the actual hands on portion in the shop would use the demonstration-performance method.

In the shop, the instructor would first demonstrate a procedure and then the student would have an opportunity to perform the same procedure. In the demonstration-performance method, the steps must be sequenced in the proper order so the students get a correct picture of each separate process or operation, as well as the overall procedure.

Another form of presentation is the **guided discussion** which is used in a classroom situation. It is a good method for encouraging active participation of the students. It is especially helpful in teaching subjects such as safety and emergency procedures where students can use initiative and imagination in addressing problem areas. All three forms of presentation will be addressed in greater depth in Chapter 5.

APPLICATION

Application is where the student uses what the instructor has presented. After a classroom presentation, the student may be asked to explain the new material. The student also may be asked to perform a procedure or operation that has just been demonstrated. For example, after an instructor has demonstrated and explained the use of the flight computer, the student may be asked to use the flight computer to compute groundspeed, drift correction, or time en route. In most instructional situations, the instructor's explanation and demonstration activities are alternated with student performance efforts. The instructor makes a presentation and then asks the student to try the same procedure or operation.

Usually the instructor will have to interrupt the student's efforts for corrections and further demonstrations. This is necessary, because it is very important that each student perform the maneuver or operation the right way the first few times. This is when habits are established. Faulty habits are difficult to correct and must be addressed as soon as possible. Flight instructors in particular must be aware of this problem since students do a lot of their practice without an instructor. Only after reasonable competence has been demonstrated should the student be allowed to practice certain maneuvers on solo flights. Then, the student can practice the maneuver again and again until correct performance becomes almost automatic. Periodic review and evaluation by the instructor is necessary to ensure that the student has not acquired any bad habits.

REVIEW AND EVALUATION

Before the end of the instructional period, the instructor should review what has been covered during the lesson and require the students to demonstrate how well the lesson objectives have been met. Evaluation is an integral part of each classroom, shop, or flight lesson. The instructor's evaluation may be informal and recorded only for the instructor's own use in planning the next lesson for the students, or it may be formal. More likely, the evaluation will be formal and results recorded to certify the student's progress in the course. In Chapter 5, methods of integrating training syllabi and record keeping will be introduced.

In either case, students should be made aware of their progress. Any advances and deficiencies should be noted at the conclusion of the lesson. Failure to make students aware of their progress, or lack of it, may create a barrier that could impede further instruction. [Figure 4-3]

Figure 4-3. If students understand that performance is measured against task standards, they will be less likely to become discouraged with their progress.

In aviation training programs, the instructor should remember that it often is difficult for students to get a clear picture of their progress. Students in flight training seldom have a chance to compare their performance with other students. However, they are in a competitive situation with an unseen competitor—competency—and they are normally able to compare their performance only with that of their instructor. The instructor's feedback must adequately compare the students' performance to the completion standards of the lesson plan so the students really know how they are doing. Otherwise, the students may become discouraged when their only visible competition, their instructor, is doing well and they are not.

In addition to a review of knowledge and skills learned during the instruction period just completed, each lesson should include a selective **review and evaluation** of things previously learned. If the evaluation reveals a deficiency in the knowledge or performance, it must be corrected before new material is presented.

If deficiencies or faults not associated with the present lesson are revealed, they should be carefully noted and pointed out to the student. Corrective measures that are practicable within the limitations of the current lesson should be taken immediately. Remedial actions, which are beyond the scope of the immediate lesson, must be included in future lessons in order to minimize unsafe practices or other discrepancies.

The evaluation of student performance and accomplishment during a lesson should be based on the objectives and goals that were established in the instructor's lesson plan. Review and evaluation allow both the instructor and the students to have a valid picture of where the student stands in respect to the established standard. Review and evaluation in every lesson provides opportunities for both positive feedback and correction of faults.

Chapter 5

Teaching Methods

The information presented in previous chapters has been largely theoretical, emphasizing concepts and principles pertinent to the learning process, human behavior, and effective communication in education and training programs. This knowledge, if properly used, will enable instructors to be more confident, efficient, and successful. The discussion which follows departs from the theoretical with some specific recommendations for the actual conduct of the teaching process. Included are methods and procedures which have been tested and found to be effective.

Teaching methods in common use, such as the lecture method, the guided discussion method, and the demonstration-performance method are covered in this chapter. A discussion on cooperative or group learning also is included since this type of learning may be useful in conjunction with either the lecture or guided discussion methods. A teaching method is seldom used by itself. In a typical lesson, an effective instructor normally uses more than one method. For example, a demonstration is usually accompanied by a thorough explanation, which is essentially a lecture.

Personal computers are a part of every segment of our society today. Since a number of computer-based programs are currently available from publishers of aviation training materials, a brief description of new technologies and how to use them effectively is provided near the end of the chapter.

ORGANIZING MATERIAL

Regardless of the teaching method used, an instructor must properly organize the material. The lessons do not stand alone within a course of training. There must be a plan of action to lead instructors and their students through the course in a logical manner toward the desired goal. Usually the goal for students is a certificate or rating. It could be a private pilot certificate, an instrument rating, or an aviation maintenance technician certificate or rating. In all cases, a systematic plan of action requires the use of an appropriate training syllabus. Generally, the syllabus must contain a description of each lesson, including objectives and completion standards. Refer to Chapter 10, *Planning Instructional Activity*, for detailed information on requirements for an aviation training syllabus, and the building-block concept for curriculum development.

Although some schools and independent instructors may develop their own syllabus, in practice, many instructors use a commercially developed syllabus that already has been selected by a school for use in their aviation training program. Thus, the main concern of the instructor usually is the more manageable task of organizing a block of training with integrated lesson plans. The traditional way of organizing a lesson plan is—introduction, development, and conclusion.

INTRODUCTION

ELEMENT	PURPOSE
• **Attention**	– Establish common ground between instructor and student – Capture and hold the attention of the class – Specify benefits the student can expect from the lesson
• **Motivation**	– Establish receptive attitude toward lesson – Create smooth transition into lesson
• **Overview**	– Indicate what is to be covered and relate this information to the overall course

Figure 5-1. The introduction prepares the students to receive the information in the lesson.

INTRODUCTION

The introduction sets the stage for everything to come. Efforts in this area pay great dividends in terms of quality of instruction. In brief, the introduction is made up of three elements—attention, motivation, and an overview of what is to be covered. [Figure 5-1]

ATTENTION

The purpose of the attention element is to focus each student's attention on the lesson. The instructor may begin by telling a story, making an unexpected or surprising statement, asking a question, or telling a joke. Any of these may be appropriate at one time or another. Regardless of which is used, it should relate to the subject and establish a background for developing the learning outcomes. Telling a story or a joke that is not related in some way to the subject can only distract from the lesson. The main concern is to gain the attention of everyone and concentrate on the subject. [Figure 5-2]

Figure 5-2. The attention element causes students to focus on the upcoming lesson.

MOTIVATION

The purpose of the motivation element is to offer the students specific reasons why the lesson content is important to know, understand, apply, or perform. For example, the instructor may talk about an occurrence where the knowledge in the lesson was applied. Or the instructor may remind the students of an upcoming test on the material. This motivation should appeal to each student personally and engender a desire to learn the material.

OVERVIEW

Every lesson introduction should contain an overview that tells the group what is to be covered during the period. A clear, concise presentation of the objective and the key ideas gives the students a road map of the route to be followed. A good visual aid can help the instructor show the students the path that they are to travel. The introduction should be free of stories, jokes, or incidents that do not help the students focus their attention on the lesson objective. Also, the instructor should avoid a long apologetic introduction, because it only serves to dampen the students' interest in the lesson.

DEVELOPMENT

Development is the main part of the lesson. Here, the instructor develops the subject matter in a manner that helps the students achieve the desired learning outcomes. The instructor must logically organize the material to show the relationships of the main points. The instructor usually shows these primary relationships by developing the main points in one of the following ways: from past to present, simple to complex, known to unknown, and most frequently used to least frequently used.

PAST TO PRESENT

In this pattern of development, the subject matter is arranged chronologically, from the present to the past or from the past to the present. Time relationships are most suitable when history is an important consideration, as in tracing the development of radio navigation systems.

SIMPLE TO COMPLEX

The simple-to-complex pattern helps the instructor lead the student from simple facts or ideas to an understanding of involved phenomena or concepts. In studying jet propulsion, for example, the student might begin by considering the action involved in releasing air from a toy balloon and finish by taking part in a discussion of a complex gas turbine engine.

KNOWN TO UNKNOWN

By using something the student already knows as the point of departure, the instructor can lead into new ideas and concepts. For example, in developing a lesson on heading indicators, the instructor could begin with a discussion of the vacuum-driven heading indicator before proceeding to a description of the radio magnetic indicator (RMI).

MOST FREQUENTLY USED
TO LEAST FREQUENTLY USED

In some subjects, certain information or concepts are common to all who use the material. This fourth organizational pattern starts with common usage before progressing to the rarer ones. When learning navigation, students should study frequently used pilotage, dead reckoning, and basic VOR/NDB radio navigation procedures before going on to area navigation procedures such as global positioning system (GPS) or inertial navigation system (INS).

Under each main point in a lesson, the subordinate points should lead naturally from one to the other. With this arrangement, each point leads logically into, and serves as a reminder of, the next. Meaningful transitions from one main point to another keep the students oriented, aware of where they have been, and where they are going. This permits effective sorting or categorizing chunks of information in the working or short-term memory. Organizing a lesson so the students will grasp the logical relationships of ideas is not an easy task, but it is necessary if the students are to learn and remember what they have learned. Poorly organized information is of little or no value to the student because it cannot be readily understood or remembered.

CONCLUSION

An effective conclusion retraces the important elements of the lesson and relates them to the objective. This review and wrap-up of ideas reinforces student learning and improves the retention of what has been learned. New ideas should not be introduced in the conclusion because at this point they are likely to confuse the students.

By organizing the lesson material into a logical format, the instructor has maximized the opportunity for students to retain the desired information. However, each teaching situation is unique. The setting and purpose of the lesson will determine which teaching method—lecture, guided discussion, demonstration-performance, cooperative or group learning, computer-based training, or a combination—will be used.

LECTURE METHOD

The lecture method is the most widely used form of presentation. Every instructor should know how to develop and present a lecture. They also should understand the advantages and limitations of this method. Lectures are used for introduction of new subjects, summarizing ideas, showing relationships between theory and practice, and reemphasizing main points. The lecture method is adaptable to many different settings, including either small or large groups. Lectures also may be used to introduce a unit of instruction or a complete training program. Finally, lectures may be combined with other teaching methods to give added meaning and direction.

The lecture method of teaching needs to be very flexible since it may be used in different ways. For example, there are several types of lectures such as the **illustrated talk** where the speaker relies heavily on visual aids to convey ideas to the listeners. With a **briefing**, the speaker presents a concise array of facts to the listeners who normally do not expect elaboration of supporting material. During a **formal lecture**, the speaker's purpose is to inform, to persuade, or to entertain with little or no verbal participation by the students. When using a **teaching lecture**, the instructor plans and delivers an oral presentation in a manner that allows some participation by the students and helps direct them toward the desired learning outcomes.

TEACHING LECTURE

The teaching lecture is favored by aviation instructors because it allows some active participation by the students. The instructor must determine the method to be used in developing the subject matter. The instructor also should carefully consider the class size and the depth of the presentation. As mentioned in Chapter 3, covering a subject in too much detail is as bad or worse than sketchy coverage. Regardless of the method of development or depth of coverage, the success of the teaching lecture depends upon the instructor's ability to communicate effectively with the class.

In other methods of teaching such as demonstration-performance or guided discussion, the instructor receives direct reaction from the students, either verbally or by some form of body language. However, in the teaching lecture, the feedback is not nearly as obvious and is much harder to interpret. In the teaching lecture, the instructor must develop a keen perception for subtle responses from the class—facial expressions, manner of taking notes, and apparent interest or disinterest in the lesson. The successful instructor will be able to interpret the meaning of these reactions and adjust the lesson accordingly.

PREPARING THE TEACHING LECTURE

The competent instructor knows that careful preparation is one key to successful performance as a classroom lecturer. This preparation should start well in advance of the presentation. The following four steps should be followed in the planning phase of preparation:

- Establishing the objective and desired outcomes;
- Researching the subject;
- Organizing the material; and
- Planning productive classroom activities.

In all stages of preparing for the teaching lecture, the instructor should support any point to be covered with meaningful examples, comparisons, statistics, or testimony. The instructor should consider that the student may neither believe nor understand any point without the use of testimony from subject area experts or without meaningful examples, statistics, or comparisons. While developing the lesson, the instructor also should strongly consider the use of examples and personal experiences related to the subject of the lesson.

After completing the preliminary planning and writing of the lesson plan, the instructor should rehearse the lecture to build self-confidence. Rehearsals, or dry runs, help smooth out the mechanics of using notes, visual aids, and other instructional devices. If possible, the instructor should have another knowledgeable person, preferably another instructor, observe the practice sessions and act as a critic. This critique will help the instructor judge the adequacy of supporting materials and visual aids, as well as the presentation. [Figure 5-3]

Figure 5-3. Instructors should try a dry run with another instructor to get a feel for the lecture presentation.

SUITABLE LANGUAGE

In the teaching lecture, simple rather than complex words should be used whenever possible. Good newspapers offer examples of the effective use of simple words. Picturesque slang and free-and-easy colloquialisms, if they suit the subject, can add variety and vividness to a teaching lecture. The instructor should not, however, use substandard English. Errors in grammar and vulgarisms detract from an instructor's dignity and reflect upon the intelligence of the students.

If the subject matter includes technical terms, the instructor should clearly define each one so that no student is in doubt about its meaning. Whenever possible, the instructor should use specific rather than general words. For example, the specific words, a leak in the fuel line, tell more than the general term, mechanical defect.

Another way the instructor can add life to the lecture is to vary his or her tone of voice and pace of speaking. In addition, using sentences of different length helps, since consistent use of short sentences results in a choppy style. Unless long sentences are carefully constructed, they are difficult to follow and can easily become tangled. To ensure clarity and variety, the instructor should normally use sentences of short and medium length.

TYPES OF DELIVERY

Lectures may include several different types of delivery. However, depending on the requirements of any particular circumstances, a lecture is usually delivered in one of four ways:

- Reading from a typed or written manuscript.
- Reciting memorized material without the aid of a manuscript.
- Speaking extemporaneously from an outline.
- Speaking impromptu without preparation.

The teaching lecture is probably best delivered in an extemporaneous manner. The instructor speaks from a mental or written outline, but does not read or memorize the material to be presented. Because the exact words to express an idea are spontaneous, the lecture is more personalized than one that is read or spoken from memory.

Since the instructor talks directly to the students, their reactions can be readily observed, and adjustments can be made based on their responses. The instructor has better control of the situation, can change the approach to meet any contingency, and can tailor each idea to suit the responses of the students. For example, if the instructor realizes from puzzled expressions that a number of students fail to grasp an idea, that point can be elaborated on until the reactions of the students indicate they understand. The extemporaneous presentation reflects the instructor's personal enthusiasm and is more flexible than other methods. For these reasons, it is likely to hold the interest of the students.

USE OF NOTES

An instructor who is thoroughly prepared or who has made the presentation before can usually speak effectively without notes. If the lecture has been carefully prepared, and the instructor is completely familiar with the outline, there should be no real difficulty.

Notes used wisely can ensure accuracy, jog the memory, and dispel the fear of forgetting. They are essential for reporting complicated information. For an instructor who tends to ramble, notes are a must because they help keep the lecture on track. The instructor who requires notes should use them sparingly and unobtrusively, but at the same time should make no effort to hide them from the students. Notes may be written legibly or typed, and they should be placed where they can be consulted easily, or held, if the instructor walks about the room. [Figure 5-4]

Figure 5-4. Notes allow the accurate dissemination of complicated information.

FORMAL VERSUS INFORMAL LECTURES

The lecture may be conducted in either a formal or an informal manner. The informal lecture includes active student participation. The primary consideration in the lecture method, as in all other teaching methods, is the achievement of desired learning outcomes. Learning is best achieved if students participate actively in a friendly, relaxed atmosphere. Therefore, the use of the informal lecture is encouraged. At the same time, it must be realized that a formal lecture is still to be preferred on some subjects and occasions, such as lectures introducing new subject matter.

The instructor can achieve active student participation in the informal lecture through the use of questions. In this way, the students are encouraged to make contributions that supplement the lecture. The instructor can use questions to determine the experience and background of the students in order to tailor the lecture to their needs, and/or to add variety, stimulate interest, and check student understanding. However, it is the instructor's responsibility to plan, organize, develop, and present the major portion of a lesson.

ADVANTAGES AND DISADVANTAGES OF THE LECTURE

There are a number of advantages to lectures. For example, a lecture is a convenient way to instruct large groups. If necessary, a public address system can be used to amplify the speaker's voice. Lectures can be used to present information that would be difficult for the student to get in other ways, particularly if the students do not have the time required for research, or if they do not have access to reference material. Lectures also can usefully and successfully supplement other teaching devices and methods. A brief introductory lecture can give direction and purpose to a demonstration or prepare students for a discussion by telling them something about the subject matter to be covered.

In a lecture, the instructor can present many ideas in a relatively short time. Facts and ideas that have been logically organized can be concisely presented in rapid sequence. Lecturing is unquestionably the most economical of all teaching methods in terms of the time required to present a given amount of material.

The lecture is particularly suitable for introducing a new subject and for explaining the necessary background information. By using a lecture in this way, the instructor can offer students with varied backgrounds a common understanding of essential principles and facts.

Although the lecture method can help the instructor meet special challenges, it does have several drawbacks. Too often the lecture inhibits student participation and, as a consequence, many students willingly let the instructor do all the work. Learning is an active process, and the lecture method tends to foster passiveness and teacher-dependence on the part of the students. As a teaching method, the lecture does not bring about maximum attainment of certain types of learning outcomes. Motor skills, for example, can seldom be learned by listening to a lecture. The only effective way students can perfect such skills is through hands-on practice.

The lecture does not easily allow the instructor to estimate the students' understanding as the material is covered. Within a single period, the instructor may unwittingly present more information than students can absorb, and the lecture method provides no accurate means of checking student progress.

Many instructors find it difficult to hold the attention of all students in a lecture throughout the class period. To achieve desired learning outcomes through the lecture method, an instructor needs considerable skill in speaking. As indicated in Chapter 1, a student's rate of retention drops off significantly after the first 10-15 minutes of a lecture and picks back up at the end. In addition, the retention rate for a lecture is about five percent after 24 hours. In comparison, the rate of retention for active learning goes up dramatically. An instructor who can introduce some form of active student participation in the middle of a lecture will greatly increase retention. One form of active learning that has been successfully used is cooperative or group learning.

COOPERATIVE OR GROUP LEARNING METHOD

Cooperative or group learning is an instructional strategy which organizes students into small groups so that they can work together to maximize their own and each other's learning. Numerous research studies in diverse school settings, and across a wide range of subject areas, indicate promising possibilities for academic achievement with this strategy. For example, advocates have noted that students completing cooperative learning group tasks tend to have higher test scores, higher self-esteem, improved social skills, and greater comprehension of the subjects they are studying. Numerous other benefits for students have been attributed to these programs. Perhaps the most significant characteristic of group learning is that it continually requires active participation of the student in the learning process.

CONDITIONS AND CONTROLS

In spite of its many advantages, cooperative or group learning is not a panacea for education or training. Virtually all studies and literature carefully mention that success depends on conditions that must be met and certain controls that must be in place. First of all, instructors need to begin planning early to determine what the student group is expected to learn and be able to do on their own. The end result of a curriculum unit or group task may emphasize academic achievement, cognitive abilities, or physical skills, but the instructor must describe in very unambiguous language the specific knowledge and/or abilities the students are to acquire and then demonstrate on their own. In addition

to clear and specific learning outcomes or objectives, some of the other conditions and controls that may apply are discussed in the following paragraphs.

HETEROGENEOUS GROUPS

Instructors should organize small groups of approximately 3 to 6 members so that students are mixed heterogeneously, considering academic abilities, ethnic backgrounds, race, and gender. Students should not be allowed to form their own groups based on friendship or cliques. The main advantages with heterogeneous groups are that students tend to interact and achieve in ways and at levels that are rarely found with other instructional strategies. They also tend to become tolerant of diverse viewpoints, to consider the thoughts and feelings of others, and to seek more support and clarification of various opinions.

CLEAR, COMPLETE DIRECTIONS AND INSTRUCTIONS

Instructors need to provide directions and instructions that contain in clear, precise terms exactly what students are to do, in what order, with what materials, and when appropriate, what students are to generate as evidence of their mastery of targeted content and skills. These directions need to be given to the students before they engage in their group learning efforts.

ALL STUDENTS IN THE GROUP MUST BUY INTO THE TARGETED OBJECTIVES

Students must perceive these objectives as their own. They must understand and believe that everyone in the group needs to master the essential information and/or skills. In cases where groups select their own objectives, all members of the group must accept the objectives as ones they have agreed to achieve.

POSITIVE INTERDEPENDENCE

Instructors must structure learning tasks so students will believe that they sink or swim together. Thus, access to rewards is through membership in the group where all members receive a reward or no member does. This means tasks are structured so that students must depend upon one another for their group's success in completing and mastering the targeted objectives.

OPPORTUNITY FOR SUCCESS

Every student must believe that he or she has an equal chance of learning the content and/or abilities, and earning the group rewards for success, regardless of the group he or she is in. In other words, the student must not feel penalized by being placed in a particular group.

ACCESS TO MUST-LEARN INFORMATION

Instructors must structure the tasks so that students have access to and comprehend the specific information that they must learn. The focus of learning tasks must be aligned with the specific objectives, as well as any test items that will be used to measure their achievement.

SUFFICIENT TIME FOR LEARNING

Each student and group should be provided the amount of time needed to learn the targeted information and/or abilities. If students do not spend sufficient time learning, the benefits will be limited. Research suggests that many of the positive values, social skills, and academic advantages of cooperative learning tend to emerge and be retained only after students have spent several weeks together in the same heterogeneous group.

POSITIVE SOCIAL INTERACTION BEHAVIORS AND ATTITUDES

Students should be positioned and postured to face each other for direct eye-to-eye contact and face-to-face conversations. Just because students are placed in groups and expected to use appropriate social and group skills does not mean they will automatically use these skills. To work together as a group, students need to engage in such interactive abilities as leadership, trust-building, conflict management, constructive criticism, encouragement, compromise, negotiation, and clarification. Instructors may need to describe the expected social interaction behaviors and attitudes of students, and to assign particular students specific roles to ensure that they consciously work on these behaviors in their groups.

INDIVIDUAL ACCOUNTABILITY

The main reason that students are put in cooperative learning groups is so they can individually achieve greater success than if they were to study alone. Thus, each student must be held individually responsible and accountable for doing his or her own share of the work and for learning what needs to be learned. As a result, each student must be formally and individually tested to determine mastery and retention of the targeted learning outcomes or training objectives.

RECOGNITION AND REWARDS FOR GROUP SUCCESS

Only members of groups who meet established levels for achievement receive the rewards or public recognition. The specific awards must be something valued by the students.

DEBRIEF ON GROUP EFFORTS

Students should spend time after the group tasks have been completed to systematically reflect upon how they worked together as a team—specifically how well they achieved their group objectives; how they helped each other comprehend the content, resources, and task procedures; how they used positive behaviors and attitudes to enable each individual and the entire group to be successful; and what they need to do in the future to be even more successful.

All of the preceding conditions and controls do not have to be used every time an instructor assigns students to work in groups. In practice, cooperative or group learning in aviation training is normally modified to adapt to school policy or for other valid reasons. For example, collaborative, student-led, instructor-led, or working group strategies are alternatives to a pure form of group learning. In these examples, the student leader or the instructor serves as a coach or facilitator who interacts with the group, as necessary, to keep it on track or to encourage everyone in the group to participate.

GUIDED DISCUSSION METHOD

In the guided discussion method, as is true with any group learning effort, the instructor typically relies on the students to provide ideas, experiences, opinions, and information. An instructor may use this method during classroom periods, and preflight and postflight briefings, after the students have gained some knowledge and experience. Fundamentally, the guided discussion method is almost the opposite of the lecture method. The instructor's goal is to draw out what the students know, rather than to spend the class period telling them. The instructor should remember that the more intense the discussion and the greater the participation, the more effective the learning. All members of the group should follow the discussion. The instructor should treat everyone impartially, encourage questions, exercise patience and tact, and comment on all responses. Sarcasm or ridicule should never be used, since it inhibits the spontaneity of the participants. In a guided discussion, the instructor acts as a facilitator to encourage discussion between students.

USE OF QUESTIONS IN A GUIDED DISCUSSION

In the guided discussion, learning is achieved through the skillful use of questions. Questions can be categorized by function and by characteristics. Understanding these distinctions helps the instructor become a more skilled user of questions.

The instructor often uses a question to open up an area for discussion. This is the **lead-off question** and its function is indicated by its name. The purpose is to get the discussion started. After the discussion develops, the instructor may ask a **follow-up question** to guide the discussion. The reasons for using a follow-up question may vary. The instructor may want a student to explain something more thoroughly, or may need to bring the discussion back to a point from which it has strayed.

In terms of characteristics, questions can be identified as overhead, rhetorical, direct, reverse, and relay. The **overhead question** is directed to the entire group to stimulate the thought and response from each group member. The instructor may use an overhead question to pose the lead-off question. The **rhetorical question** is similar in nature, because it also spurs group thought. However, the instructor provides the answer to the rhetorical question. Consequently, it is more commonly used in lecturing than in guided discussion.

The instructor who wants to phrase a question for follow-up purposes may choose the overhead type. If, however, a response is desired from a specific individual, a **direct question** may be asked of that student. A **reverse question** is used in response to a student's question. Rather than give a direct answer to the student's query, the instructor can redirect the question to another student to provide the answer. A **relay question** is redirected to the group instead of the individual.

Questions are so much a part of teaching that they are often taken for granted. Effective use of questions may result in more student learning than any other single technique used by instructors. In general, instructors should ask open-ended questions that are thought provoking and require more mental activity than simply remembering facts. Since most aviation training is at the understanding level of learning, or higher, questions should require students to grasp concepts, explain similarities and differences, and to infer cause-and-effect relationships. [Figure 5-5]

CHARACTERISTICS OF AN EFFECTIVE QUESTION

- Have a Specific Purpose
- Be Clear in Meaning
- Contain a Single Idea
- Stimulate Thought
- Require Definite Answers
- Relate to Previously Covered Information

Figure 5-5. If the objectives of a lesson are clearly established in advance, instructors will find it much easier to ask appropriate questions that keep the discussion moving in the planned direction.

PLANNING A GUIDED DISCUSSION

Planning a guided discussion is basically the same as planning a lecture. The instructor will find the following suggestions helpful in planning a discussion lesson.

Note that these same suggestions include many that are appropriate for planning cooperative learning.

- Select a topic the students can profitably discuss. Unless the students have some knowledge to exchange with each other, they cannot reach the desired learning outcomes by the discussion method. If necessary, make assignments that will give the students an adequate background for discussing the lesson topic.

- Establish a specific lesson objective with desired learning outcomes. Through discussion, the students develop an understanding of the subject by sharing knowledge, experiences, and backgrounds. Consequently, the objective normally is stated at the understanding level of learning. The desired learning outcomes should stem from the objective.

- Conduct adequate research to become familiar with the topic. While researching, the instructor should always be alert for ideas on the best way to tailor a lesson for a particular group of students. Similarly, the instructor can prepare the pre-discussion assignment more effectively while conducting research for the classroom period. During this research process, the instructor should also earmark reading material that appears to be especially appropriate as background material for students. Such material should be well organized and based on fundamentals.

- Organize the main and subordinate points of the lesson in a logical sequence. The guided discussion has three main parts—introduction, discussion, and conclusion. The introduction consists of three elements—attention, motivation, and overview. In the discussion, the instructor should be certain that the main points discussed build logically with the objective. The conclusion consists of the summary, remotivation, and closure. By organizing in this manner, the instructor phrases the questions to help the students obtain a firm grasp of the subject matter and to minimize the possibility of a rambling discussion.

- Plan at least one lead-off question for each desired learning outcome. In preparing questions, the instructor should remember that the purpose is to stimulate discussion, not merely to get answers. The instructor should avoid questions that require only short categorical answers, such as yes or no. Lead-off questions should usually begin with how or why. For example, it is better, to ask "Why does an airplane normally require a longer takeoff run at Denver than at New Orleans?" instead of, "Would you expect an airplane to require a longer takeoff run at Denver or at New Orleans?" Students can answer the second question by merely saying "Denver," but the first question is likely to start a discussion of air density, engine efficiency, and the effect of temperature on performance.

STUDENT PREPARATION FOR A GUIDED DISCUSSION

It is the instructor's responsibility to help students prepare themselves for the discussion. Each student should be encouraged to accept responsibility for contributing to the discussion and benefiting from it. Throughout the time the instructor prepares the students for their discussion, they should be made aware of the lesson objective. In certain instances, the instructor has no opportunity to assign preliminary work and must face the students cold for the first time. In such cases, it is practical and advisable to give the students a brief general survey of the topic during the introduction. Normally students should not be asked to discuss a subject without some background in that subject.

GUIDING A DISCUSSION— INSTRUCTOR TECHNIQUE

The techniques used to guide a discussion require practice and experience. The instructor needs to keep up with the discussion and know where to intervene with questions or redirect the group's focus. The following information provides a framework for successfully conducting the guided discussion.

INTRODUCTION

A guided discussion lesson is introduced in the same manner as the lecture. The introduction should include an attention element, a motivation element, and an overview of key points. To encourage enthusiasm and stimulate discussion, the instructor should create a relaxed, informal atmosphere. Each student should be given the opportunity to discuss the various aspects of the subject, and feel free to do so. Moreover, the student should feel a personal responsibility to contribute. The instructor should try to make the students feel that their ideas and active participation are wanted and needed.

DISCUSSION

The instructor opens the discussion by asking one of the prepared lead-off questions. After asking a question, the instructor should be patient. The students should be given a chance to react. The instructor should have the answer in mind before asking the question, but the students have to think about the question before answering. Sometimes an instructor finds it difficult to be patient while students figure out answers. Keep in mind that it takes time to recall data, determine how to answer, or to think of an example.

The more difficult the question, the more time the students will need to produce an answer. Sometimes students do not understand the question. Whenever the instructor sees puzzled expressions, the question should be rephrased in a slightly different form. The nature of the questions should be determined by the lesson objective and desired learning outcomes.

Once the discussion is underway, the instructor should listen attentively to the ideas, experiences, and examples contributed by the students during the discussion. Remember that during the preparation, the instructor listed some of the anticipated responses that would, if discussed by the students, indicate that they had a firm grasp of the subject. As the discussion proceeds, the instructor may find it necessary to guide the direction, to stimulate the students to explore the subject in greater depth, or to encourage them to discuss the topic in more detail. By using how and why follow-up questions, the instructor should be able to guide the discussion toward the objective of helping students understand the subject.

When it appears the students have discussed the ideas that support this particular part of the lesson, the instructor should summarize what the students have accomplished. In a guided discussion lesson, the interim summary is one of the most effective tools available to the instructor. To bring ideas together and help in transition, an interim summary can be made immediately after the discussion of each learning outcome. This will summarize the ideas developed by the group and show how they relate to, and support, the idea discussed. The interim summary may be omitted after discussing the last learning outcome when it is more expedient for the instructor to present the first part of the conclusion. An interim summary reinforces learning in relation to a specific learning outcome. In addition to its uses as a summary and transitional device, the interim summary may also be used to keep the group on the subject or to divert the discussion to another member.

CONCLUSION

A guided discussion is closed by summarizing the material covered. In the conclusion the instructor should tie together the various points or topics discussed, and show the relationships between the facts brought forth and the practical application of these facts. For example, in concluding a discussion on density altitude, an instructor might give a fairly complete description of an accident which occurred due to a pilot attempting to take off in an overloaded airplane from a short runway at a high-altitude airport on a hot day.

The summary should be succinct, but not incomplete. If the discussion has revealed that certain areas are not understood by one or more members of the group, the instructor should clarify or cover this material again.

DEMONSTRATION–PERFORMANCE METHOD

This method of teaching is based on the simple, yet sound principle that we learn by doing. Students learn physical or mental skills by actually performing those skills under supervision. An individual learns to write by writing, to weld by welding, and to fly an aircraft by actually performing flight maneuvers. Students also learn mental skills, such as speed reading, by this method. Skills requiring the use of tools, machines, and equipment are particularly well suited to this instructional method.

Every instructor should recognize the importance of student performance in the learning process. Early in a lesson that is to include demonstration and performance, the instructor should identify the most important learning outcomes. Next, explain and demonstrate the steps involved in performing the skill being taught. Then, allow students time to practice each step, so they can increase their ability to perform the skill.

The demonstration-performance method is widely used. The science teacher uses it during laboratory periods, the aircraft maintenance instructor uses it in the shop, and the flight instructor uses it in teaching piloting skills. [Figure 5-6]

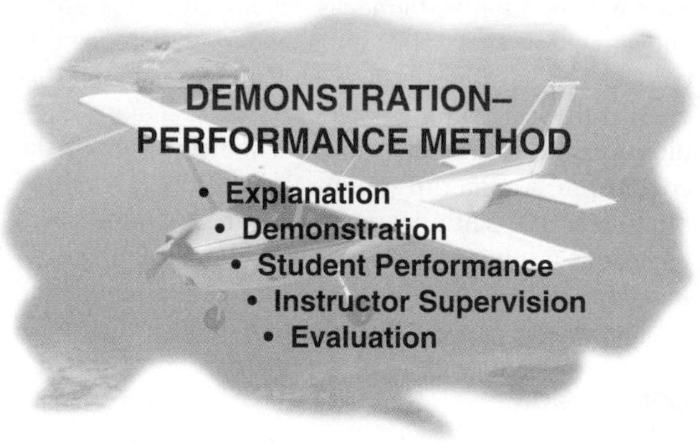

DEMONSTRATION–PERFORMANCE METHOD
- Explanation
- Demonstration
- Student Performance
- Instructor Supervision
- Evaluation

Figure 5-6. The demonstration-performance method of teaching has five essential phases.

EXPLANATION PHASE

Explanations must be clear, pertinent to the objectives of the particular lesson to be presented, and based on the known experience and knowledge of the students. In teaching a skill, the instructor must convey to the students the precise actions they are to perform. In addition to the necessary steps, the instructor should describe the end result of these efforts. Before leaving this phase, the instructor should encourage students to ask questions about any step of the procedure that they do not understand.

DEMONSTRATION PHASE

The instructor must show students the actions necessary to perform a skill. As little extraneous activity as possible should be included in the demonstration if students are to clearly understand that the instructor is accurately performing the actions previously explained. If, due to some unanticipated circumstances the demonstration does not closely conform to the explanation, this deviation should be immediately acknowledged and explained.

STUDENT PERFORMANCE AND INSTRUCTOR SUPERVISION PHASES

Because these two phases, which involve separate actions, are performed concurrently, they are discussed here under a single heading. The first of these phases is the student's performance of the physical or mental skills that have been explained and demonstrated. The second activity is the instructor's supervision.

Student performance requires students to act and do. To learn skills, students must practice. The instructor must, therefore, allot enough time for meaningful student activity. Through doing, students learn to follow correct procedures and to reach established standards. It is important that students be given an opportunity to perform the skill as soon as possible after a demonstration. In flight training, the instructor may allow the student to follow along on the controls during the demonstration of a maneuver. Immediately thereafter, the instructor should have the student attempt to perform the maneuver, coaching as necessary. In another example, students have been performing a task, such as a weight and balance computation, as a group. Prior to terminating the performance phase, they should be allowed to independently complete the task at least once, with supervision and coaching as necessary.

EVALUATION PHASE

In this phase, the instructor judges student performance. The student displays whatever competence has been attained, and the instructor discovers just how well the skill has been learned. To test each student's ability to perform, the instructor requires students to work independently throughout this phase and makes some comment as to how each performed the skill relative to the way it was taught. From this measurement of student achievement, the instructor determines the effectiveness of the instruction.

COMPUTER–BASED TRAINING METHOD

Many new and innovative training technologies are available today. One of the most significant is **computer-based training (CBT)**—the use of the personal computer as a training device. CBT is sometimes called computer-based instruction (CBI). The terms CBT and CBI are synonymous and may be used interchangeably.

The personal computer or PC has revolutionized the way businesses function and promises the same for education and training. The new generation is as comfortable with the PC as they are with the telephone. As a result, educators today are using personal computers as part of educational programs of all types.

For example, major aircraft manufacturers allocate considerable resources to developing CBT programs that are used to teach aircraft systems and maintenance procedures. As a result, the amount of manpower necessary to train aircrews and maintenance technicians on the new equipment has been significantly reduced. End users of the aircraft, such as the major airlines, can purchase the package of CBT materials along with the aircraft in order to accomplish both initial and recurrent training of their personnel. One of the major advantages of CBT is that students can progress at a rate which is comfortable for them. The students also are often able to access the CBT at their own convenience rather than that of the instructor.

Computers are now used for training at many different levels. One example that is very significant is the high technology flight training devices and flight simulators in use by everyone from flight schools to major airlines, as well as the military. Fixed-base operators (FBOs) who offer instrument training may use **personal computer-based aviation training devices (PCATDs)** or **flight training devices (FTDs)** for a portion of the instrument time a pilot needs for the instrument rating. Major airlines have high-level flight simulators that are so realistic that transitioning captains meet all qualifications in the flight simulator. Likewise, military pilots use flight training devices or flight simulators to prepare for flying aircraft, such as the A-10, for which there are no two-seat training versions.

Other common examples of CBT include the computer versions of the test prep study guides which are useful for preparation for the FAA knowledge tests. These programs typically allow the students to select a test, complete the questions, and find out how they did on the test. The student may then conduct a review of questions missed.

Some of the more advanced CBT applications allow students to progress through a series of interactive segments where the presentation varies as a result of their responses. If students wish to learn about a particular area, they do so by clicking the mouse on a particular portion of the screen. They can focus on the area they either need to study or want to study. For example, a maintenance student who wants to find information on the refueling of a specific aircraft could use a CBT program to access the refueling section, and study the entire procedure. If the student wishes to repeat a section or a portion of the section, it can be done at any time merely by clicking on the appropriate icon.

Another term in computer training is **computer assisted instruction**—the use of the computer as a tool. This is much more descriptive of the way instructors should utilize the computer in aviation training. The computer may be used as described in the previous paragraph, as well as in many other ways. However, since aviation training is all encompassing and dynamic, entrusting an entire training program to a computer is not practical. Even airline simulator programs require tailoring and hands-on interaction with a human instructor.

For most aviation training, the computer should be thought of as a very valuable tool to be used to aid the instructor. For example, in teaching aircraft maintenance, CBT programs produced by various aircraft manufacturers can be used to expose students to equipment not normally found at a maintenance school. Another use of computers would be to allow students to review procedures at their own pace while the instructor is involved in hands-on training with other students. The major advantage of CBT over other forms of instructional aid is that it is interactive—the computer responds in different ways, depending on the student's input.

While computers provide many training advantages, they also have limitations. Improper or excessive use of CBT should be avoided. For example, a flight instructor should not rely exclusively on a CBT program on traffic patterns and landings to do the ground instruction for a student pilot, then expect the student to demonstrate patterns and landings in the aircraft. Likewise, it would be improper to expect a maintenance student to be able to safely and properly perform a compression check on an aircraft engine if the only training the student received was via CBT. Computer-based training should not be used by the instructor as stand-alone training any more than a textbook or video. Like video or a textbook, CBT is an aid to the instructor. The instructor must be actively involved with the students when using instructional aids. This involvement should include close supervision, questions, examinations, quizzes, or guided discussions on the subject matter.

In teaching flight students, CBT programs can be used by the instructor as simply another form of reference for students to study. Just as a student can reread a section in a text, a student can review portions of a CBT program until it is understood. The instructor must continue to monitor and evaluate the progress of the student as usual. This is necessary to be certain a student is on track with the training syllabus. At times, instructors may feel that they are doing more one-on-one instruction than in a normal classroom setting, but repetitive forms of teaching may be accomplished by computer.

This actually gives the instructor more time for one-on-one teaching. Remember, the computer has no way of knowing when a student is having difficulty, and it will always be the responsibility of the instructor to provide monitoring and oversight of student progress and to intervene when necessary. [Figure 5-7]

A successful instructor needs to be familiar with as many teaching methods as possible. Although lecture and demonstration-performance may be the methods used most often, being aware of other methods and teaching tools such as guided discussion, cooperative learning, and computer-based instruction will better prepare an instructor for a wide variety of teaching situations.

Obviously the aviation instructor is the key to effective teaching. An experienced instructor's knowledge and skill regarding methods of instruction may be compared to a maintenance technician's toolbox. The instructor's tools are teaching methods. Just as the technician uses some tools more than others, the instructor will use some methods more often than oth-

Figure 5-7. The instructor must continually monitor student performance when using CBT, as with all instructional aids.

ers. As is the case with the technician, there will be times when a less used tool will be the exact tool needed for a particular situation. The instructor's success is determined to a large degree by the ability to organize material and to select and utilize a teaching method appropriate to a particular lesson.

Chapter 6

Critique and Evaluation

The emphasis in previous chapters centered on learning, communicating, and the teaching process. In this chapter, we will discuss the instructor's role as a critic, describe several methods of evaluation, and show how to conduct effective evaluations.

Since every student is different and each learning situation is unique, the actual outcome may not be entirely as expected. The instructor must be able to appraise student performance and convey this information back to the student. This is an informal critique, which is a part of each lesson. The critique should be used by the instructor to summarize and close out one lesson, and prepare the student for the next lesson. Formal evaluations are used periodically throughout a course, and at the end of course, to measure and document whether or not the course objectives have been met.

THE INSTRUCTOR AS A CRITIC

Although this chapter deals with the critique primarily from the standpoint of the instructor in the classroom, the techniques and methods described also apply to the aircraft maintenance instructor in the shop and to the flight instructor in the aircraft or in the briefing area. No skill is more important to an instructor than the ability to analyze, appraise, and judge student performance. The student quite naturally looks to the instructor for guidance, analysis, appraisal, as well as suggestions for improvement and encouragement. This feedback from instructor to student is called a critique.

A critique may be oral, written, or both. It should come immediately after a student's performance, while the details of the performance are easy to recall. An instructor may critique any activity which a student performs or practices to improve skill, proficiency, and learning. A critique may be conducted in private or before the entire class. A critique presented before the entire class can be beneficial to every student in the classroom as well as to the student who performed the exercise or assignment. In this case, however, the instructor should be judicious and avoid embarrassing the student in front of the whole class.

Two common misconceptions about the critique should be corrected at the outset. First, a critique is not a step in the grading process. It is a step in the learning process. Second, a critique is not necessarily negative in content. It considers the good along with the bad, the individual parts, relationships of the individual parts, and the overall performance. A critique can, and usually should, be as varied in content as the performance being critiqued.

PURPOSE OF A CRITIQUE

A critique should provide the students with something constructive upon which they can work or build. It should provide direction and guidance to raise their level of performance. Students must understand the purpose of the critique; otherwise, they will be unlikely to accept the criticism offered and little improvement will result.

A critique also can be used as a tool for reteaching. Although not all critiques lend themselves to reteaching, the instructor should be alert to the possibility and take advantage of the opportunity when it arises. If, for example, several students falter when they reach the same step in a weight-and-balance problem, the instructor might recognize the need for a more detailed explanation, another demonstration of the step, or special emphasis in the critiques of subsequent performance.

CHARACTERISTICS OF AN EFFECTIVE CRITIQUE

In order to provide direction and raise the students' level of performance, the critique must be factual and be aligned with the completion standards of the lesson. This, of course, is because the critique is a part of the learning process. Some of the requirements for an effective critique are shown in figure 6-1.

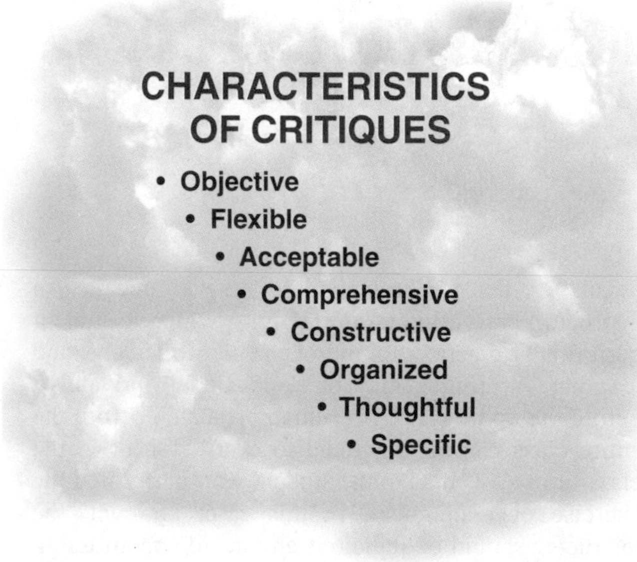

CHARACTERISTICS OF CRITIQUES

- Objective
- Flexible
- Acceptable
- Comprehensive
- Constructive
- Organized
- Thoughtful
- Specific

Figure 6-1. Effective critiques share a number of characteristics.

OBJECTIVE

The effective critique is focused on student performance. It should be objective, and not reflect the personal opinions, likes, dislikes, and biases of the instructor. For example, if a student accomplishes a complicated flight planning problem, it would hardly be fair for the instructor to criticize the student's personality traits unless they interfered with the performance itself. Instructors sometimes permit their judgment to be influenced by their general impression of the student, favorable or unfavorable. Sympathy or over-identification with a student, to such a degree that it influences objectivity, is known as "halo error." A conflict of personalities can also distort an opinion. If a critique is to be objective, it must be honest; it must be based on the performance as it was, not as it could have been, or as the instructor and student wished that it had been.

FLEXIBLE

The instructor needs to examine the entire performance of a student and the context in which it is accom-

plished. Sometimes a good student will turn in a poor performance and a poor student will turn in a good one. A friendly student may suddenly become hostile, or a hostile student may suddenly become friendly and cooperative. The instructor must fit the tone, technique, and content of the critique to the occasion, as well as the student. A critique should be designed and executed so that the instructor can allow for variables. Again and again, the instructor is faced with the problem of what to say, what to omit, what to stress, and what to minimize. The challenge of the critique for an instructor is to determine what to say at the proper moment. An effective critique is one that is flexible enough to satisfy the requirements of the moment.

ACCEPTABLE

Before students willingly accept their instructor's criticism, they must first accept the instructor. Students must have confidence in the instructor's qualifications, teaching ability, sincerity, competence, and authority. Usually, instructors have the opportunity to establish themselves with their students before the formal critiquing situation arises. If this is not the case, however, the instructor's manner, attitude, and readily apparent familiarity with the subject at hand must serve instead. Critiques do not have to be all sweetness and light, nor do they have to curry favor with students. If a critique is presented fairly, with authority, conviction, sincerity, and from a position of recognizable competence, the student probably will accept it as such. Instructors should not rely on their position to make a critique more acceptable to their students. While such factors usually operate to the instructor's advantage, acceptability depends on more active and demonstrable qualities than on simply being the instructor.

COMPREHENSIVE

A comprehensive critique is not necessarily a long one, nor must it treat every aspect of the performance in detail. The instructor must decide whether the greater benefit will come from a discussion of a few major points or a number of minor points. The instructor might critique what most needs improvement, or only what the student can reasonably be expected to improve. An effective critique covers strengths as well as weaknesses. How to balance the two is a decision that only the instructor can make. To dwell on the excellence of a performance while neglecting the portion that should be improved is a disservice to the student.

CONSTRUCTIVE

A critique is pointless unless the student profits from it. Praise for praise's sake is of no value, but praise should be included to show how to capitalize on things that are done well. The praise can then be used to inspire the student to improve in areas of lesser accomplishment. By the same token, it is not enough to identify a fault or weakness. The instructor should give positive guidance for correcting the fault and strengthening the weakness. Negative criticism that does not point toward improvement or a higher level of performance should be omitted from a critique altogether.

ORGANIZED

Unless a critique follows some pattern of organization, a series of otherwise valid comments may lose their impact. Almost any pattern is acceptable as long as it is logical and makes sense to the student as well as to the instructor. An effective organizational pattern might be the sequence of the performance itself. Sometimes a critique can profitably begin at the point where a demonstration failed and work backward through the steps that led to the failure. A success can be analyzed in similar fashion. Sometimes a defect is so glaring or the consequences so great that it overshadows the rest of the performance and can serve as the core of a critique. Breaking the whole into parts or building the parts into a whole has strong possibilities. Whatever the organization of the critique, the instructor should be flexible enough to change so the student can follow and understand it.

THOUGHTFUL

An effective critique reflects the instructor's thoughtfulness toward the student's need for self-esteem, recognition, and approval from others. The instructor should never minimize the inherent dignity and importance of the individual. Ridicule, anger, or fun at the expense of the student have no place in a critique. On occasion, an instructor may need to criticize a student in private. In some cases, discretion may rule out any criticism at all. For example, criticism does not help a student whose performance is impaired by a physiological defect. While being straightforward and honest, the instructor should always respect the student's personal feelings.

SPECIFIC

The instructor's comments and recommendations should be specific, rather than general. The student needs to focus on something concrete. A statement such as, "Your second weld wasn't as good as your first," has little constructive value. Instead, tell the student why it was not as good and how to improve the weld. If the instructor has a clear, well-founded, and supportable idea in mind, it should be expressed with firmness and authority in terms that cannot be misunderstood. Students cannot act on recommendations unless they know specifically what the recommendations are. At the conclusion of a critique, students should have no doubt what they did well and what they did poorly and, most importantly, specifically how they can improve.

METHODS OF CRITIQUE

The critique of student performance is always the instructor's responsibility, and it can never be delegated in its entirety. The instructor can add interest and variety to the criticism through the use of imagination and by drawing on the talents, ideas, and opinions of others. There are several useful methods of conducting a critique.

INSTRUCTOR/STUDENT CRITIQUE

The instructor leads a group discussion in which members of the class are invited to offer criticism of a performance. This method should be controlled carefully and directed with a firm purpose. It should be organized and not allowed to degenerate into a random free-for-all.

STUDENT-LED CRITIQUE

The instructor asks a student to lead the critique. The instructor can specify the pattern of organization and the techniques or can leave it to the discretion of the student leader. Because of the inexperience of the participants in the lesson area, student-led critiques may not be efficient, but they can generate student interest and learning and, on the whole, be effective.

SMALL GROUP CRITIQUE

For this method, the class is divided into small groups and each group is assigned a specific area to analyze. These groups must present their findings to the class. Frequently, it is desirable for the instructor to furnish the criteria and guidelines. The combined reports from the groups can result in a comprehensive critique.

INDIVIDUAL STUDENT CRITIQUE BY ANOTHER STUDENT

The instructor also may require another student to present the entire critique. A variation is for the instructor to ask a number of students questions about the manner and quality of performance. Discussion of the performance, and of the critique, can often allow the group to accept more ownership of the ideas expressed. As with all critiques incorporating student participation, it is important that the instructor maintain firm control over the process.

SELF-CRITIQUE

A student is required to critique personal performance. Like all other methods, a self-critique must be controlled and supervised by the instructor. Whatever the methods employed, the instructor must not leave controversial issues unresolved, nor erroneous impressions uncorrected. The instructor must make allowances for the student's relative inexperience. Normally, the instructor should reserve time at the end of the student critique to cover those areas that might have been omitted, not emphasized sufficiently, or considered worth repeating.

WRITTEN CRITIQUE

Written critiques have three advantages. First, the instructor can devote more time and thought to it than to an oral critique in the classroom. Second, the students can keep written critiques and refer to them whenever they wish. Third, when the instructor requires all the students to write a critique of a performance, the student-performer has the permanent record of the suggestions, recommendations, and opinions of all the other students. The disadvantage of a written critique is that other members of the class do not benefit.

GROUND RULES FOR CRITIQUING

There are a number of rules and techniques to keep in mind when conducting a critique. The following list can be applied, regardless of the type of critiquing activity.

- Except in rare and unusual instances, do not extend the critique beyond its scheduled time and into the time allotted for other activities. A point of diminishing returns can be reached quickly.

- Avoid trying to cover too much. A few well-made points will usually be more beneficial than a large number of points that are not developed adequately.

- Allow time for a summary of the critique to reemphasize the most important things a student should remember.

- Avoid dogmatic or absolute statements, remembering that most rules have exceptions.

- Avoid controversies with the class, and do not get into the delicate position of taking sides with group factions.

- Never allow yourself to be maneuvered into the unpleasant position of defending criticism. If the criticism is honest, objective, constructive, and comprehensive, no defense should be necessary.

- If part of the critique is written, make certain that it is consistent with the oral portion.

Although, at times, a critique may seem like an evaluation, it is not. Both student and instructor should consider it as an integral part of the lesson. It normally is a wrap-up of the lesson. A good critique closes the chapter on the lesson and sets the stage for the next lesson. Since the critique is a part of the lesson, it should be limited to what transpired during that lesson. In contrast, an evaluation is more far reaching than a critique because it normally covers several lessons.

EVALUATION

Whenever learning takes place, the result is a definable, observable, measurable change in behavior. The purpose of an evaluation is to determine how a student is progressing in the course. Evaluation is concerned with defining, observing, and measuring or judging this new behavior. Evaluation normally occurs before, during, and after instruction; it is an integral part of the learning process. During instruction, some sort of evaluation is essential to determine what the students are learning and how well they are learning it. The instructor's evaluation may be the result of observations of the students' overall performance, or it may be accomplished as either a spontaneous or planned evaluation, such as an oral quiz, written test, or skill performance test. [Figure 6-2]

EVALUATION

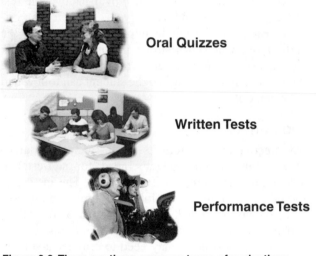

Oral Quizzes

Written Tests

Performance Tests

Figure 6-2. There are three common types of evaluations that instructors may use.

ORAL QUIZZES

The most used means of evaluation is the direct or indirect oral questioning of students by the instructor. Questions may be loosely classified as fact questions and thought questions. The answer to a fact question is based on memory or recall. This type of question usually concerns who, what, when, and where. Thought questions usually involve why or how, and require the student to combine knowledge of facts with an ability to analyze situations, solve problems, and arrive at conclusions. Proper quizzing by the instructor can have a number of desirable results.

- Reveals the effectiveness of the instructor's training procedures.

- Checks the student's retention of what has been learned.

- Reviews material already covered by the student.

- Can be used to retain the student's interest and stimulate thinking.

- Emphasizes the important points of training.

- Identifies points that need more emphasis.

- Checks the student's comprehension of what has been learned.

- Promotes active student participation, which is important to effective learning.

CHARACTERISTICS OF EFFECTIVE QUESTIONS

An effective oral quiz requires some preparation. The instructor should devise and write pertinent questions in advance. One method is to place them in the lesson plan. Prepared questions merely serve as a framework, and as the lesson progresses, should be supplemented by such impromptu questions as the instructor considers appropriate. Usually an effective question has only one correct answer. This is always true of good questions of the objective type and generally will be true of all good questions, although the one correct answer to a thought question may sometimes be expressed in a variety of ways. To be effective, questions must apply to the subject of instruction. Unless the question pertains strictly to the particular training being conducted, it serves only to confuse the students and divert their thoughts to an unrelated subject. An effective question should be brief and concise, but also clear and definite. Enough words must be used to establish the conditions or significant circumstances exactly, so that instructor and students will have the same mental picture.

To be effective, questions must be adapted to the ability, experience, and stage of training of the students. Effective questions center on only one idea. A single question should be limited to who, what, when, where, how, or why, not a combination. Effective questions must present a challenge to the students. Questions of suitable difficulty serve to stimulate learning. Effective questions demand and deserve the use of proper English.

TYPES OF QUESTIONS TO AVOID

Asking, "Do you understand?" or "Do you have any questions?" has no place in effective quizzing. Assurance by the students that they do understand or that they have no questions provides no evidence of their comprehension, or that they even know the subject under discussion. Other typical types of questions that must be avoided are provided in the following list.

- **Puzzle**— "What is the first action you should take if a conventional gear airplane with a weak right brake is swerving left in a right crosswind during a full-flap, power-on wheel landing?"

- **Oversize**— "What do you do before beginning an engine overhaul?"

- **Toss-up**— "In an emergency, should you squawk 7700 or pick a landing spot?"

- **Bewilderment**— "In reading the altimeter—you know you set a sensitive altimeter for the nearest station pressure—if you take temperature into account, as when flying from a cold air mass through a warm front, what precaution should you take when in a mountainous area?"

- **Trick questions**—These questions will cause the students to develop the feeling that they are engaged in a battle of wits with the instructor, and the whole significance of the subject of the instruction involved will be lost.

An example of a trick question would be where the alternatives are 1, 2, 3, and 4, but they are placed in the following form.

A. 4
B. 3
C. 2
D. 1

The only reason for reversing the order of choices is to trick the student to inadvertently answering incorrectly. Instructors often justify use of trick questions as testing for attention to detail. If attention to detail is an objective, detailed construction of alternatives is preferable to trick questions.

- **Irrelevant questions**—The teaching process must be an orderly procedure of building one block of learning upon another in logical progression, until a desired goal is reached. Diversions, which introduce unrelated facts and thoughts, will only obscure this orderly process and slow the student's progress. Answers to unrelated questions are not helpful in evaluating the student's knowledge of the subject at hand. An example of an irrelevant question would be to ask a question about tire inflation during a test on the timing of magnetos.

ANSWERING QUESTIONS FROM STUDENTS

Responses to student questions must also conform with certain considerations if answering is to be an effective teaching method. The question must be clearly understood by the instructor before an answer is attempted. The instructor should display interest in the student's question and frame an answer that is as direct and accurate as possible. After the instructor completes a response, it should be determined whether or not the student's request for information has been completely answered, and if the student is satisfied with the answer.

Sometimes it may be unwise to introduce the more complicated or advanced considerations necessary to completely answer a student's question at the current point in training. In this case, the instructor should carefully explain to the student that the question was good and pertinent, but that a detailed answer would, at this time, unnecessarily complicate the learning tasks. The instructor should advise the student to reintroduce the question later at the appropriate point in training, if it does not become resolved in the normal course of instruction.

Occasionally, a student asks a question that the instructor cannot answer. In such cases, the instructor should freely admit not knowing the answer, but should promise to get the answer or, if practicable, offer to help the student look it up in available references.

In all quizzing conducted as a portion of the instruction process, "yes" and "no" answers should be avoided. Questions should be framed so that the desired answers are specific and factual. Questions should also be constructed to avoid one-word answers, since such answers might be the product of a good guess and not be truly representative of student learning or ability. If a one-word answer is received, the instructor should follow up with additional questions to get a better idea of the student's comprehension of the material.

WRITTEN TESTS

As evaluation devices, written tests are only as good as the knowledge and proficiency of the test writer. This section is intended to provide the aviation instructor with only the basic concepts of written test design. There are many excellent publications available to the aviation instructor on test administration, test scoring, grade assignment, whole test analysis, and test item analysis. Refer to the reference section at the end of this handbook for testing and test writing publications.

CHARACTERISTICS OF A GOOD TEST

A **test** is a set of questions, problems, or exercises for determining whether a person has a particular knowledge or skill. A test can consist of just one test item, but it usually consists of a number of test items. A **test item** measures a single objective and calls for a single response. The test could be as simple as the correct answer to an essay question or as complex as completing a knowledge or practical test. Regardless of the underlying purpose, effective tests share certain characteristics. [Figure 6-3]

Reliability is the degree to which test results are consistent with repeated measurements. If identical measurements are obtained every time a certain instrument is applied to a certain dimension, the instrument is considered reliable. An unreliable instrument cannot be depended upon to yield consistent results. An altimeter

CHARACTERISTICS OF A GOOD TEST

- Reliability
- Validity
- Usability
- Objectivity
- Comprehensiveness
- Discrimination

Figure 6-3. Effective tests have six primary characteristics.

that has worn moving parts, a steel tape that expands and contracts with temperature changes, or cloth tapes that are affected by humidity cannot be expected to yield reliable measurements. While no instrument is perfectly reliable, it is obvious that some instruments are more reliable than others. For example, a laboratory balance is more reliable than a bathroom scale for measuring weight.

The reliability of an instrument can be estimated by numerous measurements of the same object. For example, a rough measure of the reliability of a thermometer can be obtained by taking several, consecutive readings of the temperature of a fluid held at a constant temperature. Except for the errors made by the person taking the readings, the difference between the highest and lowest readings can be considered a range of unreliability in the thermometer.

Reliability has the same meaning whether applied to written tests or to balances, thermometers, and altimeters. The reliability of a written test is judged by whether it gives consistent measurement to a particular individual or group. Measuring the reliability of a written test is, however, not as straightforward as it is for the measuring devices we have discussed. In an educational setting, knowledge, skills, and understanding do not remain constant. Students can be expected to improve their scores between attempts at taking the same test because the first test serves as a learning device. The student gains new knowledge and understanding. If a written test consistently rates the members of a group in a certain rank order, the reliability is probably acceptable, even though the scores of the students have increased overall.

Validity is the extent to which a test measures what it is supposed to measure. If a maintenance technician intends to measure the diameter of a bearing with a micrometer, it must be determined that the contacting surfaces of the bearing and the micrometer are free of grease and dirt. Otherwise, the measurement will include the diameter of the bearing and the thickness of the extraneous matter, and it will be invalid.

A test used in educational evaluation follows the same principles of validity. Evaluations used in the classroom are valid only to the extent that they measure achievement of the objectives of instruction.

A rough estimate of the content validity of a classroom test may be obtained from the judgments of several competent instructors. To estimate validity, they should read the test critically and consider its content relative to the stated objectives of the instruction. Items that do not pertain directly to the objectives of the course should be modified or eliminated. Validity is the most important consideration in test evaluation. The instructor must carefully consider whether the test actually measures what it is supposed to measure.

Usability refers to the functionality of tests. A usable written test is easy to give if it is printed in a type size large enough for the students to read easily. The wording of both the directions for taking the test and of the test items themselves needs to be clear and concise. Graphics, charts, and illustrations, which are appropriate to the test items, must be clearly drawn, and the test should be easily graded.

Objectivity describes singleness of scoring of a test; it does not reflect the biases of the person grading the test. Later in the discussion, you will find that supply-type test items are very difficult to grade with complete objectivity. An example of this is essay questions. It is nearly impossible to prevent an instructor's own knowledge and experience in the subject area, writing style, or grammar from affecting the grade awarded. Selection-type test items, such as true-false or multiple-choice, are much easier to grade objectively.

Comprehensiveness is the degree to which a test measures the overall objectives. Suppose, for example, an aircraft maintenance technician wants to measure the compression of an aircraft engine. Measuring the compression on a single cylinder would not provide an indication of the entire engine. Only by measuring the compression of every cylinder would the test be comprehensive enough to indicate the compression condition of the engine.

In classroom evaluation, a test must sample an appropriate cross-section of the objectives of instruction. The comprehensiveness of a test is the degree to which the scope of the course objectives is tested. Sometimes it will not be possible to have test questions measuring all objectives of the course. At these times, the evaluation is but a sample of the entire course. Just as the owner of the wheat has to select samples of wheat from scattered positions in the car, the instructor has to make certain that the evaluation includes a representative and comprehensive sampling of the objectives of the course. In both instances, the evaluators must deliberately take comprehensive samples in order to realistically measure the overall achievement of the course objectives.

Discrimination is the degree to which a test distinguishes the difference between students. For example, a machinist wishes to measure six bearings that are slightly graduated in size. If a ruler is used to measure the diameters of the bearings, little difference will be found between the smallest bearing and the second smallest one. If the machinist compares the third bearing with the first bearing, slight differences in size might be detected, but the ruler could not be depended on for accurately assorting the six bearings. However, if the machinist measures with a micrometer, which can measure very fine graduations, the diameters of the first and second bearing, the second and third bearing, and so on, can be easily differentiated.

In classroom evaluation, a test must be able to measure small differences in achievement in relation to the objectives of the course. When a test is constructed to identify the difference in the achievement of students, it has three features.

- There is a wide range of scores.

- All levels of difficulty are included.

- Each item distinguishes between the students who are low and those who are high in achievement of the course objectives.

TEST DEVELOPMENT

When testing aviation students, the instructor is usually concerned more with criterion-referenced testing than norm-referenced testing. **Norm-referenced testing** measures a student's performance against the performance of other students. **Criterion-referenced testing** evaluates each student's performance against a carefully written, measurable, standard or criterion. There is little or no concern about the student's performance in relation to the performance of other students. The FAA knowledge and practical tests for pilots and aircraft maintenance technicians are all criterion referenced because in aviation training, it is necessary to measure student performance against a high standard of proficiency consistent with safety.

The aviation instructor constructs tests to measure progress toward the standards that will eventually be measured at the conclusion of the training. For example, during an early stage of flight training, the flight instructor must administer a presolo written exam to student pilots. Since tests are an integral part of the instructional process, it is important for the aviation instructor to be well informed about recommended testing procedures.

Aviation instructors can follow a four-step process when developing a test. This process is useful for tests that apply to the cognitive and affective domains of learning, and also can be used for skill testing in the psychomotor domain. The development process for criterion-referenced tests follows a general-to-specific pattern.[Figure 6-4]

TEST DEVELOPMENT STEPS

- Determine Level-of-Learning Objectives

- List Indicators/Samples of Desired Behavior

- Establish Criterion Objectives

- Develop Criterion-Referenced Test Items

Figure 6-4. There are four steps to test development.

DETERMINE LEVEL-OF-LEARNING OBJECTIVES

The first step in developing a test is to state the individual objectives as general, level-of-learning objectives. The objectives should measure one of the learning levels of the cognitive, affective, or psychomotor domains described in Chapter 1. The levels of cognitive learning include knowledge, comprehension, application, analysis, synthesis, and evaluation. For the comprehension or understanding level, an objective could be stated as, "Describe how to perform a compression test on an aircraft reciprocating engine." This objective requires a student to explain how to do a compression test, but not necessarily perform a compression test (application level). Further, the student would not be expected to compare the results of compression tests on different engines (analysis level), design a compression test for a different type of engine (synthesis or correlation level), or interpret the results of the compression test (evaluation level). A general level-of-learning objective is a good starting point for developing a test because it defines the scope of the learning task.

LIST INDICATORS/SAMPLES OF DESIRED BEHAVIOR

The second step is to list the indicators or samples of behavior that will give the best indication of the achievement of the objective. Some level-of-learning objectives often cannot be directly measured. As a result, behaviors that can be measured are selected in order to give the best evidence of learning. For example, if the instructor is expecting the student to display the comprehension level-of-learning on compression testing, some of the specific test question answers should describe appropriate tools and equipment, the proper equipment setup, appropriate safety procedures, and the steps used to obtain compression readings. The overall test must be comprehensive enough to give a true representation of the learning to be measured. It is not usually feasible to measure every aspect of a level-of-learning objective, but by carefully choosing samples of behavior, the instructor can obtain adequate evidence of learning.

ESTABLISH CRITERION OBJECTIVES

The next step in the test development process is to define criterion (performance-based) objectives. In addition to the behavior expected, criterion objectives state the conditions under which the behavior is to be performed and the criteria that must be met. If the instructor developed performance-based objectives during the creation of lesson plans, criterion objectives have already been formulated. The criterion objective provides the framework for developing the test items used to measure the level-of-learning objectives. In the compression test example, a criterion objective to measure the comprehension level of learning might be stated as, "The student will demonstrate comprehension of compression test procedures for reciprocating aircraft engines by completing a quiz with a minimum passing score of 70%."

DEVELOP CRITERION-REFERENCED TEST ITEMS

The last step is to develop criterion-referenced test items. The actual development of the test questions is covered in the remainder of this chapter. While developing questions, the instructor should attempt to measure the behaviors described in the criterion objective(s). The questions in the exam for the compression test example should cover all of the areas necessary to give evidence of comprehending the procedure. The results of the test (questions missed) identify areas that were not adequately covered.

Performance-based objectives serve as a reference for the development of test items. If the test is the presolo knowledge test, the objectives are for the student to comprehend the regulations, the local area, the aircraft type, and the procedures to be used. The test should measure the student's knowledge in these specific areas. Individual instructors should develop their own tests to measure the progress of their students. If the test is to measure the readiness of a student to take a knowledge test, it should be based on the objectives of all the lessons the student has received.

Another source of test items includes FAA knowledge test guides for a particular knowledge test. These sample questions are designed to measure the level-of-learning desired for pilots or aviation maintenance technicians. As a result, they are a good source of example questions to be used in measuring a student's preparedness to take the knowledge test.

However, care must be taken not to teach questions to ensure the student does not merely memorize answers or the letter of the answer. When using questions from any source, whether from a publisher or developed by individual instructors, periodically revising the questions used and changing the letters and positions of the answers will encourage learning the material rather than learning the test.

WRITTEN TEST ITEMS

Written questions include two general categories, the supply-type item and the selection-type item. **Supply-type test items** require the student to furnish a response in the form of a word, sentence, or paragraph. **Selection-type test items** require the student to select from two or more alternatives. See Appendix A for sample test items.

SUPPLY TYPE

The supply-type item may be required where a selection-type cannot be devised to properly measure student knowledge. The supply-type requires the students to organize their knowledge. It demands an ability to express ideas that is not required for a selection-type item. This type item is valuable in measuring the students' generalized understanding of a subject.

On the other hand, a supply-type item may evaluate the students' ability to write rather than their specific knowledge of the subject matter. It places a premium on neatness and penmanship. The main disadvantage of supply-type tests is that they cannot be graded with uniformity. There is no assurance that the grade assigned is the grade deserved by the student. The same test graded by different instructors would probably be assigned different scores. Even the same test graded by the same instructor on consecutive days might be assigned altogether different scores. Still another disadvantage of a supply-type test is the time required by the student to complete it and the time required by the instructor to grade it. Everything considered, the disadvantages of the supply-type test appear to exceed the advantages to such an extent that instructors prefer to use the selection-type test. It should be noted that although selection-type tests are best in many cases, there are times where the supply-type is desirable. This would

be when there is a need to thoroughly determine the knowledge of a person in a particular subject area. An example of this would be the presolo knowledge exam where it would be difficult to determine knowledge of procedures strictly with selection-type test items.

SELECTION TYPE

Written tests made up of selection-type items are highly objective. That is, the results of such a test would be graded the same regardless of the student taking the test or the person grading it. Tests that include only selection-type items make it possible to directly compare student accomplishment. For example, it is possible to compare the performance of students within one class to students in a different class, or students under one instructor with those under another instructor. By using selection-type items, the instructor can test on many more areas of knowledge in a given time than could be done by requiring the student to supply written responses. This increase in comprehensiveness can be expected to increase validity and discrimination. Another advantage is that selection-type tests are well adapted to statistical item analysis.

True-False

The **true-false test item** consists of a statement followed by an opportunity for the student to determine whether the statement is true or false. This item-type, with all its variations, has a wide range of usage. It is well adapted for testing knowledge of facts and details, especially when there are only two possible answers. The chief disadvantage is that true-false questions create the greatest probability of guessing.

True-false test items are probably used and misused more than any other selection-type item. Frequently, instructors select sentences more or less at random from textual material and make half of them false by inserting negatives. When tests are constructed in this way, the principal attribute being measured is rote memory rather than knowledge of the subject. Such test construction has aroused antagonism toward selection tests in general and true-false questions in particular. It has also decreased the validity of educational evaluations. Some of the principles that should be followed in the construction of true-false items are contained in the accompanying list.

- Include only one idea in each statement.

- Use original statements rather than verbatim text.

- Statements should be entirely true or entirely false.

- Avoid the unnecessary use of negatives. They tend to confuse the reader.

- If negatives must be used, underline or otherwise emphasize the negative.

- Avoid involved statements. Keep wording and sentence structure as simple as possible. Make statements both definite and clear.

- Avoid the use of ambiguous words and terms (some, any, generally, most times, etc.)

- Whenever possible, use terms which mean the same thing to all students.

- Avoid absolutes (all, every, only, no, never, etc.) These words are known as **determiners** and provide clues to the correct answer. Since unequivocally true or false statements are rare, statements containing absolutes are usually false.

- Avoid patterns in the sequence of correct responses because students can often identify the patterns. Instructors sometimes deliberately use patterns to make hand scoring easier. This is a poor practice.

- Make statements brief and about the same length. Some instructors unconsciously make true statements longer than false ones. Students are quick to take advantage of this tendency.

- If a statement is controversial (sources have differing information), the source of the statement should be listed.

Multiple-Choice

A **multiple-choice** test item consists of two parts; the **stem** which includes the question, statement, or problem, and a list of alternatives or **responses**. Incorrect answers are called **distractors**. When properly devised and constructed, multiple-choice items offer several advantages that make this type more widely used and versatile than either the matching or the true-false items. [Figure 6-5]

Multiple-choice test questions may be used to determine student achievement, ranging from acquisition of facts to understanding, reasoning, and ability to apply what has been learned. It is appropriate to use when the question, statement, or problem has the following characteristics.

- Has a built-in and unique solution such as a specific application of laws or principles.

- May be clearly limited by the wording of the item so that the student must choose the best of several offered solutions rather than a universal solution.

- Is such that several options are plausible, or even scientifically accurate, but the student may be asked to identify the one most pertinent.

- Has several pertinent solutions, and the student may be asked to identify the most appropriate solution.

Three major difficulties are common in the construction of multiple-choice test items. One is the development of a question or an item stem that must be expressed clearly and without ambiguity. Another requirement is that the statement of an answer or correct response cannot be refuted. Finally, the distractors must be written in such a way that they will be attractive to those students who do not possess the knowledge or understanding necessary to recognize the keyed response.

As mentioned previously, a multiple-choice item stem may take several basic forms.

- It may be a direct question followed by several possible answers.

- It may be an incomplete sentence followed by several possible phrases that complete the sentence.

- It may be a stated problem based on an accompanying graph, diagram, or other artwork followed by the correct response and the distractors.

The student may be asked to select the one choice which is the correct answer or completion, the one choice that is an incorrect answer or completion, or the one choice which is best of the answers presented in the test item. Beginning test writers find it easier to write items in the question form. In general, the form with the options as answers to a question is preferable to the form that uses an incomplete statement as the stem. It is more easily phrased and is more natural for the student to read. Less likely to contain ambiguities,

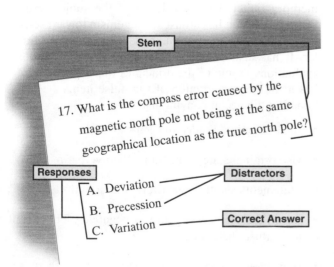

Figure 6-5. Sample multiple-choice test item.

it usually results in more similarity between the options and gives fewer clues to the correct response. Samples of multiple-choice questions can be found in Appendix A.

When multiple-choice questions are used, three or four alternatives are generally provided. It is usually difficult to construct more than four convincing responses; that is, responses which appear to be correct to a person who has not mastered the subject matter.

Students are not supposed to guess the correct option; they should select an alternative only if they know it is correct. Therefore it is considered ethical to mislead the unsuccessful student into selecting an incorrect alternative. An effective and valid means of diverting the student from the correct response is to use common student errors as distractors. For example, if writing a question on the conversion of degrees Celsius to degrees Fahrenheit, providing alternatives derived by using incorrect formulas would be logical, since using the wrong formula is a common student error.

Items intended to measure the knowledge level of learning should have only one correct alternative; all other alternatives should be clearly incorrect. When items are to measure achievement at a higher level of learning, some or all of the alternatives should be acceptable responses—but one should be clearly better than the others. In either case, the instructions given should direct the student to select the best alternative. Some of the principles that should be followed in the construction of multiple-choice items are contained in the following list.

• Make each item independent of every other item in the test. Do not permit one question to reveal, or depend on, the correct answer to another question. If items are to be interrelated, it becomes impossible to pinpoint specific deficiencies in either students or instructors.

• Design questions that call for essential knowledge rather than for abstract background knowledge or unimportant facts.

• State each question in language appropriate to the students. Failure to do so can result in decreased validity of the test, since the ability to understand the language will be measured as well as the subject-matter knowledge or achievement.

• Include sketches, diagrams, or pictures when they can present a situation more vividly than words. They generally speed the testing process, add interest, and help to avoid reading difficulties and technical language. A common criticism of written tests is the reliance placed on the reading ability of the student. The validity of the examination may be decreased unless reading ability is an objective of the course or test.

• When a negative is used, emphasize the negative word or phrase by underlining, bold facing, italicyzing, or printing in a different color. A student who is pressed for time may identify the wrong response simply because the negative form is overlooked. To whatever extent this occurs, the validity of the test is decreased.

• Questions containing double negatives invariably cause confusion. If a word, such as "not" or "false," appears in the stem, avoid using another negative word in the stem or any of the responses.

• Trick questions, unimportant details, ambiguities, and leading questions should be avoided, since they do not contribute to effective evaluation in any way. Instead, they tend to confuse and antagonize the student. Instructors often justify use of trick questions as testing for attention to detail. If attention to detail is an objective, detailed construction of alternatives is preferable to trick questions.

Stems

In preparing the stem of a multiple-choice item, the following general principles should be applied. These principles will help to ensure that the test item is valid. [Figure 6-6]

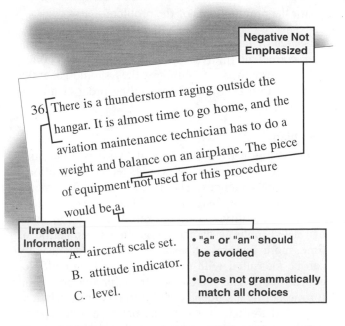

Figure 6-6. This is an example of a multiple-choice question with a poorly written stem.

- The stem of the question should clearly present the central problem or idea. The function of the stem is to set the stage for the alternatives that follow.

- The stem should contain only material relevant to its solution, unless the selection of what is relevant is part of the problem.

- The stem should be worded in such a way that it does not give away the correct response. Avoid the use of determiners such as clue words or phrases.

- Put everything that pertains to all alternatives in the stem of the item. This helps to avoid repetitious alternatives and saves time.

- Generally avoid using "a" or "an" at the end of the stem. They may give away the correct choice. Every alternative should grammatically fit with the stem of the item.

Alternatives

The alternatives in a multiple-choice test item are as important as the stem. They should be formulated with care; simply being incorrect should not be the only criterion for the distracting alternatives. Some distractors which can be used are listed below.

- An incorrect response which is related to the situation and which sounds convincing to the untutored.

- A common misconception.

- A statement which is true but does not satisfy the requirements of the problem.

- A statement which is either too broad or too narrow for the requirements of the problem.

Research of instructor-made tests reveals that, in general, correct alternatives are longer than incorrect ones. When alternatives are numbers, they should generally be listed in ascending or descending order of magnitude or length.

Matching

A **matching** test item consists of two lists which may include a combination of words, terms, illustrations, phrases, or sentences. The student is asked to match alternatives in one list with related alternatives in a second list. In reality, matching exercises are a collection of related multiple-choice items. In a given period of time, more samples of a student's knowledge usually can be measured with matching rather than multiple-choice items. The matching item is particularly good for measuring a student's ability to recognize relationships and to make associations between terms, parts, words, phrases, clauses, or symbols listed in one column with related items in another column. Matching

reduces the probability of guessing correct responses, especially if alternatives may be used more than once. The testing time can also be used more efficiently. Some of the principles that should be followed in the construction of matching items are included below.

- Give specific and complete instructions. Do not make the student guess what is required.

- Test only essential information; never test unimportant details.

- Use closely related materials throughout an item. If students can divide the alternatives into distinct groups, the item is reduced to several multiple-choice items with few alternatives, and the possibility of guessing is distinctly increased.

- Make all alternatives credible responses to each element in the first column, wherever possible, to minimize guessing by elimination.

- Use language the student can understand. By reducing language barriers, both the validity and reliability of the test will be improved.

- Arrange the alternatives in some sensible order. An alphabetical arrangement is common.

Matching-type test items are either equal column or unequal column. An equal column test item has the same number of alternatives in each column. When using this form, always provide for some items in the response column to be used more than once, or not at all, to preclude guessing by elimination. Unequal column type test items have more alternatives in the second column than in the first and are generally preferable to equal columns. Samples of the two forms of matching-item questions can be found in Appendix A.

DEVELOPING A TEST ITEM BANK

Developing a test item bank is one of the instructor's most difficult tasks. Besides requiring considerable time and effort, this task demands a mastery of the subject, an ability to write clearly, and an ability to visualize realistic situations for use in developing problems. Because it is so difficult to develop good test items, a semipermanent record of items that have been developed is desirable. One way of preserving test items is to record the test item, along with the analysis of each question, on a set of cards. If questions are maintained on a computer, provisions could be made to include appropriate analysis gathered, thus creating a useful database. In either case, a pool of test questions is created after a large group of questions has been assembled. As long as precautions are taken to safeguard the security of items in the pool, the existence of the pool lightens the instructor's burden of continuously preparing new items. [Figure 6-7]

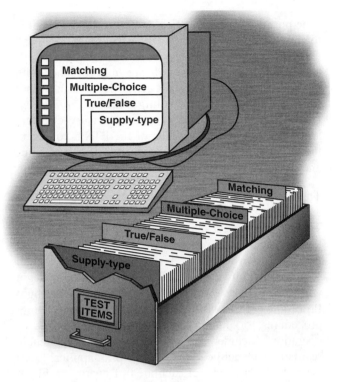

Figure 6-7. A bank of test items makes it easier to construct new tests.

PRINCIPLES TO FOLLOW

Regardless of item type or form, the following principles should be followed in writing new items. The list also applies to reviewing and revising existing items.

• Each item should test a concept or idea that is important for the student to know, understand, or be able to apply.

• Each item must be stated so that everyone who is competent in the subject-matter area would agree on the correct response.

• Each item should be stated in language the student will understand.

• The wording of the item should be simple, direct, and free of ambiguity. The wording should be edited for brevity. Unnecessary words merely delay the student.

• Sketches, diagrams, or pictures should be included when they are necessary for the student to visualize the problem correctly or when they will add realism.

• Each item should present a problem that demands knowledge of the subject or course. No item that can be responded to solely on the basis of general knowledge should be included in an achievement test.

PRESOLO KNOWLEDGE TESTS

Title 14 of the Code of Federal Regulations (14 CFR) part 61 requires the satisfactory completion of a presolo knowledge test prior to solo flight. The presolo knowledge test is required to be administered, graded, and all incorrect answers reviewed by the instructor providing the training prior to endorsing the student pilot certificate and logbook for solo flight. The regulation states that the presolo knowledge test must include questions applicable to 14 CFR parts 61 and 91 and on the flight characteristics and operational limitations of the make and model aircraft to be flown. This allows the flight instructor the flexibility to develop a presolo written test which not only evaluates the student's knowledge on general operating rules, but on the specific environment in which the student will be operating and on the particular make and model of aircraft to be flown.

The content and number of test questions are to be determined by the flight instructor. An adequate sampling of the general operating rules should be included. In addition, a sufficient number of specific questions should be asked to ensure the student has the knowledge to safely operate the aircraft in the local environment.

The regulation requires a presolo knowledge test for each make and model of aircraft to be soloed. Because of the varying complexity of aircraft and operating environments, the flight instructor will have to use good judgment in developing the test. For instance, a student who would be operating from a controlled airport located near a terminal control area or airport radar service area should have adequate knowledge to operate safely in the environment prior to solo. Likewise, a student operating from a high elevation airport might need emphasis placed on the effects of density altitude. Specific questions should be asked to fit the situation. [Figure 6-8]

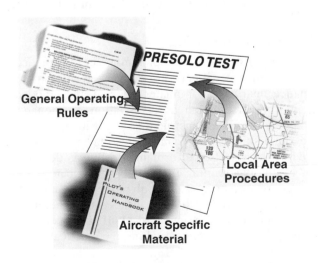

Figure 6-8. The presolo test must include questions on general operating rules, aircraft to be flown, and local area procedures.

The specific procedures for developing test questions have been covered earlier in this chapter, but a review of some items as they apply to the presolo knowledge test are in order. Though selection-type test items are easier to grade, it is recommended that supply-type test items be used for the portions of the presolo knowledge test where specific knowledge is to be tested. One problem with supply-type test items is difficulty in assigning the appropriate grade. Since the purpose of this test is to determine if a student pilot is ready to solo, no specific grade is assigned. The purpose of the test is to determine fitness for solo and not to assign a grade relative to a student's peers. Since solo flight requires a thorough working knowledge of the different conditions likely to be encountered on the solo flight, it is important that the test properly evaluate this area. In this way, the instructor can see any areas that are not adequately understood and can then cover them in the review of the test. Selection-type test items do not allow the instructor to evaluate the student's knowledge beyond the immediate scope of the test items. An example of a supply-type test question would be to ask the student to, "Explain the procedures for entering the traffic pattern for Runway 26." The supply-type test item measures much more adequately the knowledge of the student, and lends itself very well to presolo testing.

Though supply-type test items allow broad questions to be asked, it is probably not possible to cover every conceivable circumstance to be encountered on a solo flight. The instructor must devise the test so the general operating rules are adequately sampled to ensure the overall objective of a safe solo flight is measured. The test also should ask a sufficient number of specific questions to determine that the student has the knowledge to safely operate the aircraft in the local area.

The instructor should keep a record of the test results for at least three (3) years. The record should at least include the date, name of the student, and the results of the test.

PERFORMANCE TESTS

The flight instructor does not administer the practical test for a pilot certificate, nor does the aviation maintenance instructor administer the oral and practical exam for certification as an aviation maintenance technician. Aviation instructors do get involved with the same skill or performance testing that is measured in these tests. Performance testing is desirable for evaluating training that involves an operation, a procedure, or a process. The job of the instructor is to prepare the student to take these tests. Therefore, each element of the practical test will have been evaluated prior to an applicant taking the practical exam.

Practical tests for maintenance technicians and pilots are criterion-referenced tests. The practical tests are criterion-referenced because the objective is for all successful applicants to meet the high standards of knowledge, skill, and safety required by the Federal Aviation Regulations.

The purpose of the **practical test standards (PTS)** is to delineate the standards by which FAA inspectors and designated pilot examiners conduct tests for ratings and certificates. The standards are in accordance with the requirements of 14 CFR parts 61, 91, and other FAA publications including the *Aeronautical Information Manual* and pertinent advisory circulars and handbooks. The objective of the PTS is to ensure the certification of pilots at a high level of performance and proficiency, consistent with safety.

The practical test standards for aeronautical certificates and ratings include **AREAS OF OPERATION** and **TASKS** that reflect the requirements of the FAA publications mentioned above. Areas of operation define phases of the practical test arranged in a logical sequence within each standard. They usually begin with Preflight Preparation and end with Postflight Procedures. Tasks are titles of knowledge areas, flight procedures, or maneuvers appropriate to an area of operation. Included are references to the applicable regulations or publications. Private pilot applicants are evaluated in all tasks of each area of operation. Flight instructor applicants are evaluated on one or more tasks in each area of operation. In addition, certain tasks are required to be covered and are identified by notes immediately following the area of operation titles. [Figure 6-9]

Figure 6-9. Practical test standards are made up of areas of operation and tasks.

An instructor is responsible for training the applicants to acceptable standards in all subject matter areas, procedures, and maneuvers included in the TASKS within each AREA OF OPERATION in the appropriate practical test standard. Because of the impact of their teaching activities in developing safe, proficient pilots, flight instructors should exhibit a high level of knowledge, skill, and the ability to impart that knowledge and skill to the students.

Since every task in the PTS may be covered on the check ride, the instructor must evaluate all of the tasks before certifying the applicant to take the practical test. While this evaluation will not be totally formal in nature, it should adhere to criterion-referenced testing. Practical test standards are available from several aviation publishers and are a good reference to use when preparing a student for the practical test. Although the instructor should always train the student to the very highest level possible, the evaluation of the student is only in relation to the standards listed in the PTS. The instructor, and the examiner, should also keep in mind that the standards are set at a level that is already very high. They are not minimum standards and they do not represent a floor of acceptability. In other words, the standards are the acceptable level that must be met and there are no requirements to exceed them.

Chapter 7

Instructional Aids and Training Technologies

Instructional aids should not be confused with training media. Educators generally describe **training media** as any physical means that communicates an instructional message to students. For example, the instructor's voice, printed text, video cassettes, interactive computer programs, part-task trainers, flight training devices or flight simulators, and numerous other types of training devices are considered training media. **Instructional aids**, on the other hand, are devices that assist an instructor in the teaching-learning process. Instructional aids are not self-supporting; they are supplementary training devices. The key factor is that instructional aids support, supplement, or reinforce.

In general, the coverage of instructional aids in the first part of this chapter applies to a classroom setting with one instructor and several students. The discussion about types of instructional aids begins with the most basic aids and progresses to the more complex and expensive aids. The last segment is about new training technologies which may apply to a typical classroom environment, as well as other training environments.

While instructors may become involved in the selection and preparation of instructional aids, usually they are already in place. Instructors simply need to learn how to effectively use them.

INSTRUCTIONAL AID THEORY

For many years, educators have theorized about how the human brain and the memory function during the communicative process. There is general agreement about certain theoretical factors that seem pertinent to understanding the use of instructional aids.

- During the communicative process, the sensory register of the memory acts as a filter. As stimuli are received, the individual's sensory register works to sort out the important bits of information from the routine or less significant bits. Within seconds, what is perceived as the most important information is passed to the working or short-term memory where it is processed for possible storage in the long-term memory. This complex process is enhanced by the use of appropriate instructional aids that highlight and emphasize the main points or concepts.

- The working or short-term memory functions are limited by both time and capacity. Therefore, it is essential that the information be arranged in useful bits or chunks for effective coding, rehearsal, or recording. The effectiveness of the instructional aid is critical for this process. Carefully selected charts, graphs, pictures, or other well-organized visual aids are examples of items that help the student understand, as well as retain, essential information.

- Ideally, instructional aids should be designed to cover the key points and concepts. In addition, the coverage should be straightforward and factual so it is easy for students to remember and recall. Generally, instructional aids that are relatively simple are best suited for this purpose.

REASONS FOR USE OF INSTRUCTIONAL AIDS

In addition to helping students remember important information, instructional aids have other advantages. When properly used, they help gain and hold the attention of students. Audio or visual aids can be very useful in supporting a topic, and the combination of both audio and visual stimuli is particularly effective since the two most important senses are involved. Instructors should keep in mind that they often are salesmen of ideas, and many of the best sales techniques that attract the attention of potential clients are well worth considering. One caution—the instructional aid should keep student attention on the subject; it should not be a distracting gimmick.

Clearly, a major goal of all instruction is for the student to be able to retain as much knowledge of the subject as possible, especially the key points. Numerous studies have attempted to determine how well instructional aids serve this purpose. Indications from the studies vary greatly—from modest results, which show a 10 to 15 percent increase in retention, to more optimistic results in which retention is increased by as much as 80 percent. [Figure 7-1]

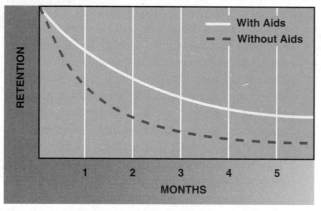

Figure 7-1. Studies generally agree that measurable improvement in student retention of information occurs when instruction is supported by appropriate instructional aids.

Good instructional aids also can help solve certain language barrier problems. Consider the continued expansion of technical terminology in everyday usage. This, coupled with culturally diverse backgrounds of today's students, makes it necessary for instructors to be precise in their choice of terminology. Words or terms used in an instructional aid should be carefully selected to convey the same meaning for the student as they do for the instructor. They should provide an accurate visual image and make learning easier for the student.

Another use for instructional aids is to clarify the relationships between material objects and concepts. When relationships are presented visually, they often are much easier to understand. For example, the subsystems within a physical unit are relatively easy to relate to each other through the use of schematics or diagrams. Symbols, graphs, and diagrams can also show relationships of location, size, time, frequency, and value. By symbolizing the factors involved, it is even possible to visualize abstract relationships.

Instructors are frequently asked to teach more and more in a smaller time frame. Instructional aids can help them do this. For example, instead of using many words to describe a sound, object, or function, the instructor plays a recording of the sound, shows a picture of the object, or presents a diagram of the function. Consequently, the student learns faster and more accurately, and the instructor saves time in the process.

GUIDELINES FOR USE OF INSTRUCTIONAL AIDS

The use of any instructional aid must be planned, based on its ability to support a specific point in a lesson. A simple process can be used to determine if and where instructional aids are necessary.

- Clearly establish the lesson objective. Be certain of what is to be communicated.

- Gather the necessary data by researching for support material.

- Organize the material into an outline or a lesson plan. The plan should include all key points that need to be covered. This may include important safety considerations.

- Select the ideas to be supported with instructional aids. The aids should be concentrated on the key points. Aids are often appropriate when long segments of technical description are necessary, when a point is complex and difficult to put into words, when instructors find themselves forming visual images, or when students are puzzled by an explanation or description.

Aids should be simple and compatible with the learning outcomes to be achieved. Obviously, an explanation of elaborate equipment may require detailed schematics or mockups, but less complex equipment may lend itself to only basic shapes or figures. Since aids are normally used in conjunction with a verbal presentation, words on the aid should be kept to a minimum. In many cases, visual symbols and slogans can replace extended use of verbiage. The instructor should avoid the temptation to use the aids as a crutch. The tendency toward unnecessarily distracting artwork also should be avoided.

Instructional aids should appeal to the student and be based on sound principles of instructional design. When practical, they should encourage student participation. They also should be meaningful to the student, lead to the desired behavioral or learning objectives, and provide appropriate reinforcement. Aids that involve learning a physical skill should guide students toward mastery of the skill or task specified in the lesson objective.

Instructional aids have no value in the learning process if they cannot be heard or seen. Recordings of sounds and speeches should be tested for correct volume and quality in the actual environment in which they will be used. Visual aids must be visible to the entire class. All lettering and illustrations must be large enough to be seen easily by the students farthest from the aids. Colors, when used, should provide clear contrast and easily be visible.

The usefulness of aids can be improved by proper sequencing to build on previous learning. Frequently, good organization and natural patterns of logic dictate the sequence. However, use of standardized materials, including a syllabus, is recommended. Sequencing also can be enhanced simply by using overlays on transparencies, stripping techniques on charts and chalk or marker boards, and by imaginative use of magnetic boards. Sequencing can be emphasized and made clearer by the use of contrasting colors.

The effectiveness of aids and the ease of their preparation can be increased by initially planning them in rough draft form. Revisions and alterations are easier to make at that time than after their completion. The rough draft should be carefully checked for technical accuracy, proper terminology, grammar, spelling, basic balance, clarity, and simplicity. Instructional aids should also be reviewed to determine whether their use is feasible in the training environment and whether they are appropriate for the students. [Figure 7-2]

In practice, the choice of instructional aids depends on several factors. Availability, feasibility, or cost may impose realistic limitations. The number of students in a class and the existing facilities are other considerations. In some school situations, the designers of the curriculum determine the use of instructional aids. In this case, the instructor may have little control over their use. On the other hand, an independent instructor may have considerable latitude, but limited resources.

GUIDELINES FOR INSTRUCTIONAL AIDS

Support the lesson objective.

Be student centered.

Build on previous learning.

Contain useful and meaningful content that is consistent with sound principles of learning.

Appeal to students.

Maintain student attention and interest.

Encourage student participation, when appropriate.

Lead students in the direction of the behavior or learning outcomes specified in the learning objective.

Provide proper stimuli and reinforcement.

Contain quality photos, graphs, and text, as required.

Be checked prior to use for completeness and technical accuracy.

Contain appropriate terminology for the student.

Be properly sequenced.

Be easy to understand.

Include appropriate safety precautions.

Figure 7-2. The listing shown here summarizes guidelines for effective instructional aids.

Often, instructors must improvise and adapt to the existing circumstances in order to incorporate quality instructional aids.

TYPES OF INSTRUCTIONAL AIDS

Some of the most common and economical aids are chalk or marker boards, and supplemental print materials, including charts, diagrams, and graphs. Other aids, which usually are more expensive, are projected materials, video, computer-based programs, and models, mock-ups, or cut-aways.

CHALK OR MARKER BOARD

The chalk or marker board is one of the most widely used tools for instructors. Its versatility and effectiveness provide several advantages for most types of instruction. First, the material presented can be erased, allowing the surface to be used again and again; and second, the boards serve as an excellent medium for joint student-instructor activity in the classroom. The following practices are fundamental in the use of the chalk or marker board:

- Keep the chalk or marker board clean.

- Erase all irrelevant material.

- Keep chalk, markers, erasers, cleaning cloths, rulers, and related items readily available to avoid interruption of the presentation.

- Organize and practice the chalk or marker board presentation in advance.

- Write or draw large enough for everyone in the group to see.

- Leave a margin around the material and sufficient space between lines of copy so the board is not overcrowded.

- Present material simply and briefly.

- Make only one point at a time. A complete outline tends to distract students and makes a logical presentation difficult. If writing has been previously prepared, it should be covered and then revealed one step at a time.

- If necessary, use the ruler, compass, or other devices in making drawings.

- Use colored chalk or marker for emphasis.

- Underline statements for emphasis.

- Use the upper part of the board. In many classrooms, students may not be able to see the lower half.

- Stand to one side of the board to avoid hiding the essential information.

- Use a pointer when appropriate.

- Adjust lighting as necessary to remove glare.

SUPPLEMENTAL PRINT MATERIAL

Print media, including photographs, reproductions of pictures, drawings, murals, cartoons, and other print materials are valuable supplemental aids. Charts, diagrams, and graphs are also in this category. Many of these items are suitable for long-term use on bulletin boards and in briefing areas. Pictures, drawings, and photographs are especially effective because they provide common visual imagery for both instructors and students. In addition, they also provide realistic details necessary for visual recognition of important subject material. In many cases, this type of supplemental training media may be reproduced in a format for projection on a screen or other clear surface.

Charts, diagrams, and graphs include any printed material which gives information in tabular form. There are several types of charts which can be used in presenting data such as the pie chart, the flow chart, and the organizational chart, among others. The type of chart selected for use depends largely on the type of information the instructor wants to convey. An important factor is the chart's format. Since charts may consist of a series of single sheets or be tied together in a flip-chart format with several pages, the location and handling of them should be planned in advance.

A graph is a symbolic drawing which shows relationships or makes comparisons. The most common types are the line graph and the bar graph. The selection of a graph for use in any given situation depends upon the type of information the instructor wants to convey.

Charts, diagrams, and graphs can be used effectively to show relationships, chronological changes, distributions, components, and flow. They are easy to construct and can be produced in the same manner as pictures. In addition, they can be drawn on a chalk or marker board and can be duplicated. Care must be taken to display only a small amount of material and to make the material as simple but meaningful as possible.

Numerous other useful print items may be considered as supplemental training aids. Some of these include study guides, exercise books, course outlines, and syllabi. Well-designed course outlines are especially useful to students because they list the key points and help students organize note taking during a lecture.

ENHANCED TRAINING MATERIALS

Aviation instructors must cover a broad range of aeronautical knowledge and skill training for pilots and aviation maintenance technicians. The actual training requirements are based in the Federal Aviation Regulations and other publications used by designated pilot and maintenance examiners when they conduct practical tests. While aviation instructors are expected to be familiar with all regulatory training requirements, use of instructor-oriented training materials which are enhanced for regulatory compliance can be very beneficial for ensuring required training is being accomplished, endorsed, and properly documented. Whether working as an individual instructor or employed by a flight or maintenance school, the instructor must ensure that each student accomplishes a number of important benchmarks. Enhanced training materials, which include these benchmarks, can help aviation instructors to complete, endorse, and document required training.

One example of these types of materials includes training syllabi, which have provisions for instructor endorsements and record keeping. Such syllabi not only present the course of training in a logical step-by-step, building block sequence, they contain provisions to remind both students and instructors of critical regulatory training benchmarks which are approaching. Blocks for instructor endorsements also may be included at appropriate points. Provisions for logging training time can be incorporated so the syllabus could also serve as the training record for the student, instructor, or school. When required endorsements and record keeping provisions are designed into training syllabi, it is much easier, from the instructors' standpoint, to conduct required training, track student progress, and certify records. In case the student transfers to another school or instructor, the training record can be reviewed and the student's training status easily assessed.

Another example of enhanced, instructor-oriented material for pilot training is a maneuvers guide or handbook which includes the practical test standards as an integral part of the description of maneuvers and procedures. Students learn from the beginning how to perform the maneuver or procedure and also become familiar with the performance criteria. Instructors need not refer to another document to evaluate the student's performance. The examiner for the Oral and Practical (O&P) is required to ask four questions in each of the subject areas, which are required by the regulations to be taught. The examiner also is required to assign a practical project from each subject area. Individual maintenance instructors, as well as publishers, have compiled lists of typical questions and projects. Use of these questions and projects as part of the syllabus helps an instructor ensure that all subject areas for a particular class have been covered.

There are many ways to incorporate design features in training materials in order to facilitate regulatory compliance, required endorsements, and record keeping. Computer-based training also can be designed so the progress of the student can be tracked and documented. As training becomes more detailed and complex, instructor-oriented materials can be a valuable instructional aid for all aviation instructors. More information on enhanced training materials is presented in Chapter 10.

PROJECTED MATERIAL

Traditional aids in this group include motion pictures, filmstrips, slides of various sizes, transparencies for overhead projection, and specialized equipment such as rear screen projection or an opaque projector. However, the use of motion pictures and filmstrips for training has declined, mostly because of availability of more user-friendly media such as video. The essential factor governing continued use is that the content must be current and support the lesson.

Use of projected materials requires planning and practice. The instructor should set up and adjust the equipment and lighting beforehand and then preview the presentation. During a classroom session, the instructor should provide students with an overview of the presentation before showing it. After the presentation, the instructor should allow time for questions and a summary of key points.

Aside from a chalk or marker board, the overhead transparency and projector is still one of the more convenient and cost effective instructional aids. With acetate or plastic, instructors can easily create their own overhead transparencies, or they may purchase commercially produced ones.

The equipment can be placed at the front of the room, allowing the instructor to maintain eye contact with students. The brilliant light source concentrated at a short distance makes it possible to use the projector in lighted areas. The instructor also can write on a blank transparency as the lesson progresses, much like a chalk or marker board. Additional transparencies can be overlaid onto the original to show development or buildup of an event or display. Overlays can also be cut into various shapes and moved about in relation to the base transparency. This is a useful technique for displaying dial indications or fitting

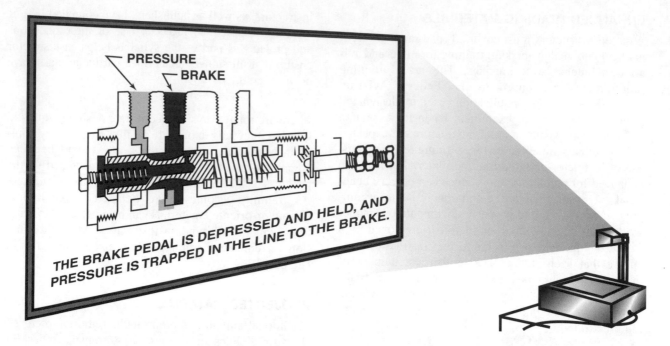

Figure 7-3. The overhead projector is self-contained, portable, and adaptable to large or small classrooms.

several parts of a component together so relative motion can be simulated. [Figure 7-3]

As with any projection equipment, instructors should ensure that the projector does not obstruct the students' line of sight. The projector usually works better on a low stand, chair, or table. The projection angle should be adjusted to eliminate image distortion. Finally, although the overhead projector is simple to operate and requires little maintenance, it has disadvantages. Most projectors are bulky to handle and store, and the fan used for cooling the projector may be noisy.

Although vastly different from other projection equipment, the opaque projector reflects light from the surface of the picture or three-dimensional object onto a regular projection screen. The height of usable objects is limited to the space between the top of the lowered projection plate and the body of the projector, usually about two or three inches. The area of the picture or object is limited to approximately 10 inches by 10 inches.

Items which may be projected are practically limitless. A postage stamp, typed material, textbook illustrations, or a defective spark plug are representative of the items that may be projected. This equipment is especially adapted to enlarging diagrams and small charts for display purposes. Since the material projected requires no special preparation, the cost is very low. Many of the

limitations of the overhead projector are also true of the opaque projector.

VIDEO

As indicated previously, video has become one of the most popular of all instructional aids. The initial discussion of video, which follows, is limited to passive video. Interactive video is covered separately.

PASSIVE VIDEO

Passive video cassettes provide motion, color, sound, and in many cases, special effects with advanced graphic and animation techniques. High-quality, commercially produced video cassettes are available for almost every subject pertaining to aviation training. Consequently, video has replaced many of the projection-type instructional aids.

Advantages of video are well documented. The current generation of students is sometimes referred to as the video generation. Some educators have theorized that TV has produced a visual culture that has actually changed the way people learn. In any case, it is apparent that most, if not all, students are familiar with and receptive to video.

For instructors, the convenience of video is certainly an advantage. The capability to easily stop, freeze, rewind, and replay is particularly helpful for both instructors and students. The cost of a video cassette and the associated equipment, although higher than some of the more basic instructional aid equipment, is fairly economical. In addition, the video cassette recorder and television can be used for other than instructional purposes.

Instructors also should be aware of certain disadvantages with video. Students are often accustomed to dramatic, action-packed film or video that is designed as entertainment. At the same time, they tend to watch film or TV in a passive way without attempting to absorb what they are seeing and hearing. Instructional video, in comparison, normally is perceived as much less exciting and less stimulating visually. This, coupled with an inattentive viewing style, can diminish the instructional value of the video.

As is true with any instructional aid, instructors need to follow some basic guidelines when using video. For example, the video presentation is not designed to replace the instructor. Prior planning and rehearsal will help determine the important points and concepts that should be stressed, either during the presentation or as part of a summary. Instructors should also try to prepare students for viewing video programs by telling them what to watch carefully, what is important, or possibly, what is incorrect. In addition, instructors should be available to summarize the presentation and answer any questions students may have regarding content.

INTERACTIVE VIDEO

Interactive video refers broadly to software that responds quickly to certain choices and commands by the user. A typical system consists of a combination of a compact disk, computer, and video technology. A **compact disk (CD)** is a format for storing information digitally. A major advantage of a CD is the capability to store enormous amounts of information. As an example, a single compact disk may contain all pertinent aviation regulations, plus the complete AIM. With search and find features incorporated, a CD is a powerful information source.   The software may include additional features such as image banks with full color photos and graphics, as well as questions or directions which are programmed to create interactivity for students as they progress through the course.

The questions or directions are programmed using a **branching** technique, which provides several possible courses of action for the user to choose in order to move from one sequence to another. For example, a program may indicate, "That was incorrect. Go back to . . . and try again."

Interactive video solves one of the main problems of passive video in that it increases involvement of the student in the learning process. Well-designed interactive video, when properly used, is highly effective as an instructional aid. Each student essentially receives a customized learning experience.

Distance learning, or distance education, is another trend applicable to aviation. In general terms, distance learning is the use of print or electronic media to deliver instruction when the instructor and student are separated. It also may be defined as a system and process that connects students with resources for learning. As sources for access to information expand, the possibilities for distance learning increases.

COMPUTER-BASED MULTIMEDIA

Interactive video is one form of computer-based multimedia. However, in recent years, the terms computer-based training (CBT), or multimedia training, have become very popular. The term multimedia is not new. Multimedia has been used for decades in some form or other. In a basic form, **multimedia** is a combination of more than one instructional media, but it could include several forms of media—audio, text, graphics, and video (or film). Multimedia in a more current context generally implies a computer-based media that is shown on personal computers (PCs). With computer-based multimedia, information access is simplified. Sophisticated databases can organize vast amounts of information which can be quickly sorted, searched, found, and cross-indexed.

Real interactivity with computer-based training means the student is fully engaged with the instruction by doing something meaningful which makes the subject of study come alive. For example, the student frequently is able to control the pace of instruction, review previous material, jump forward, and receive instant feedback. With advanced tracking features, computer-based training also can be used to test the student's achievement, compare the results with past performance, and indicate the student's weak or strong areas.

Although computers are often used on an individual basis by students, equipment is available that can project images from a computer screen. This allows the instructor to use a computer in conjunction with specially designed software programs to

Figure 7-4. Software programs are available which allow instructors to use computers to create unique presentations for an entire class through on-screen projection.

create presentations for an entire class. The instructor can tailor the presentation for the class, if necessary, and also include graphics at appropriate points. [Figure 7-4]

With computer-based training, the role of both the student and the instructor changes. Students become more involved in their own learning, and instructors may no longer occupy a center-stage position in a typical classroom setting. Instead, instructors become supportive facilitators of the computer-based multimedia program. As such, they serve as guides or resource experts and circulate among students who are working individually or in small groups. This results in considerable one-on-one instructor/student interaction. Thus, the instructor provides assistance, reinforcement, and answers questions for those who need it most.

In this situation, the computer-based training should still be considered as an add-on instructional aid to improve traditional classroom instruction. The instructor, although no longer the center of attention, must continue to maintain complete control over the learning environment to ensure learning objectives are being achieved.

A more advanced application of computer-based training may involve less instructor control. For example, a laboratory-type environment may be configured with separate study areas for each student. With this setup, the physical facility is usually referred to as a learning center or training center. Students in these centers are often monitored by a teacher's aid, or other trained personnel, who can provide guidance, answer questions, and act as a conduit to the instructor who is responsible for the training. In this case, the responsible instructor needs to establish procedures to make sure the required training is accomplished, since he or she must certify student competency at the end of the course.

Numerous advantages are attributed to computer-based multimedia training. It is widely used in airline training for both pilots and aviation maintenance technicians. Due to the active nature of CBT, the overall learning process is enhanced in several ways. Well-designed programs allow students to feel like they are in control of what they are learning and how fast they learn it. They can explore areas that interest them and discover more about a subject on their own. In addition, learning often seems more enjoyable than learning from a regular classroom lecture. The main advantages are less time spent on instruction compared to traditional classroom training, and higher levels of mastery and retention.

Disadvantages include the lack of peer interaction and personal feedback. For the instructor, maintaining control of the learning situation may be difficult. It also may be difficult to find good CBT programs for certain subject areas, and the expense associated with the equipment, software, and facilities must be considered. In addition, instructors and students may lack sufficient experience with personal computers to take full advantage of the CBT programs that are available.

MODELS, MOCK-UPS, AND CUT-AWAYS

Models, mock-ups, and cut-aways are additional instructional aids. A **model** is a copy of a real object. It can be an enlargement, a reduction, or the same size as the original. The scale model represents an exact reproduction of the original, while simplified models do not represent reality in all details. Some models are solid and show only the outline of the object they portray, while others can be manipulated or operated. Still others, called **cut-aways**, are built in sections and can be taken apart to reveal the internal structure. Whenever possible, the various parts should be labeled or colored to clarify relationships.

Although a model may not be a realistic copy of an actual piece of equipment, it can be used effectively in explaining operating principles of various types of equipment. Models are especially adaptable to small group discussions in which students are encouraged to ask questions. A model is even more effective if it works like the original, and if it can be taken apart and reassembled. With the display of an operating model, the students can observe how each part works in relation to the other parts. When the instructor points to each part of the model while explaining these relationships, the students can better understand the mechanical principles involved. As instructional aids, models are usually more practical than originals because they are lightweight and easy to manipulate.

A **mock-up** is a three-dimensional or specialized type of working model made from real or synthetic materials. It is used for study, training, or testing in place of the real object, which is too costly or too dangerous, or which is impossible to obtain. The mock-up may emphasize or highlight elements or components for learning and eliminate nonessential elements. [Figure 7-5]

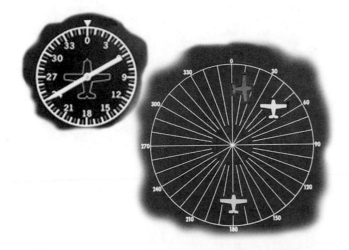

Figure 7-5. This mock-up, which includes moveable pointers, a rotatable compass card, and other moveable indicators, is designed to teach instrument navigation procedures.

Production and equipment costs are limiting factors to consider in developing and using models, mock-ups, and cut-aways. Depending on the nature of the representation, costs can vary from low to high. For instance, scale replicas are often very expensive. In general, if a two-dimensional representation will satisfy the instructor's requirement, it should be used.

TEST PREPARATION MATERIAL

Test preparation material applies to an array of paper-based, video, and computer-based products that are designed by commercial publishers to help student applicants prepare for FAA tests. While test preparation materials may be effective in preparing students for FAA tests, the danger is that students may learn to pass a given test, but fail to learn other critical information essential to safe piloting and maintenance practices. In addition, FAA inspectors and designated examiners have found that student applicants often exhibit a lack of knowledge during oral questioning, even though many have easily passed the FAA knowledge test. A major shortcoming of test preparation materials is that the emphasis is on rote learning, which is the lowest of all levels of learning.

Test preparation materials, as well as instructors, that dwell on teaching the test are shortchanging student applicants. All instructors who use test preparation publications should stress that these materials are not designed as stand-alone learning tools. They should be considered as a supplement to instructor-led training.

FUTURE DEVELOPMENTS

While no one person can accurately predict the future, most will agree that new technological advances will affect practically everyone. In aviation training, the increased use of computer technology, such as CBT, simulation, and virtual reality will continue to expand. The proliferation of sources for information has prompted writers to refer to the current era as the information age. Electronic communications, including use of computer databases, voice mail, e-mail, the Internet, the World Wide Web, and satellite-based, wireless communications, have become routine. This explosion of information access has already affected aviation training, and it will be even more significant in the future.

Emerging computer technology includes improved voice-recognition software and miniature electro-optical devices. Voice-recognition technology, which lets computers accept spoken rather than keyed input, is expected to be highly effective for technical training. Miniature electro-optical devices have also advanced beyond the science fiction stage. With these devices, computer-aided information is projected electronically on sunglass-style eyewear which is connected to a lightweight, belt-mounted computer. The computer-aided information would be particularly useful for aviation maintenance activities. For example, it would be possible for a technician's eyes to easily move back and forth from computer-generated technical data to the actual hardware while diagnosing and correcting a maintenance problem.

Trends in training indicate a shift from the typical classroom to more extensive use of a lab-type environment with computer work or study stations. This is part of the learning or training center concept in which students become more actively involved and responsible for their own training. In these centers, students will have access to simulation devices, computer networks, and multimedia programs. As a related part of this concept, training system designers advocate more use of group or collaborative learning techniques, cable or closed circuit TV, interactive multimedia, and electronic communications. Aviation-related learning centers are usually associated with colleges, universities, and research centers. The airlines, as well as aeronautical programs at some colleges and universities, have used similar facilities for many years. Further growth in this type of training is likely.

One other type of computer-based technology is virtual reality. **Virtual reality (VR)** actually is a separate form of computer-based technology. It creates a sensory experience that allows a participant to believe and barely distinguish a virtual experience from a real one. VR uses graphics with animation systems, sounds, and images to reproduce electronic versions of real-life experience. Despite enormous potential, VR, in its current stage of development, has drawbacks. It is extremely expensive, and versions with a head-mounted display sometimes produce unfavorable side effects.

For those engaged in aviation training, the implications of ongoing technological advances should be apparent. The challenge will be to learn how to stay abreast of the changes that apply to training and adopt those that are the most useful and cost effective. Since much of the new technology will be based on computer technology, instructors with well-developed computer skills will be in demand. In the new century, much of the existing technology will become obsolete. New, more efficient, and probably more complex technology will appear and replace the old.

Although the explosion of training technology offers new opportunities, instructors must remember their main teaching goals and be selectively receptive to new possibilities. Electronic information on computer networks and bulletin boards is from commercial providers, as well as community, state, and national government agencies. There is no guarantee that all of this information is current, or even accurate.

Professional instructors need to be resourceful and discriminating. They should study and research extensively in professional journals and other publications as well as use the Internet. Above all, they should use creativity and imagination. There is always a better way to help students learn what they really need to know. In the next chapter, the broad scope of aviation instructor responsibilities is fully covered. Among these are the need for instructors to continue to update and expand their existing levels of knowledge and skill. The subject of professionalism, along with several methods for enhancing the instructor's professional image, also is discussed.

Chapter 8

Instructor Responsibilities and Professionalism

Students look to aviation instructors as authorities in their respective areas. It is important that aviation instructors not only know how to teach, but they also need to project a knowledgeable and professional image. In addition, aviation instructors are on the front lines of efforts to improve the safety record of the industry. This chapter addresses the scope of responsibilities for aviation instructors and enumerates methods they can use to enhance their professional image and conduct.

AVIATION INSTRUCTOR RESPONSIBILITIES

The job of an aviation instructor, or any instructor, is to teach. Previous chapters have discussed how people learn, the teaching process, and teaching methods. As indicated, the learning process can be made easier by helping students learn, providing adequate instruction, demanding adequate standards of performance, and emphasizing the positive. [Figure 8-1]

RESPONSIBILITIES FOR ALL AVIATION INSTRUCTORS

- **Helping Students Learn**
- **Providing Adequate Instruction**
- **Demanding Adequate Standards of Performance**
- **Emphasizing the Positive**

Figure 8-1. There are four main responsibilities for aviation instructors.

HELPING STUDENTS LEARN

Learning should be an enjoyable experience. By making each lesson a pleasurable experience for the student, the instructor can maintain a high level of student motivation. This does not mean the instructor must make things easy for the student or sacrifice standards of performance to please the student. The student will experience satisfaction from doing a good job or from successfully meeting the challenge of a difficult task.

The idea that people must be led to learning by making it easy is a fallacy. People are not always attracted to something simply because it is pleasant and effortless. Though they might initially be drawn to less difficult tasks, they ultimately devote more effort to activities that bring rewards, such as self-enhancement and personal satisfaction. People want to feel capable; they are proud of the successful achievement of difficult goals.

Learning should be interesting. Knowing the objective of each period of instruction gives meaning and interest to the student as well as the instructor. Not knowing the objective of the lesson often leads to confusion, disinterest, and uneasiness on the part of the student.

Learning to fly should provide students with an opportunity for exploration and experimentation. As part of this, students should be allowed time to explore and evaluate the various elements of each lesson. This encourages them to discover their own capabilities and it helps build self-confidence. Since students learn at different rates and in different ways, it usually is necessary to adjust presentations for some students.

Learning to fly should be a habit-building period during which students devote their attention, memory, and judgment to the development of correct habit patterns. Any objective other than to learn the right way is likely to make students impatient. The instructor should keep the students focused on good habits both by example and by a logical presentation of learning tasks.

Because aviation instructors have full responsibility for all phases of required training, they must be clear regarding the objectives. For ground and flight training, the objectives reflect the knowledge and skill required to train safe pilots who can complete the knowledge and practical tests for the appropriate certificate or rating. In the case of the flight student studying for the practical test, the objectives will come from the practical test standards (PTS) for the desired certificate or rating. Maintenance students will likewise be facing objectives aligned with the knowledge tests and the Oral and Practical. After the objectives have been established, the sequence of training, teaching methods, and related activities must be organized to best achieve them.

To accomplish these objectives, instructors need to take specific actions. The following measures should result in a positive and efficient learning experience.

• Devise a plan of action.

• Create a positive student-instructor relationship.

• Present information and guidance effectively.

• Transfer responsibility to the student as learning occurs.

• Evaluate student learning and thereby measure teaching effectiveness.

As noted in the list, the instructor must devise a plan of action, and present information and guidance effectively. Knowing the objectives is one part of accomplishing these tasks and knowing the student is the other. For example, the plan of action for a lesson on reciprocating engines for maintenance students would be different for a student transitioning from automotive maintenance than it would for a student with no maintenance background. In theory, the transitioning student would have less need for basic information. The best way to confirm this is with a pretest. Until the students are tested, the instructor does not know for sure where each student stands in relation to the objectives. A **pretest** is a criterion-referenced test constructed to measure the knowledge and skills that are necessary to begin the course. Pretests also may be used to determine the student's current level of knowledge and skill in relation to the material that will be presented in the course.

The pretest measures whether or not the student has the prerequisite knowledge and skills necessary to proceed with the course of instruction. Examples of skills that might be required of a student pilot would be knowledge of basic math, understanding the English language, and having certain spatial skills to understand maps and the relationship of maps to the earth. A pretest can expose deficiencies in these and other areas. The instructor could then base the plan of action accordingly. In the extreme, it might be necessary for the prospective student to get more training or education before beginning flight training.

The second part of a pretest is measuring the level of knowledge or skill the student has in relation to the material that is going to be taught. Typically, one or two questions for each of the key knowledge areas or skills in the course are included. The instructor will then be able to identify how much the student knows and tailor the instruction accordingly. Knowing where a student is at the beginning helps the instructor present the information and offer guidance more effectively.

Helping the student learn does not mean that the instructor has the responsibility for performing learning tasks which students need to do for themselves. This is not effective instruction. The best instructors provide information, guidance, and opportunity for student learning, and support the student's motivation while they are in a learning situation.

PROVIDING ADEQUATE INSTRUCTION

The flight instructor should attempt to carefully and correctly analyze the student's personality, thinking, and ability. No two students are alike, and the same methods of instruction cannot be equally effective for each student. The instructor must talk with a student at some length to learn about the student's background, interests, temperament, and way of thinking. The instructor's methods also may change as the student advances through successive stages of training.

An instructor who has not correctly analyzed a student may soon find that the instruction is not producing the desired results. For example, this could mean that the instructor has analyzed a student as a slow thinker, who is actually a quick thinker but is hesitant to act. Such a student may fail to act at the proper time due to lack of self-confidence, even though the situation is correctly understood. In this case, instruction would obviously be directed toward developing student self-confidence, rather than drill on flight fundamentals. In another case, too much criticism may completely subdue a timid person, whereas brisk instruction may force a more diligent application to the learning task. A slow student requires instructional methods that combine tact, keen perception, and delicate handling. If such a student receives too much help and encouragement, a feeling of incompetence may develop.

A student whose slow progress is due to discouragement and a lack of confidence should be assigned subgoals that can be attained more easily than the normal learning goals. For this purpose, complex lessons can be separated into elements, and each element practiced until an acceptable performance is achieved before the whole maneuver or operation is attempted. As an example, instruction in S-turns may begin with consideration for headings only. Elements of altitude control, drift correction, and coordination can be introduced one at a time. As the student gains confidence and ability, goals should be increased in difficulty until progress is normal.

Students who are fast learners can also create problems for the instructor. Because they make few mistakes, they may assume that the correction of errors is unimportant. Such overconfidence may soon result in faulty performance. For such students, the instructor should constantly raise the standard of performance for each lesson, demanding greater effort. Individuals learn when they are aware of their errors. Students who are permitted to complete every flight lesson without corrections and guidance will not retain what they have practiced as well as those students who have their attention constantly directed to an analysis of their performance. On the other hand, deficiencies should not be invented solely for the students' benefit because unfair criticism immediately destroys their confidence in the instructor.

The demands on an instructor to serve as a practical psychologist are much greater than is generally realized. As discussed in Chapters 1 and 2, an instructor can meet this responsibility through a careful analysis of the students and through a continuing deep interest in them.

STANDARDS OF PERFORMANCE

Flight instructors must continuously evaluate their own effectiveness and the standard of learning and performance achieved by their students. The desire to maintain pleasant personal relationships with the students must not cause the acceptance of a slow rate of learning or substandard flight performance. It is a fallacy to believe that accepting lower standards to please a student will produce a genuine improvement in the student-instructor relationship. An earnest student does not resent reasonable standards that are fairly and consistently applied.

Instructors fail to provide competent instruction when they permit their students to get by with a substandard performance, or without learning thoroughly some item

of knowledge pertinent to safe piloting. More importantly, such deficiencies may in themselves allow hazardous inadequacies in student performance later on.

EMPHASIZING THE POSITIVE

Aviation instructors have a tremendous influence on their students' perception of aviation. The way instructors conduct themselves, the attitudes they display, and the manner in which they develop their instruction all contribute to the formation of either positive or negative impressions by their students. The success of an aviation instructor depends, in large measure, on the ability to present instruction so that students develop a positive image of aviation. [Figure 8-2]

Figure 8-2. Students learn more when instruction is presented in a positive manner.

Chapter 1 emphasized that a negative self-concept inhibits the perceptual process, that fear adversely affects the students' perceptions, that the feeling of being threatened limits the ability to perceive, and that negative motivation is not as effective as positive motivation. Merely knowing about these factors is not enough. Instructors must be able to detect these factors in their students and strive to prevent negative feelings from becoming part of the instructional process.

Consider how the following scenario for the first lesson might impress a new student pilot without previous experience in aviation:

• An exhaustive indoctrination in preflight procedures with emphasis on the extreme precautions which must be taken before every flight because "... mechanical failures in flight are often disastrous."

• Instruction in the extreme care which must be taken in taxiing an airplane, because "... if you go too fast, it's likely to get away from you."

- A series of stalls, because ". . . this is how so many people lose their lives in airplanes."

- A series of simulated forced landings, because ". . . one should always be prepared to cope with an engine failure."

These are a series of new experiences that might make the new student wonder whether or not learning to fly is a good idea. The stall series may even cause the student to become airsick. In contrast, consider a first flight lesson in which the preflight inspection is presented to familiarize the student with the airplane and its components, and the flight consists of a perfectly normal flight to a nearby airport and return. Following the flight, the instructor can call the student's attention to the ease with which the trip was made in comparison with other modes of transportation, and the fact that no critical incidents were encountered or expected.

This by no means proposes that preflight inspections, stalls, and emergency procedures should be omitted from training. It only illustrates the positive approach in which the student is not overwhelmed with the critical possibilities of aviation before having an opportunity to see its potential and pleasurable features. The introduction of emergency procedures after the student has developed an acquaintance with normal operations is not so likely to be discouraging and frightening, or to inhibit learning by the imposition of fear.

There is nothing in aviation that demands that students must suffer as part of their instruction. This has often been the case because of overemphasis on negative motivation and explanations. Every reasonable effort should be made to ensure that instruction is given under the most favorable conditions.

Although most student pilots have been exposed to air travel in one form or another, they may not have flown in light, training aircraft. Consequently, students may experience unfamiliar noises, vibrations, eerie sensations due to G-forces, or a woozy feeling in the stomach. To be effective, instructors cannot ignore the existence of these negative factors, nor should they ridicule students who are adversely affected by them. These negative sensations can usually be overcome by understanding and positive instruction.

When emphasizing to a student that a particular procedure must be accomplished in a certain manner, an instructor might be tempted to point out the consequences of doing it differently. The instructor may even tell the student that to do it otherwise is to flirt with disaster or to suffer serious consequences. Justifications such as these may be very convenient,

and the instructor may consider the negative approach necessary to ensure that the point is committed to memory. However, the final test must be whether the stated reasons contribute to the learning situation.

Most new instructors tend to adopt those teaching methods used by their own instructors. These methods may or may not have been good. The fact that one has learned under one system of instruction does not mean that this is necessarily the best way it can be done, regardless of the respect one retains for the ability of their original instructor. Some students learn in spite of their instruction, rather than because of it. Emphasize the positive because positive instruction results in positive learning.

FLIGHT INSTRUCTOR RESPONSIBILITIES

All aviation instructors shoulder an enormous responsibility because their students will ultimately be flying and servicing or repairing aircraft. Flight instructors have some additional responsibilities including the responsibility of evaluating student pilots and making a determination of when they are ready to solo. Other flight instructor responsibilities are based on Title 14 of the Code of Federal Regulations (14 CFR) part 61, and advisory circulars (ACs). [Figure 8-3]

ADDITIONAL RESPONSIBILITIES FOR FLIGHT INSTRUCTORS

- Evaluation of Student Piloting Ability
- Pilot Supervision
- Practical Test Recommendations
- Flight Instructor Endorsements
- Additional Training and Endorsements
- Pilot Proficiency

Figure 8-3. The flight instructor has many additional responsibilities.

EVALUATION OF STUDENT PILOTING ABILITY

Evaluation is one of the most important elements of instruction. In flight instruction, the instructor initially determines that the student understands the procedure or maneuver. Then the instructor demonstrates the maneuver, allows the student to practice the maneuver under direction, and finally evaluates student accomplishment by observing the performance.

Evaluation of demonstrated ability during flight instruction must be based upon established standards of performance, suitably modified to apply to the student's experience and stage of development as a pilot. The evaluation must consider the student's mastery of the elements involved in the maneuver, rather than merely the overall performance.

Demonstrations of performance directly apply to the qualification of student pilots for solo and solo cross-country privileges. Also associated with pilot skill evaluations during flight training are the stage checks conducted in FAA-approved school courses and the practical tests for pilot certificates and ratings.

In evaluating student demonstrations of piloting ability, it is important for the flight instructor to keep the student informed of progress. This may be done as each procedure or maneuver is completed or summarized during postflight critiques. When explaining errors in performance, instructors should point out the elements in which the deficiencies are believed to have originated and, if possible, suggest appropriate corrective measures.

Correction of student errors should not include the practice of taking the controls away from students immediately when a mistake is made. Safety permitting, it is frequently better to let students progress part of the way into the mistake and find their own way out. It is difficult for students to learn to do a maneuver properly if they seldom have the opportunity to correct an error. On the other hand, students may perform a procedure or maneuver correctly and not fully understand the principles and objectives involved. When the instructor suspects this, students should be required to vary the performance of the maneuver slightly, combine it with other operations, or apply the same elements to the performance of other maneuvers. Students who do not understand the principles involved will probably not be able to do this successfully.

PILOT SUPERVISION

Flight instructors have the responsibility to provide guidance and restraint with respect to the solo operations of their students. This is by far the most important flight instructor responsibility because the instructor is the only person in a position to make the determination that a student is ready for solo operations. Before endorsing a student for solo flight, the instructor should require the student to demonstrate consistent ability to perform all of the fundamental maneuvers. The student should also be capable of handling ordinary problems that might occur, such as traffic pattern congestion, change in active runway, or unexpected crosswinds. The instructor must remain in control of the situation. By requiring the first solo flight to consist of landings to a full stop, the instructor has the opportunity to stop the flight if unexpected conditions or poor performance warrant such action.

PRACTICAL TEST RECOMMENDATIONS

Provision is made on the airman certificate or rating application form for the written recommendation of the flight instructor who has prepared the applicant for the practical test involved. Signing this recommendation imposes a serious responsibility on the flight instructor. A flight instructor who makes a practical test recommendation for an applicant seeking a certificate or rating should require the applicant to thoroughly demonstrate the knowledge and skill level required for that certificate or rating. This demonstration should in no instance be less than the complete procedure prescribed in the applicable practical test standards (PTS).

A practical test recommendation based on anything less risks the presentation of an applicant who may be unprepared for some part of the actual practical test. In such an event, the flight instructor is logically held accountable for a deficient instructional performance. This risk is especially great in signing recommendations for applicants who have not been trained by the instructor involved. 14 CFR parts 61 and 141 require a minimum of three hours of flight training preparation within 60 days preceding the date of the test for a recreational, private, or commercial certificate. The same training requirement applies to the instrument rating. The instructor signing the endorsement is required to have conducted the training in the applicable areas of operation stated in the regulations and the PTS, and certify that the person is prepared for the required practical test. In most cases, the conscientious instructor will have little doubt concerning the applicant's readiness for the practical test.

FAA inspectors and designated pilot examiners rely on flight instructor recommendations as evidence of qualification for certification, and proof that a review has been given of the subject areas found to be deficient on the appropriate knowledge test. Recommendations also provide assurance that the applicant has had a thorough briefing on the practical test standards and the associated knowledge areas, maneuvers, and procedures. If the flight instructor has trained and prepared the applicant competently, the applicant should have no problem passing the practical test.

FLIGHT INSTRUCTOR ENDORSEMENTS

The authority and responsibility for endorsing student pilot certificates and logbooks for solo and solo cross-country flight privileges are granted in 14 CFR part 61. These endorsements are further explained in AC 61-65, *Certification: Pilots and Flight Instructors*. Failure to ensure that a student pilot meets the requirements of regulations prior to making endorsements allowing solo flight is a serious deficiency in performance for which an instructor is held accountable. Providing a solo endorsement for a student pilot who is not fully prepared to accept the responsibility for solo flight operations also is a breach of faith with the student.

Flight instructors also have the responsibility to make logbook endorsements for pilots who are already certificated. Included are additional endorsements for recreational, private, commercial, and instrument-rated pilots as well as flight instructors. Typical examples include endorsements for flight reviews, instrument proficiency checks, and the additional training required for high performance, high altitude, and tailwheel aircraft. Completion of prerequisites for a practical test is another instructor task that must be documented properly. Examples of all common endorsements can be found in the current issue of AC 61-65, Appendix 1. This appendix also includes references to 14 CFR part 61 for more details concerning the requirements that must be met to qualify for each respective endorsement. The examples shown contain the essential elements of each endorsement, but it is not necessary for all endorsements to be worded exactly as those in the AC. For example, changes to regulatory requirements may affect the wording, or the instructor may customize the endorsement for any special circumstances of the student. Any time a flight instructor gives ground or flight training, a logbook entry is required. [Figure 8-4]

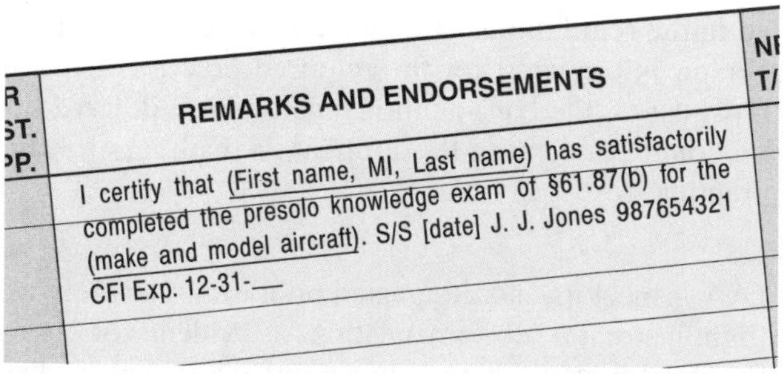

Figure 8-4. This is a sample logbook endorsement for presolo aeronautical knowledge.

14 CFR part 61 also requires that the instructor maintain a record in a logbook or some separate document that includes information on the type of endorsement, the name of the person receiving the endorsement, and the date of the endorsement. For a knowledge or practical test endorsement, the record must include the kind of test, the date, and the results. Records of endorsements must be maintained for at least three years.

FAA FORM 8710-1

After ensuring that an applicant for a certificate is prepared for the test and has met all the knowledge, proficiency, and experience requirements, it is advisable for the flight instructor to assist the applicant in filling out FAA Form 8710-1, *Airman Certificate and/or Rating Application*. The instructor's certification that the applicant is ready to take the test is on the reverse of the form, but the applicant will likely need the assistance of the instructor in filling out the front.

FAA Form 8710-1 comes with instructions attached for completing it. The example shown is for a private pilot applicant who received training under 14 CFR part 61. This is only an example, since the form is periodically revised to reflect changes in the applicable rules and regulations. If the current form is a later edition than shown here, the instructions must be read very carefully to ensure all areas of the form are filled out correctly. The example shown is annotated with additional guidance to clarify or reinforce certain areas that are frequently found incomplete by the FAA during the certification process. [Figure 8-5]

ADDITIONAL TRAINING AND ENDORSEMENTS

Flight instructors often provide required training and endorsements for certificated pilots. AC 61-98, *Currency and Additional Qualification Requirements for Certificated Pilots*, contains information to assist the instructor in providing training/endorsements for flight reviews, instrument proficiency checks, and transitions to other makes and models of aircraft. Included in the AC is general guidance in each of these areas, references to other related documents, and sample training plans that are pertinent to this type of training.

FLIGHT REVIEWS

The conduct of **flight reviews** for certificated pilots is not only a responsibility of the flight instructor, but it can also be an excellent opportunity to expand on the instructor's professional services. The flight review is intended to be an industry-managed, FAA-monitored currency program. The flight instructor must remember that the flight review is not a test or a check ride, but an instructional service designed to assess a pilot's knowledge and skills. As stated in 14 CFR part 61, no person may act as pilot in command of an aircraft unless a flight review has been accomplished within the preceding 24 calendar months.

Effective pilot refresher training must be based on specific objectives and standards. The objectives should

Middle name must be spelled out; if no middle name, the letters "NMN" must be indicated. DO NOT USE MIDDLE INITIAL.

Type or print in ink when filling out 8710-1.

Spell out color.

Must include city or county and state within the U.S. Include city and country outside the U.S.

Do not use P.O.Box or Rural Route, UNLESS a statement of physical location is provided.

Enter class shown on medical certificate (i.e. 1st, 2nd, 3rd), if required.

Check that flight time is sufficient for certificate or rating.

Make sure applicant signs form.

TYPE OR PRINT ALL ENTRIES IN INK

Form Approved OMB No: 2120-0021

Airman Certificate and/or Rating Application

U.S. Department of Transportation
Federal Aviation Administration

I. Application Information ☐ Student ☐ Recreational ☒ Private ☐ Commercial ☐ Airline Transport ☐ Instrument
☐ Additional Aircraft Rating ☒ Airplane Single-Engine ☐ Airplane Multiengine ☐ Rotorcraft ☐ Glider ☐ Lighter-Than-Air
☐ Flight Instructor ____ Initial ____ Renewal ____ Reinstatement ☐ Additional Instructor Rating ☐ Ground Instructor
☐ Medical Flight Test ☐ Reexamination ☐ Reissuance of ____ Certificate ☐ Other ____

A. Name (Last, First, Middle)	B. SSN (US Only)	C. Date of Birth Mo. Day Year	D. Place of Birth
Doe, John David	223-45-6678	11/25/	Bakersfield, CA

E. Address (Please See Instructions Before Completing)	F. Nationality (Citizenship) Specify	G. Do you read, speak and understand English?
1234 North Street	☒ USA ☐ Other	☒ Yes ☐ No

City, State, Zip Code	H. Height	I. Weight	J. Hair	K. Eyes	L. Sex
Alltown, PA 62534	68 In.	165 Lbs.	Blonde	Blue	☒ Male ☐ Female

M. Do you now hold, or have you ever held an FAA Pilot Certificate?	N. Grade Pilot Certificate	O. Certificate Number	P. Date Issued
☒ Yes ☐ No	Student	BB07138	06-15-___

Q. Do you hold a Medical Certificate?	R. Class of Certificate	S. Date Issued	T. Name of Examiner
☒ Yes ☐ No	Third	6-15-	Thomas C. Smith, MD

U. Have you been convicted for violation of Federal or State statutes relating to narcotic drugs, marijuana, or depressant or stimulant drugs or substances ☐ Yes ☒ No V. Date of Final Conviction

W. Glider or Free Balloon Pilots only:	Medical Statement: I have no known physical defect which makes me unable to pilot a glider or free balloon.	Signature	X. Date

II. Certificate or Rating Applied For on Basis of:

☒ A. Completion of Required Test	1. Aircraft to be used (if flight test required) Cessna 152	2a. Total time in this aircraft 55 hours	2b. Pilot in command 24 hours

Items U. and V. DO NOT apply to alcohol related offenses (DWI or DUI).

☐ B. Military Competence Obtained in	1. Service	2. Date Rated	3. Rank or Grade and Service Number
	4. Has flown at least 10 hours as pilot in command during the past 12 months in the following military aircraft.		

☐ C. Graduate of Approved Course	1. Name and Location of Training Agency or Training Center		1a Certification Number
	2. Curriculum From Which Graduated		3. Date

☐ D. Holder of Foreign License issued By	1. Country	2. Grade of License	3. Number
	4. Ratings		

☐ E. Completion of Air Carrier's Approved Training Program	1. Name of Air Carrier	2. Date	3. Which Curriculum ☐ Initial ☐ Upgrade ☐ Transition

III. Record of Pilot time (Do not write in the shaded areas.)

	Total	Instruction Received	Solo	Pilot in Command	Second in Command	Cross Country Instruction Received	Cross Country Solo	Cross Country Pilot in Command	Instrument	Night Instruction Received	Night Take-off/ Landing	Night Pilot in Command	Night Take-off/ Landing Pilot in Command	Number of Flights	Number of Aero-Tows	Number of Ground Launches	Number of Powered Launches	Number of Free Flights
Airplanes	55	31	24	24		5	12	12	3	4	12							
Rotor-craft																		
Gliders																		
Lighter than Air																		
Training Device Simulator																		

IV. Have you failed a test for this certificate or rating? ☐ Yes ☒ No   **Within the Past 30 days?** ☐ Yes ☒ No

V. Applicant's Certification — I certify that all statements and answers provided by me on this application form are complete and true to the best of my knowledge, and I agree that they are to be considered as part of the basis for issuance of any FAA certificate to me. I have also read and understand the Privacy Act statement that accompanies this form.

Signature of Applicant	Date
John David Doe John David Doe	04-12-

FAA Use Only

EMP	REG	D.O.	SEAL	CON	ISS	ACT	LEV	TR	S.H.	SRCH	#RTE	RATING (1)

Date signed by applicant should be within 60 days prior to date of practical test.

Figure 8-5. This sample FAA Form 8710-1 (front page) has been completed for a private pilot applicant.

Practical test date must be within 60 days after date of recommendation.

Full printed name should be included with signature.

Instructor's certificate must be current on date of recommendation.

Instructor's Recommendation

I have personally instructed the applicant and consider this person ready to take the test.

Date	Instructor's Signature		Certificate No:	Certificate Expires
4-11-	*James E. Jones* James E. Jones		1234567 CFI	05-31-

Air Agency's Recommendation

The applicant has successfully completed our _____ course, and is recommended for certification or rating without further _____ test.

Date	Agency Name and Number	Official's Signature
		Title

Designated Examiner's Report

☐ Student Pilot Certificate Issued *(Copy attached)*

☒ I have personally reviewed this applicant's pilot logbook, and certify that the individual meets the pertinent requirements of FAR 61 for the pilot certificate or rating sought.

☐ I have personally reviewed this applicant's graduation certificate, and found it to be appropriate and in order, and have returned the certificate.

☒ I have personally tested and/or verified this applicant in accordance with pertinent procedures and standards with the result indicated below.

    ☒ Approved—Temporary Certificate Issued *(Copy Attached)*

    ☐ Disapproved—Disapproval Notice Issued *(Copy Attached)*

Location of Test *(Facility, City, State)*	Duration of Test		
	Ground	Simulator	Flight
Alltown, PA	2.6	0	2.1

Certificate or Rating for Which Tested	Type(s) of Aircraft Used	Registration No.(s)
Private Pilot	Cessna 152	N12345

Date	Examiner's Signature		Certificate No.	Designation No.	Designation Expires
04-12-	Henry L. Smith	*Henry L. Smith*	332345678	AE-01-1123	01-31-

Evaluator's Record For Airline Transport Certificate/Rating Only

	Inspector	Examiner	Signature	Date
Oral	☐	☐		
Approved Simulator/Training Device Check	☐	☐		
Aircraft Flight Check	☐	☐		
Advanced Qualification Program	☐	☐		

Inspector's Report

I have personally tested this applicant in accordance with or have otherwise verified that this applicant complies with pertinent procedures, standards, policies, and or necessary requirements with the result indicated below.

    ☐ **Approved**—Temporary Certificate Issued   ☐ **Disapproved**—Disapproval Notice Issued

Location of Test *(Facility, City, State)*	Duration of Test		
	Ground	Simulator	Flight

Certificate or Rating for Which Tested	Type(s) of Aircraft Used	Registration No.(s)

☐ Student Pilot Certificate issued   ☐ Certificate or Rating Based on   ☐ Instructor ☐ Flight ☐ Ground

☐ Examiner's Recommendation   ☐ Military Competence   ☐ Renewal ☐ Approved

  ☐ ACCEPTED ☐ REJECTED   ☐ Foreign License   ☐ Reinstatement ☐ Disapproved

☐ Reissue or Exchange of Pilot Certificate   ☐ Approved Course Graduate   **Instructor Renewal Based on**

☐ Special medical test conducted—report forwarded to Aeromedical Certification Branch, AAM-130   ☐ Other Approved FAA Qualification Criteria ☐ Activity ☐ Training Course

    ☐ Certificate Issued ☐ Acquaintance ☐ Test

    ☐ Certificate Denied

Training Course (FIRC) Name	Graduation Certificate No.	Date

Date	Inspector's Signature	FAA District Office

Attachments:

☐ Student Pilot Certificate (copy)   ☒ Airmans Identification (ID)   ☐ Notice of Disapproval

☒ Report of Written Examination   Pennsylvania Drivers License   ☐ Superseded Pilot Certificate

☒ Temporary Pilot Certificate (copy)   Form of ID 223456678   ☐ Answer Sheet Graded

    Number 11-25-   ☐ Answer Sheet Graded (Foreign Instrument)

    Expiration Date

FAA Form 8710-1 (7-95) Supersedes Previous Edition

NSN: 0052-00-682-5006

☆ U.S. GOVERNMENT PRINTING OFFICE: 1997-668-108

Figure 8-5. This sample FAA Form 8710-1 (back page) has been completed for a private pilot applicant.

include a thorough checkout appropriate to the pilot certificate and aircraft ratings held, and the standards should be at least those required for the issuance of that pilot certificate. Before beginning any training, the pilot and the instructor should agree fully on these objectives and standards, and, as training progresses, the pilot should be kept appraised of progress toward achieving those goals.

AC 61-98, Chapter 1, provides guidance for conducting the flight review. Appendix 1 is a sample flight review plan and checklist. Appendix 2 is a sample list of flight review knowledge, maneuvers, and procedures. It contains recommended procedures and standards for general pilot refresher courses. At the conclusion of a successful flight review, the logbook of the pilot should be endorsed. [Figure 8-6]

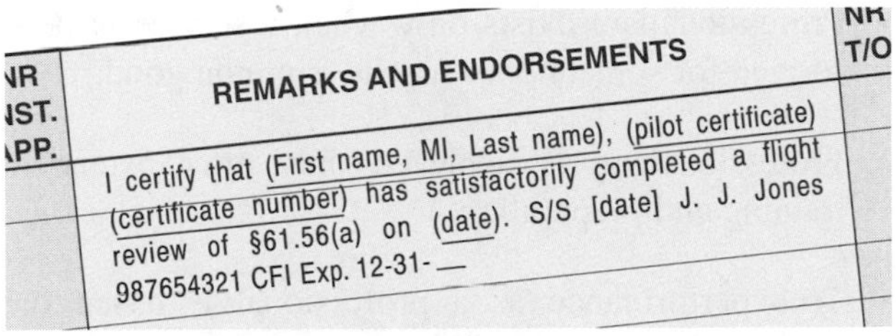

Figure 8-6. This sample logbook endorsement is for completion of a flight review.

INSTRUMENT PROFICIENCY CHECKS

Instrument rated pilots who have not met instrument currency requirements in the preceding six months or for six months thereafter are required by 14 CFR part 61 to pass an instrument proficiency check in order to regain their instrument flying privileges.

AC 61-98 contains guidance for the conduct of an **instrument proficiency check,** including a sample plan of action and checklist. When conducting an instrument proficiency check, the flight instructor should use the Instrument Rating Practical Test Standards as the primary reference for specific maneuvers and any associated tolerances. A pilot taking an instrument proficiency check should be expected to meet the criteria of the specific tasks selected in the Instrument Rating Practical Test Standards.

The flight instructor must hold aircraft and instrument ratings on his or her instructor certificate appropriate to the aircraft being flown. Part or all of the check may be conducted in a flight training device or flight simulator that meets 14 CFR section 141.41 requirements. The FAA FSDO having jurisdiction over the area where the device is used must specifically approve each flight training device or flight simulator. If planning to use a flight training device or flight simulator to conduct all or part of an instrument proficiency check, instructors should contact the local FSDO to verify the approval status of the device.

AIRCRAFT CHECKOUTS/TRANSITIONS

Certificated pilots look to flight instructors for **aircraft checkouts** and **transition training** including high performance airplanes, tailwheel airplanes, and aircraft capable of flight at high altitudes. The flight instructor who checks out and certifies the competency of a pilot in an aircraft for which a type rating is not required by regulations is accepting a major responsibility for the safety of future passengers. Many newer light airplanes are comparable in performance and complexity to transport airplanes. For these, the flight instructor's checkout should be at least as thorough as an official type rating practical test.

AC 61-98 provides a list of requirements for transitioning to other makes and models of aircraft along with a sample training plan. This AC also lists other publications that can be helpful in conducting checkouts. All checkouts should be conducted to the performance standards required by the appropriate practical test standards for the pilot certificate.

For the conduct of an aircraft checkout, it is essential that the flight instructor be fully qualified in the aircraft to be used and be thoroughly familiar with its operating procedures, approved flight manual, and operating limitations. An instructor who does not meet the recent flight experience prescribed by regulations for the aircraft concerned should not attempt to check out another pilot.

For the benefit of the pilot concerned, and for the instructor's protection in the case of later questions, the flight instructor should record in the pilot's logbook the exact extent of any checkout conducted. This can be done most easily by reference to the appropriate PTS.

In the event the instructor finds a pilot's performance to be insufficient to allow sign off, the pilot should be thoroughly debriefed on all problem areas, and further instruction scheduled. In some cases, a referral to another instructor may be appropriate.

PILOT PROFICIENCY

Professional flight instructors know the importance of maintaining knowledge and skill both as instructors and as pilots. Only by keeping themselves at top proficiency can they be true professionals. The flight instructor is at the leading edge of the aviation industry's efforts to improve aviation safety through additional training. One of the ways the FAA attempts to improve proficiency is through the requirement for having a flight review within the past 24 months. Another method of encouraging pilot proficiency is through provisions of AC 61-91, *Pilot Proficiency Award Program.*

The objective of the program is to provide pilots with the opportunity to establish and participate in a personal recurrent training program. It is open to all pilots holding a recreational pilot certificate or higher and a current medical certificate when required. Pilots of qualified ultralight vehicles are also eligible. For airplanes, the program requires three hours of flight training which includes one hour directed toward basic airplane control and mastery of the airplane; one hour devoted to patterns, approaches, and landings; and one hour of instrument training either in an airplane, approved flight training device, or flight simulator. The program also requires attending at least one sanctioned aviation safety seminar, or industry-conducted recurrent training program. AC 61-91 contains requirements for other categories/classes of aircraft, as well as additional detailed requirements for all aircraft.

Incentives to participate include distinctive pins and certificates of completion for Phases I through X. A certificate is awarded for Phases XI through XX. Work toward another phase can begin as soon as one phase is completed, but 12 months must pass between completion of one phase and application for the award of the next phase. Another incentive to participate is that the completion of a phase substitutes for the flight review and restarts the 24-month clock.

Flight instructors may also participate in the program. By giving instruction leading to phase completion for three pilots (nine hours of instruction) and attendance at a safety seminar or clinic, an instructor can earn Phases I through III. Phases IV through XX are each earned by completion of an evaluation or proficiency flight with a designated examiner or FAA inspector and attendance at a safety seminar or clinic.

Flight instructors can substantially improve their own proficiency and that of their students and other pilots by participating and encouraging participation in the Pilot Proficiency Award Program. When an instructor has conducted the appropriate training toward the completion of a phase, a logbook endorsement is required. [Figure 8-7]

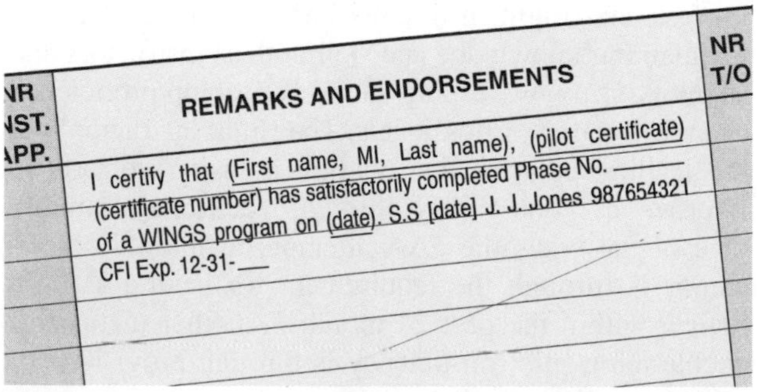

Figure 8-7. This is an example of an instructor's logbook endorsement for a pilot who has completed a phase of training according to requirements of the Pilot Proficiency Award Program.

PROFESSIONALISM

The aviation instructor is the central figure in aviation training and is responsible for all phases of required training. The instructor must be fully qualified as an aviation professional, either as a pilot or aircraft maintenance technician; however, the instructor's ability must go far beyond this if the requirements of professionalism are to be met. Although the word "professionalism" is widely used, it is rarely defined. In fact, no single definition can encompass all of the qualifications and considerations that must be present before true professionalism can exist.

Though not all inclusive, the following list gives some major considerations and qualifications that should be included in the definition of professionalism.

• Professionalism exists only when a service is performed for someone, or for the common good.

• Professionalism is achieved only after extended training and preparation.

• True performance as a professional is based on study and research.

• Professionals must be able to reason logically and accurately.

• Professionalism requires the ability to make good judgmental decisions. Professionals cannot limit their actions and decisions to standard patterns and practices.

• Professionalism demands a code of ethics. Professionals must be true to themselves and to those they service. Anything less than a sincere performance is quickly detected, and immediately destroys their effectiveness.

Aviaton instructors should carefully consider this list. Failing to meet these qualities may result in poor performance by the instructor and students. Preparation and performance as an instructor with these qualities constantly in mind will command recognition as a professional in aviation instruction. Professionalism includes an instructor's public image.

SINCERITY

The professional instructor should be straightforward and honest. Attempting to hide some inadequacy behind a smokescreen of unrelated instruction will make it impossible for the instructor to command the respect and full attention of a student. Teaching an aviation student is based upon acceptance of the instructor as a competent, qualified teacher and an expert pilot or aircraft maintenance technician. Any facade of instructor pretentiousness, whether it is real or mistakenly assumed by the student, will immediately cause the student to lose confidence in the instructor and learning will be adversely affected.

ACCEPTANCE OF THE STUDENT

With regard to students, the instructor must accept them as they are, including all their faults and problems. The student is a person who wants to learn, and the instructor is a person who is available to help in the learning process. Beginning with this understanding, the professional relationship of the instructor with the student should be based on a mutual acknowledgement that the student and the instructor are important to each other, and that both are working toward the same objective.

Under no circumstance should the instructor do anything which implies degrading the student. Acceptance, rather than ridicule, and support rather than reproof will encourage learning. Students must be treated with respect, regardless of whether the student is quick to learn or is slow and apprehensive. Criticizing a student who does not learn rapidly is similar to a doctor reprimanding a patient who does not get well as rapidly as predicted.

PERSONAL APPEARANCE AND HABITS

Personal appearance has an important effect on the professional image of the instructor. Today's aviation customers expect their instructors to be neat, clean, and appropriately dressed. Since the instructor is engaged in a learning situation, the attire worn should be appropriate to a professional status. [Figure 8-8]

Figure 8-8. The aviation instructor should always present a professional appearance.

Personal habits have a significant effect on the professional image. The exercise of common courtesy is perhaps the most important of these. An instructor who is rude, thoughtless, and inattentive cannot hold the respect of students, regardless of ability as a pilot or aviation maintenance technician. Personal cleanliness is important to aviation instruction. Frequently, an instructor and a student work in close proximity, and even little annoyances such as body odor or bad breath can cause serious distractions from learning the tasks at hand.

DEMEANOR

The attitude and behavior of the instructor can contribute much to a professional image. The instructor should avoid erratic movements, distracting speech habits, and capricious changes in mood. The professional image requires development of a calm, thoughtful, and disciplined, but not somber, demeanor.

The instructor should avoid any tendency toward frequently countermanding directions, reacting differently to similar or identical errors at different times, demanding unreasonable performance or progress, or criticizing a student unfairly. A forbidding or overbearing manner is as much to be avoided as is an air of flippancy. Effective instruction is best conducted in a calm, pleasant, thoughtful approach that puts the student at ease. The instructor must constantly portray competence in the subject matter and genuine interest in the student's well being.

SAFETY PRACTICES AND ACCIDENT PREVENTION

The safety practices emphasized by instructors have a long lasting effect on students. Generally, students consider their instructor to be a model of perfection whose habits they attempt to imitate, whether consciously or unconsciously. The instructor's advocacy and description of safety practices mean little to a student if the instructor does not demonstrate them consistently.

For this reason, instructors must meticulously observe the safety practices being taught to students. A good example is the use of a checklist before takeoff. If a student pilot sees the flight instructor start an airplane and take off without referring to a checklist, no amount of instruction in the use of a checklist will convince that student to faithfully use one when solo flight operations begin.

To maintain a professional image, a flight instructor must carefully observe all regulations and recognized safety practices during all flight operations. An instructor who is observed to fly with apparent disregard for loading limitations or weather minimums creates an image of irresponsibility that many hours of scrupulous flight instruction can never correct. Habitual observance of regulations, safety precautions, and the precepts of courtesy will enhance the instructor's image of professionalism. Moreover, such habits make the instructor more effective by encouraging students to develop similar habits.

The flight instructor must go beyond the requirements of developing technically proficient students who are knowledgeable in the areas of their equipment, flight procedures, and maneuvers. The flight instructor must not only teach students to know their own and their equipment's limitations, but must also teach them to be guided by those limitations. The flight instructor must make a strenuous effort to develop good judgment on the part of the students.

The aircraft maintenance instructor must similarly make the maintenance technician student aware of the consequences of safety in the work place. If a maintenance student observes the instructor violating safety practices such as not wearing safety glasses around hazardous equipment, the student will likely not be conscientious about using safety equipment when the instructor is not around.

PROPER LANGUAGE

In aviation instruction, as in other professional activities, the use of profanity and obscene language leads to distrust or, at best, to a lack of complete confidence in the instructor. To many people, such language is actually objectionable to the point of being painful. The professional instructor must speak normally, without inhibitions, and develop the ability to speak positively and descriptively without excesses of language.

The beginning aviation student is being introduced to new concepts and experiences and encountering new terms and phrases that are often confusing. Words such as "traffic," "stall," "elevator," and "lift" are familiar, but are given entirely new meanings. Coined words, such as VORTAC, UNICOM, and PIREP cause further difficulty. Phrases such as "clear the area," "monitor ATIS," or "lower the pitch attitude" are completely incomprehensible. The language is new and strange, but the words are a part of aviation and beginning students need to learn the common terms. Normally, they are eager to learn and will quickly adopt the terminology as part of their vocabulary. At the beginning of the student's training, and before each lesson during early instruction, the instructor should carefully define the terms and phrases that will be used during the lesson. The instructor should then be careful to limit instruction to those terms and phrases, unless the exact meaning and intent of any new expression are explained immediately.

Student errors and confusion can also result from using many of the colloquial expressions of aviation. These expressions are the result of the glamorous past of aviation and often are not understood even by long time aviators. Jargon such as ". . . throw the cobs to it," or ". . . firewall it," should be avoided. A phrase such as ". . . advance the power," would be preferable, since it has wider acceptance and understanding. In all cases, terminology should be explained to the student before it is used during instruction.

SELF-IMPROVEMENT

Professional aviation instructors must never become complacent or satisfied with their own qualifications and abilities. They should be constantly alert for ways to improve their qualifications, effectiveness, and the services they provide to students. Flight instructors are considered authorities on aeronautical matters and are the experts to whom many pilots refer questions concerning regulations, requirements, and new operating techniques. Likewise, aviation maintenance instructors are considered by maintenance students and other maintenance technicians to be a source of up-to-date information. They have the opportunity and responsibility of introducing new procedures and techniques to their students and other aviation professionals with whom they come in contact. Specific suggestions for self-improvement are discussed in Chapter 11.

MINIMIZING STUDENT FRUSTRATIONS

Minimizing student frustrations in the classroom, shop, or during flight training, is a basic instructor responsibility. By following some basic rules, instructors can reduce student frustrations and create a learning environment that will encourage rather than discourage learning. [Figure 8-9]

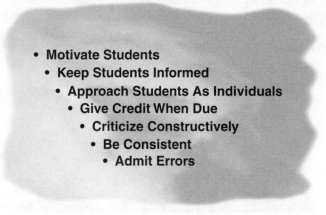

- Motivate Students
- Keep Students Informed
- Approach Students As Individuals
- Give Credit When Due
- Criticize Constructively
- Be Consistent
- Admit Errors

Figure 8-9. These are practical ways to minimize student frustration.

Motivate Students—More can be gained from wanting to learn than from being forced to learn. All too often students do not realize how a particular lesson or course can help them reach an important goal. When they can see the benefits or purpose of a lesson or course, their enjoyment and their efforts will increase.

Keep Students Informed—Students feel insecure when they do not know what is expected of them or what is going to happen to them. Instructors can minimize feelings of insecurity by telling students what is expected of them and what they can expect in return. Instructors should keep students informed in various ways, including giving them an overview of the course, keeping them posted on their progress, and giving them adequate notice of examinations, assignments, or other requirements.

Approach Students As Individuals—When instructors limit their thinking to the whole group without considering the individuals who make up that group, their efforts are directed at an average personality which really fits no one. Each group has its own personality that stems from the characteristics and interactions of its members. However, each individual within the group has a personality that is unique and that should be constantly considered.

Give Credit When Due—When students do something extremely well, they normally expect their abilities and efforts to be noticed. Otherwise, they may become frustrated. Praise or credit from the instructor is usually ample reward and provides an incentive to do even better. Praise pays dividends in student effort and achievement when deserved, but when given too freely, it becomes valueless.

Criticize Constructively—Although it is important to give praise and credit when deserved, it is equally important to identify mistakes and failures. It does not help to tell students that they have made errors and not provide explanations. If a student has made an earnest effort but is told that the work is unsatisfactory, with no other explanation, frustration occurs. Errors cannot be corrected if they are not identified, and if they are not identified, they will probably be perpetuated through faulty practice. On the other hand, if the student is briefed on the errors and is told how to correct them, progress can be made.

Be Consistent—Students want to please their instructor. This is the same desire that influences much of the behavior of subordinates toward their superiors in industry and business. Naturally, students have a keen interest in knowing what is required to please the instructor. If the same thing is acceptable one day and unacceptable the next, the student becomes confused. The instructor's philosophy and actions must be consistent.

Admit Errors—No one, including the students, expects an instructor to be perfect. The instructor can win the respect of students by honestly acknowledging mistakes. If the instructor tries to cover up or bluff, the students will be quick to sense it. Such behavior tends to destroy student confidence. If in doubt about some point, the instructor should admit it to the students.

ADDITIONAL RESPONSIBILITIES

This chapter has identified a number of areas necessary to maintain a professional appearance, demeanor, and attitude. In addition, the instructor has a number of responsibilities to the student, the public, and the FAA. Other areas aviation instructors should be deeply involved with include accident prevention and judgment training. Experience has shown that most accidents are the result of a chain of events. These events can be a mistake, but can also be a simple oversight, lack of awareness, or lack of a sense of urgency. The study of human factors in accidents is being taught throughout the aviation industry in an effort to understand why accidents occur and how training can prevent them. Concentration of this effort is in the area of how people make mistakes as a result of fatigue, stress, complacency, personal conflict, fear, or confusion. Human factors training also addresses the development of good judgment through the study of how and why people react to internal and external influences.

Flight instructors must incorporate aeronautical decision making (ADM) and judgment training into their instruction. This is a systematic approach to risk assessment and stress management in aviation. It shows how personal attitudes can influence decision making and how those attitudes can be modified to enhance safety in the cockpit. A number of FAA and industry references are available which provide instructors with methods for teaching ADM techniques and skills as a part of flight instruction. Aeronautical decision making and judgment training will be discussed more fully in Chapter 9.

Techniques of Flight Instruction

In this chapter, the demonstration-performance method is applied to the telling-and-doing technique of flight instruction, as well as the integrated technique of flight instruction. This chapter also discusses positive exchange of flight controls, use of distractions, obstacles to learning encountered during flight training, and provides an overall orientation for teaching aeronautical decision making (ADM) and judgment.

THE TELLING-AND-DOING TECHNIQUE

This technique has been in use for a long time and is very effective in teaching physical skills. Flight instructors find it valuable in teaching procedures and maneuvers. The **telling-and-doing technique** is actually a variation of the demonstration-performance method. It follows the four steps of demonstration performance discussed in Chapter 5, except for the first step. In the telling-and-doing technique, the first step is preparation. This is particularly important in flight instruction because of the introduction of new maneuvers or procedures.

The flight instructor needs to be well prepared and highly organized if complex maneuvers and procedures are to be taught effectively. The student must be intellectually and psychologically ready for the learning activity. The **preparation** step is accomplished prior to the flight lesson with a discussion of lesson objectives and completion standards, as well as a thorough preflight briefing. Students need to know not only what they will learn, but also how they will learn it—that is, how the lesson will proceed and how they will be evaluated. The preparation phase also should include coverage of appropriate safety procedures.

INSTRUCTOR TELLS—INSTRUCTOR DOES

Presentation is the second step in the teaching process. It is a continuation of preparing the student, which began in the detailed preflight discussion, and now continues by a carefully planned demonstration and accompanying verbal explanation of the procedure or maneuver. While demonstrating inflight maneuvers, the instructor should explain the required power settings, aircraft attitudes, and describe any other pertinent factors that may apply. This is the only step in which the student plays a passive role. It is important that the demonstration conforms to the explanation as closely as possible. In addition, it should be demonstrated in the same sequence in which it was explained so as to avoid confusion and provide reinforcement. Since students generally imitate the instructor's performance, the instructor must demonstrate the skill exactly the way the students are expected to practice it, including all safety procedures that the students must follow. If a deviation does occur, the instructor should point it out and discuss any differences from the initial explanation.

Most physical skills lend themselves to a sequential pattern where the skill is explained in the same step-by-step order normally used to perform it. When the skill being taught is related to previously learned procedures or maneuvers, the known to unknown strategy may be used effectively. When teaching more than one skill at the same time, the simple-to-complex strategy works well. By starting with the simplest skill, a student gains confidence and is less likely to become frustrated when faced with building skills that are more complex.

Another consideration in this phase is the language used. Instructors should attempt to avoid unnecessary jargon and technical terms that are over the heads of their students. Instructors should also take care to clearly describe the actions that students are expected to perform. Communication is the key. It is neither appropriate nor effective for instructors to try to impress students with their expertise by using language that is unnecessarily complicated.

As an example, a level turn might be demonstrated and described by the instructor in the following way:

- Use outside visual references and monitor the flight instruments.

- After clearing the airspace around the airplane, add power slightly, turn the airplane in the desired direction, and apply a slight amount of back pressure on the yoke to maintain altitude. Maintain coordinated flight by applying rudder in the direction of the turn.

- Remember, the ailerons control the roll rate, as well as the angle of bank. The rate at which the airplane rolls depends on how much aileron deflection you use. How far the airplane rolls (steepness of the bank) depends on how long you deflect the ailerons, since the airplane continues to roll as long as the ailerons are deflected. When you reach the desired angle of bank, neutralize the ailerons and trim, as appropriate.

- Lead the roll-out by approximately one-half the number of degrees of your angle of bank. Use coordinated aileron and rudder control pressures as you roll out. Simultaneously, begin releasing the back pressure so aileron, rudder, and elevator pressures are neutralized when the airplane reaches the wings-level position.

- Leading the roll-out heading by one-half your bank angle is a good rule of thumb for initial training. However, keep in mind that the required amount of lead really depends on the type of turn, turn rate, and roll-out rate. As you gain experience, you will develop a consistent roll-in and roll-out technique for various types of turns. Upon reaching a wings-level attitude, reduce power and trim to remove control pressures.

STUDENT TELLS—INSTRUCTOR DOES

This is a transition between the second and third steps in the teaching process. It is the most obvious departure from the demonstration-performance technique, and may provide the most significant advantages. In this step, the student actually plays the role of instructor, telling the instructor what to do and how to do it. Two benefits accrue from this step. First, being freed from the need to concentrate on performance of the maneuver and from concern about its outcome, the student should be able to organize his or her thoughts regarding the steps involved and the techniques to be used. In the process of explaining the maneuver as the instructor performs it, perceptions begin to develop into insights. Mental habits begin to form with repetition of the instructions previously received. Second, with the student doing the talking, the instructor is able to evaluate the student's understanding of the factors involved in performance of the maneuver.

According to the principle of primacy, it is important for the instructor to make sure the student gets it right the first time. The student should also understand the correct sequence and be aware of safety precautions for each procedure or maneuver. If a misunderstanding exists, it can be corrected before the student becomes absorbed in controlling the airplane.

STUDENT TELLS—STUDENT DOES

Application is the third step in the teaching process. This is where learning takes place and where performance habits are formed. If the student has been adequately prepared (first step) and the procedure or maneuver fully explained and demonstrated (second step), meaningful learning will occur. The instructor should be alert during the student's practice to detect any errors in technique and to prevent the formation of faulty habits.

At the same time, the student should be encouraged to think about what to do during the performance of a maneuver, until it becomes habitual. In this step, the thinking is done verbally. This focuses concentration on the task to be accomplished, so that total involvement in the maneuver is fostered. All of the student's physical and mental faculties are brought into play. The instructor should be aware of the student's thought processes. It is easy to determine whether an error is induced by a misconception or by a simple lack of motor skills. Therefore, in addition to forcing total concentration on the part of the student, this method provides a means for keeping the instructor aware of what the student is thinking. The student is not only learning to do something, but he or she is learning a self-teaching process that is highly desirable in development of a skill.

The exact procedures that the instructor should use during student practice depends on factors such as the student's proficiency level, the type of maneuver, and the stage of training. The instructor must exercise good judgment to decide how much control to use. With potentially hazardous or difficult maneuvers, the instructor should be alert and ready to take control at any time. This is especially true during a student's first attempt at a particular maneuver. On the other hand, if a student is progressing normally, the instructor should avoid unnecessary interruptions or too much assistance.

A typical test of how much control is needed often occurs during a student's first few attempts to land an aircraft. The instructor must quickly evaluate the student's need for help, and not hesitate to take control, if required. At the same time, the student should be allowed to practice the entire maneuver often enough to achieve the level of proficiency established in the lesson objectives. Since this is a learning phase rather than an evaluation phase of the training, errors or unsafe practices should be identified and corrected in a positive and timely way. In some cases, the student will not be able to meet the proficiency level specified in the lesson objectives within the allotted time. When this occurs, the instructor should be prepared to schedule additional training.

STUDENT DOES—INSTRUCTOR EVALUATES

The fourth step of the teaching process is **review and evaluation**. In this step, the instructor reviews what has been covered during the instructional flight and determines to what extent the student has met the objectives outlined during the preflight discussion. Since the student no longer is required to talk through the maneuver during this step, the instructor should be satisfied that the student is well prepared and understands the task before starting. This last step is identical to the final step used in the demonstration-performance method. The instructor observes as the student performs, then makes appropriate comments.

At the conclusion of the evaluation phase, record the student's performance and verbally advise each student of the progress made toward the objectives. Regardless of how well a skill is taught, there may still be failures. Since success is a motivating factor, instructors should be positive in revealing results. When pointing out areas that need improvement, offer concrete suggestions that will help. If possible, avoid ending the evaluation on a negative note.

In summary, the telling and doing technique of flight instruction follows the four basic steps of the teaching process and the demonstration-performance method. However, the telling-and-doing technique includes specific variations for flight instruction. [Figure 9-1]

TEACHING PROCESS	DEMONSTRATION-PERFORMANCE METHOD	TELLING-AND-DOING TECHNIQUE
Preparation	Explanation	Preparation
Presentation	Demonstration	Instructor Tells Instructor Does
		Student Tells Instructor Does
Application	Student Performance Supervision	Student Tells Student Does
Review and Evaluation	Evaluation	Student Does Instructor Evaluates

Figure 9-1. This comparison of steps in the teaching process, the demonstration-performance method, and the telling-and-doing technique shows the similarities as well as some differences. The main difference in the telling-and-doing technique is the important transition, student tells—instructor does, which occurs between the second and third step.

INTEGRATED FLIGHT INSTRUCTION

Integrated flight instruction is flight instruction during which students are taught to perform flight maneuvers both by outside visual references and by reference to flight instruments. For this type of instruction to be fully effective, the use of instrument references should begin the first time each new maneuver is introduced. No distinction in the pilot's operation of the flight controls is permitted, regardless of whether outside references or instrument indications are used for the performance of the maneuver. When this training technique is used, instruction in the control of an airplane by outside visual references is integrated with instruction in the use of flight instrument indications for the same operations.

DEVELOPMENT OF HABIT PATTERNS

The continuing observance and reliance upon flight instruments is essential for efficient, safe operations. The habit of monitoring instruments is difficult to develop after one has become accustomed to relying almost exclusively on outside references.

General aviation accident reports provide ample support for the belief that reference to flight instruments is important to safety. The safety record of pilots who hold instrument ratings is significantly better than that of pilots with comparable flight time who have never received formal flight training for an instrument rating. Student pilots who have been required to perform all normal flight maneuvers by reference to instruments, as well as by outside references, will develop from the start the habit of continuously monitoring their own and the airplane's performance.

The early establishment of proper habits of instrument cross-check, instrument interpretation, and aircraft control will be highly useful to the student pilot. The habits formed at this time also will give the student a firm foundation for later training for an instrument rating.

ACCURACY OF FLIGHT CONTROL

During early experiments with the integrated technique of flight instruction, it was soon recognized that students trained in this manner are much more precise in their flight maneuvers and operations. This applies to all flight operations, not just when flight by reference to instruments is required.

Notable among student achievements are better monitoring of power settings and more accurate control of headings, altitudes, and airspeeds. As the habit of monitoring their own performance by reference to instruments is developed, students will begin to make corrections without prompting.

The habitual attention to instrument indications leads to improved landings because of more precise airspeed control. Effective use of instruments also results in superior cross-country navigation, better coordination, and generally, a better overall pilot competency level.

OPERATING EFFICIENCY

As student pilots become more proficient in monitoring and correcting their own flight technique by reference to flight instruments, the performance obtained from an airplane increases noticeably. This is particularly true of modern, complex, or high-performance airplanes, which are responsive to the use of correct operating airspeeds.

The use of correct power settings and climb speeds and the accurate control of headings during climbs result in a measurable increase in climb performance. Holding precise headings and altitudes in cruising flight will definitely increase average cruising performance.

The use of integrated flight instruction provides the student with the ability to control an airplane in flight for limited periods if outside references are lost. This ability could save the pilot's life and those of the passengers in an actual emergency.

During the conduct of integrated flight training, the flight instructor must emphasize to the students that the introduction to the use of flight instruments does not prepare them for operations in marginal weather or instrument meteorological conditions. The possible consequences, both to themselves and to others, of experiments with flight operations in weather conditions below VFR minimums before they are instrument rated, should be constantly impressed on the students.

PROCEDURES

The conduct of integrated flight instruction is simple. The student's first briefing on the function of the flight controls should include the instrument indications to be expected, as well as the outside references which should be used to control the attitude of the airplane.

Each new flight maneuver should be introduced using both outside references and instrument references. Students should develop the ability to maneuver an aircraft equally as well by instrument or outside references. They naturally accept the fact that the manipulation of the flight controls is identical, regardless of which references are used to determine the attitude of the airplane. This practice should continue throughout the student's flight instruction for all maneuvers. To fully achieve the demonstrated benefits of this type of training, the use of visual and instrument references must be constantly integrated throughout the training. Failure to do so will lengthen the flight instruction necessary for the student to achieve the competency required for a private pilot certificate.

PRECAUTIONS

The instructor must be sure that the students develop, from the start of their training, the habit of looking for other air traffic at all times. If students are allowed to believe that the instructor assumes all responsibility for scanning and collision avoidance procedures, they will not develop the habit of maintaining a constant vigilance, which is essential to safety. Any observed tendency of a student to enter flight maneuvers without first making a careful check for other air traffic must be corrected immediately.

In earlier stages of training, students may find it easier to perform flight maneuvers by instruments than by outside references. The fact that students can perform better by reference to instruments may cause them to concentrate most of their attention on the instruments, when they should be using outside references. This must not be allowed to continue, since it will cause considerable difficulty later in training while maneuvering by reference to ground objects. This tendency will also limit vigilance for other air traffic. The instructor should carefully observe the student's performance of maneuvers during the early stages of integrated flight instruction to ensure that this habit does not develop.

During the conduct of integrated flight instruction, the instructor should make it clear that the use of instruments is being taught to prepare students to accurately monitor their own and their aircraft's performance. The instructor must avoid any indication, by word or action that the proficiency sought is intended solely for use in difficult weather situations.

FLIGHT INSTRUCTOR QUALIFICATIONS

As a prerequisite, a flight instructor must be thoroughly familiar with the functions, characteristics, and proper use of all standard flight instruments. It is the personal responsibility of each flight instructor to maintain familiarity with current pilot training techniques and certification requirements. This may be done by frequent review of new periodicals and technical publications, personal contacts with FAA inspectors and designated pilot examiners, and by participation in pilot and flight instructor clinics. The application of outmoded instructional procedures, or the preparation of student pilots using obsolete certification requirements is inexcusable.

OBSTACLES TO LEARNING DURING FLIGHT INSTRUCTION

Certain obstacles are common to flight instruction and may apply directly to the student's attitude, physical condition, and psychological make-up. These are included in the following list:

• Feeling of unfair treatment;

• Impatience to proceed to more interesting operations;

• Worry or lack of interest;

• Physical discomfort, illness, and fatigue;

• Apathy due to inadequate instruction; and

• Anxiety.

UNFAIR TREATMENT

Students who believe that their instruction is inadequate, or that their efforts are not conscientiously considered and evaluated, will not learn well. In addition, their motivation will suffer no matter how intent they are on learning to fly. Motivation will also decline when a student believes the instructor is making unreasonable demands for performance and progress. [Figure 9-2]

I said 3,000 feet . . . not 2,990!

Figure 9-2. The assignment of impossible or unreasonable goals discourages the student, diminishes effort, and retards the learning process.

Assignment of goals that the student considers difficult, but possible, usually provides a challenge, and promotes learning. In a typical flight lesson, reasonable goals are listed in the lesson objectives and the desired levels of proficiency for the goals are included in statements that contain completion standards.

IMPATIENCE

Impatience is a greater deterrent to learning pilot skills than is generally recognized. With a flight student, this may take the form of a desire to make an early solo flight, or to set out on cross-country flights before the basic elements of flight have been learned.

The impatient student fails to understand the need for preliminary training and seeks only the ultimate objective without considering the means necessary to reach it. With every complex human endeavor, it is necessary to master the basics if the whole task is to be performed competently and safely. The instructor can correct student impatience by presenting the necessary preliminary training one step at a time, with clearly stated goals for each step. The procedures and elements mastered in each step should be clearly identified in explaining or demonstrating the performance of the subsequent step.

Impatience can result from instruction keyed to the pace of a slow learner when it is applied to a motivated, fast learner. It is just as important that a student be advanced to the subsequent step as soon as one goal has been attained, as it is to complete each step before the next one is undertaken. Disinterest grows rapidly when unnecessary repetition and drill are required on operations that have already been adequately learned.

WORRY OR LACK OF INTEREST

Worry or lack of interest has a detrimental effect on learning. Students who are worried or emotionally upset are not ready to learn and derive little benefit from instruction. Worry or distraction may be due to student concerns about progress in the training course, or may stem from circumstances completely unrelated to their instruction. Significant emotional upsets may be due to personal problems, psychiatric disturbances, or a dislike of the training program or the instructor.

The experiences of students outside their training activities affect their behavior and performance in training; the two cannot be separated. When students begin flight training, they bring with them their interests, enthusiasms, fears, and troubles. The instructor cannot be responsible for these outside diversions, but cannot ignore them because they have a critical effect on the learning process. Instruction must be keyed to the utilization of the interests and enthusiasm students bring with them, and to diverting their attention from their worries and troubles to the learning tasks at hand. This is admittedly difficult, but must be accomplished if learning is to proceed at a normal rate.

Worries and emotional upsets that result from a flight training course can be identified and addressed. These problems are often due to inadequacies of the course or of the instructor. The most effective cure is prevention. The instructor must be alert to see that the students understand the objectives of each step of their training, and that they know at the completion of each lesson exactly how well they have progressed and what deficiencies are apparent. Discouragement and emotional upsets are rare when students feel that nothing is being withheld from them or is being neglected in their training.

PHYSICAL DISCOMFORT, ILLNESS, AND FATIGUE

Physical discomfort, illness, and fatigue will materially slow the rate of learning during both classroom instruction and flight training. Students who are not completely at ease, and whose attention is diverted by discomforts such as the extremes of temperature, poor ventilation, inadequate lighting, or noise and confusion, cannot learn at a normal rate. This is true no matter how diligently they attempt to apply themselves to the learning task.

A minor illness, such as a cold, or a major illness or injury will interfere with the normal rate of learning. This is especially important for flight instruction. Most illnesses adversely affect the acuteness of vision, hearing, and feeling, all of which are essential to correct performance.

Airsickness can be a great deterrent to flight instruction. A student who is airsick, or bothered with incipient airsickness, is incapable of learning at a normal rate. There is no sure cure for airsickness, but resistance or immunity can be developed in a relatively short period of time. An instructional flight should be terminated as soon as incipient sickness is experienced. As the student develops immunity, flights can be increased in length until normal flight periods are practicable.

Keeping students interested and occupied during flight is a deterrent to airsickness. They are much less apt to become airsick while operating the controls themselves. Rough air and unexpected abrupt maneuvers tend to increase the chances of airsickness. Tension and apprehension apparently contribute to airsickness and should be avoided.

The detection of student fatigue is important to efficient flight instruction. This is important both in assessing a student's substandard performance early in a lesson, and also in recognizing the deterioration of performance. Once fatigue occurs as a result of application to a learning task, the student should be given a break in instruction and practice. Fatigue can be delayed by introducing a number of maneuvers, which involve different elements and objectives.

Fatigue is the primary consideration in determining the length and frequency of flight instruction periods. The amount of training, which can be absorbed by one student without incurring debilitating fatigue, does not necessarily indicate the capacity of another student. Fatigue which results from training operations may be either physical or mental, or both. It is not necessarily a function of physical robustness or mental acuity. Generally speaking, complex operations tend to induce fatigue more rapidly than simpler procedures do, regardless of the physical effort involved. Flight instruction should be continued only as long as the student is alert, receptive to instruction, and is performing at a level consistent with experience.

APATHY DUE TO INADEQUATE INSTRUCTION

Students quickly become apathetic when they recognize that the instructor has made inadequate preparations for the instruction being given, or when the instruction appears to be deficient, contradictory, or insincere. To hold the student's interest and to maintain the motivation necessary for efficient learning, well-planned, appropriate, and accurate instruction must be provided. Nothing destroys a student's interest so quickly as a poorly organized period of instruction. Even an inexperienced student realizes immediately when the instructor has failed to prepare a lesson. [Figure 9-3]

Figure 9-3. Poor preparation leads to spotty coverage, misplaced emphasis, unnecessary repetition, and a lack of confidence on the part of the student. The instructor should always have a plan.

Instruction may be overly explicit and so elementary it fails to hold student interest, or it may be so general or complicated that it fails to evoke the interest necessary for effective learning. To be effective, the instructor must teach for the level of the student. The presentation must be adjusted to be meaningful to the person for whom it is intended. For example, instruction in the preflight inspection of an aircraft should be presented quite differently for a student who is a skilled aircraft maintenance technician compared to the instruction on the same operation for a student with no previous aeronautical experience. The inspection desired in each case is the same, but a presentation meaningful to one of these students would be inappropriate for the other.

Poor instructional presentations may result not only from poor preparation, but also from distracting mannerisms, personal untidiness, or the appearance of irritation with the student. Creating the impression of talking down to the student is one of the surest ways for an instructor to lose the student's confidence and attention. Once the instructor loses this confidence, it is difficult to regain, and the learning rate is unnecessarily diminished.

ANXIETY

Anxiety may place additional burdens on the instructor. This frequently limits the student's perceptive ability and retards the development of insights. The student must be comfortable, confident in the instructor and the aircraft, and at ease, if effective learning is to occur. Providing this atmosphere for learning is one of the first and most important tasks of the instructor. Although doing so may be difficult at first, successive accomplishments of recognizable goals and the avoidance of alarming occurrences or situations will rapidly ease the student's mind. This is true of all flight students, but special handling by the instructor may be required for students who are obviously anxious or uncomfortable.

POSITIVE EXCHANGE OF FLIGHT CONTROLS

Positive exchange of flight controls is an integral part of flight training. It is especially critical during the telling-and-doing technique of flight instruction. Due to the importance of this subject, the following discussion provides guidance for all pilots, especially student pilots, flight instructors, and pilot examiners, on the recommended procedure to use for the positive exchange of flight controls between pilots when operating an aircraft.

BACKGROUND

Incident/accident statistics indicate a need to place additional emphasis on the exchange of control of an aircraft by pilots. Numerous accidents have occurred due to a lack of communication or misunderstanding as to who actually had control of the aircraft, particularly between students and flight instructors.

Establishing the following procedure during the initial training of students will ensure the formation of a habit pattern that should stay with them throughout their flying careers. They will be more likely to relinquish control willingly and promptly when instructed to do so during flight training.

PROCEDURES

During flight training, there must always be a clear understanding between students and flight instructors of who has control of the aircraft. Prior to flight, a briefing should be conducted that includes the procedure for the exchange of flight controls. A positive three-step process in the exchange of flight controls between pilots is a proven procedure and one that is strongly recommended. When an instructor is teaching a maneuver to a student, the instructor will normally demonstrate the maneuver first, then have the student follow along on the controls during a demonstration and, finally, the student will perform the maneuver with the instructor following along on the controls. [Figure 9-4]

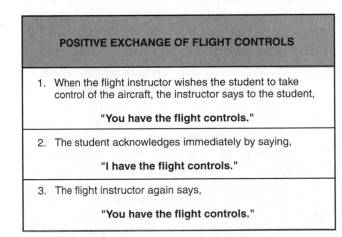

POSITIVE EXCHANGE OF FLIGHT CONTROLS
1. When the flight instructor wishes the student to take control of the aircraft, the instructor says to the student, **"You have the flight controls."**
2. The student acknowledges immediately by saying, **"I have the flight controls."**
3. The flight instructor again says, **"You have the flight controls."**

Figure 9-4. During this procedure, a visual check is recommended to see that the other person actually has the flight controls. When returning the controls to the instructor, the student should follow the same procedure the instructor used when giving control to the student. The student should stay on the controls and keep flying the aircraft until the instructor says, "I have the flight controls." There should never be any doubt as to who is flying the aircraft.

Flight instructors should always guard the controls and be prepared to take control of the aircraft. When necessary, the instructor should take the controls and calmly announce, "I have the flight controls." If an instructor allows a student to remain on the controls, the instructor may not have full and effective control of the aircraft. Anxious students can be incredibly strong and usually exhibit reactions inappropriate to the situation. If a recovery is necessary, there is absolutely nothing to be gained by having the student on the controls and having to fight for control of the aircraft.

Students should never be allowed to exceed the flight instructor's limits. Flight instructors should not exceed their own ability to perceive a problem, decide upon a course of action, and physically react within their ability to fly the aircraft.

USE OF DISTRACTIONS

National Transportation Safety Board (NTSB) statistics reveal that most stall/spin accidents occured when the pilot's attention was diverted from the primary task of flying the aircraft. Sixty percent of stall/spin accidents occured during takeoff and landing, and twenty percent were preceded by engine failure. Preoccupation inside or outside the cockpit while changing aircraft configuration or trim, maneuvering to avoid other traffic or clearing hazardous obstacles during takeoff and climb could create a potential stall/spin situation.

The intentional practice of stalls and spins seldom resulted in an accident. The real danger was inadvertent stalls induced by distractions during routine flight situations.

Pilots at all skill levels should be aware of the increased risk of entering into an inadvertent stall or spin while performing tasks that are secondary to controlling the aircraft. The FAA has also established a policy for use of certain distractions on practical tests for pilot certification. The purpose is to determine that applicants possess the skills required to cope with distractions while maintaining the degree of aircraft control required for safe flight. The most effective training is the simulation of scenarios that can lead to inadvertent stalls by creating distractions while the student is practicing certain maneuvers.

The instructor should tell the student to divide his/her attention between the distracting task and maintaining control of the aircraft. The following are examples of distractions that can be used for this training:

* Drop a pencil. Ask the student to pick it up.

* Ask the student to determine a heading to an airport using a chart.

* Ask the student to reset the clock.

* Ask the student to get something from the back seat.

* Ask the student to read the outside air temperature.

* Ask the student to call the Flight Service Station (FSS) for weather information.

* Ask the student to compute true airspeed with a flight computer.

* Ask the student to identify terrain or objects on the ground.

* Ask the student to identify a field suitable for a forced landing.

* Have the student climb 200 feet and maintain altitude, then descend 200 feet and maintain altitude.

* Have the student reverse course after a series of S-turns.

AERONAUTICAL DECISION MAKING

Aeronautical decision making (ADM) is a systematic approach to the mental process used by aircraft pilots to consistently determine the best course of action in response to a given set of circumstances. The importance of teaching students effective ADM skills can not be overemphasized. The flight instructor can make a difference! While progress is continually being made in the advancement of pilot training methods, aircraft equipment and systems, and services for pilots, accidents still occur. Despite all the changes in technology to improve flight safety, one factor remains the same—the human factor. It is estimated that approximately 75% of all aviation accidents are **human factors** related.

Historically, the term **pilot error** has been used to describe the causes of these accidents. Pilot error means that an action or decision made by the pilot was the cause of, or contributing factor which lead to, the accident. This definition also includes the pilot's failure to make a decision or take action. From a broader perspective, the phrase "human factors related" more aptly describes these accidents since it is usually not a single decision that leads to an accident, but a chain of events triggered by a number of factors.

The **poor judgment chain**, sometimes referred to as the error chain, is a term used to describe this concept of contributing factors in a human factors related accident. Breaking one link in the chain normally is all that is necessary to change the outcome of the sequence of events. The best way to illustrate this concept to students is to discuss specific situations which lead to aircraft accidents or incidents. The following is an example of the type of scenario which can be presented to students to illustrate the poor judgment chain.

A private pilot, who had logged 100 hours of flight time, made a precautionary landing on a narrow dirt runway at a private airport. The pilot lost directional control during landing and swerved off the runway into the grass. A witness recalled later that the airplane appeared to be too high and fast on final approach, and speculated the pilot was having difficulty controlling the airplane in high winds. The weather at the time of the incident was reported as marginal VFR due to rain showers and thunderstorms. When the airplane was fueled the following morning, 60 gallons of fuel were required to fill the 62-gallon capacity tanks.

By discussing the events that led to this incident, instructors can help students understand how a series of judgmental errors contributed to the final outcome of this flight. For example, one of the first elements that affected the pilot's flight was a decision regarding the weather. On the morning of the flight, the pilot was running late, and having acquired a computer printout of the forecast the night before, he did not bother to obtain a briefing from flight service before his departure.

A flight planning decision also played a part in this poor judgment chain. The pilot calculated total fuel requirements for the trip based on a rule-of-thumb figure he had used previously for another airplane. He did not use the fuel tables printed in the pilot's operating handbook for the airplane he was flying on this trip. After reaching his destination, the pilot did not request refueling. Based on his original calculations, he believed sufficient fuel remained for the flight home.

Failing to recognize his own limitations was another factor that led the pilot one step closer to the unfortunate conclusion of his journey. In the presence of deteriorating weather, he departed for the flight home at 5:00 in the afternoon. He did not consider how fatigue and lack of extensive night flying experience could affect the flight. As the flight continued, the weather along the route grew increasingly hazardous. Since the airplane's fuel supply was almost exhausted, the pilot no longer had the option of diverting to avoid rapidly developing thunderstorms. With few alternatives left, he was forced to land at the nearest airfield available, a small private airport with one narrow dirt runway. Due to the gusty wind conditions and the pilot's limited experience, the approach and landing were difficult. After touchdown, the pilot lost directional control and the

airplane finally came to a stop in the grass several yards to the side of the runway.

On numerous occasions during the flight, the pilot could have made effective decisions which may have prevented this incident. However, as the chain of events unfolded, each poor decision left him with fewer and fewer options. Teaching pilots to make sound decisions is the key to preventing accidents. Traditional pilot instruction has emphasized flying skills, knowledge of the aircraft, and familiarity with regulations. ADM training focuses on the decision-making process and the factors that affect a pilot's ability to make effective choices.

ORIGINS OF ADM TRAINING

The airlines developed some of the first training programs that focused on improving aeronautical decision making. Human factors-related accidents motivated the airline industry to implement **crew resource management (CRM)** training for flight crews. The focus of CRM programs is the effective use of all available resources; human resources, hardware, and information. Human resources include all groups routinely working with the cockpit crew (or pilot) who are involved in decisions which are required to operate a flight safely. These groups include, but are not limited to: dispatchers, cabin crewmembers, maintenance personnel, and air traffic controllers. Although the CRM concept originated as airlines developed ways of facilitating crew cooperation to improve decision making in the cockpit, CRM principles, such as workload management, situational awareness, communication, the leadership role of the captain, and crewmember coordination have direct application to the general aviation cockpit. This also includes single pilots since pilots of small aircraft, as well as crews of larger aircraft, must make effective use of all available resources—human resources, hardware, and information.

Crew resource management training has proven extremely successful in reducing accidents, and airlines typically introduce CRM concepts during initial indoctrination of new hires. Instructors in the general aviation environment can learn from this example when conducting ADM training. In the past, some students were introduced to ADM concepts toward the completion of their training or not at all. It is important that these concepts be incorporated throughout the entire training course for all levels of students; private, instrument, commercial, multi-engine, and ATP. Instructors, as well as students, also can refer to AC 60-22, *Aeronautical*

Decision Making, which provides background references, definitions, and other pertinent information about ADM training in the general aviation environment. [Figure 9-5]

THE DECISION-MAKING PROCESS

An understanding of the decision-making process provides students with a foundation for developing ADM skills. Some situations, such as engine failures, require a pilot to respond immediately using established procedures with little time for detailed analysis. Traditionally, pilots have been well trained to react to emergencies, but are not as well prepared to make decisions which require a more reflective response. Typically during a flight, the pilot has time to examine any changes which occur, gather information, and assess risk before reaching a decision. The steps leading to this conclusion constitute the decision-making process. When the decision-making process is presented to students, it is essential to discuss how the process applies to an actual flight situation. To explain the decision-making process, the instructor can introduce the following steps with the accompanying scenario that places the student in the position of making a decision about a typical flight situation.

DEFINING THE PROBLEM

Problem definition is the first step in the decision-making process. Defining the problem begins with recognizing that a change has occurred or that an expected

DEFINITIONS
ADM is a systematic approach to the mental process used by pilots to consistently determine the best course of action in response to a given set of circumstances.
ATTITUDE is a personal motivational predisposition to respond to persons, situations, or events in a given manner that can, nevertheless, be changed or modified through training as sort of a mental shortcut to decision making.
ATTITUDE MANAGEMENT is the ability to recognize hazardous attitudes in oneself and the willingness to modify them as necessary through the application of an appropriate antidote thought.
CREW RESOURCE MANAGEMENT (CRM) is the application of team management concepts in the flight deck environment. It was initially known as cockpit resource management, but as CRM programs evolved to include cabin crews, maintenance personnel, and others, the phrase crew resource management was adopted. This includes single pilots, as in most general aviation aircraft. Pilots of small aircraft, as well as crews of larger aircraft, must make effective use of all available resources; human resources, hardware, and information. A current definition includes all groups routinely working with the cockpit crew who are involved in decisions required to operate a flight safely. These groups include, but are not limited to: pilots, dispatchers, cabin crewmembers, maintenance personnel, and air traffic controllers. CRM is one way of addressing the challenge of optimizing the human/machine interface and accompanying interpersonal activities.
HEADWORK is required to accomplish a conscious, rational thought process when making decisions. Good decision making involves risk identification and assessment, information processing, and problem solving.
JUDGMENT is the mental process of recognizing and analyzing all pertinent information in a particular situation, a rational evaluation of alternative actions in response to it, and a timely decision on which action to take.
PERSONALITY is the embodiment of personal traits and characteristics of an individual that are set at a very early age and extremely resistant to change.
POOR JUDGMENT CHAIN is a series of mistakes that may lead to an accident or incident. Two basic principles generally associated with the creation of a poor judgment chain are: (1) One bad decision often leads to another; and (2) as a string of bad decisions grows, it reduces the number of subsequent alternatives for continued safe flight. ADM is intended to break the poor judgment chain before it can cause an accident or incident.
RISK ELEMENTS IN ADM take into consideration the four fundamental risk elements: the pilot, the aircraft, the environment, and the type of operation that comprise any given aviation situation.
RISK MANAGEMENT is the part of the decision making process which relies on situational awareness, problem recognition, and good judgment to reduce risks associated with each flight.
SITUATIONAL AWARENESS is the accurate perception and understanding of all the factors and conditions within the four fundamental risk elements that affect safety before, during, and after the flight.
SKILLS and PROCEDURES are the procedural, psychomotor, and perceptual skills used to control a specific aircraft or its systems. They are the stick and rudder or airmanship abilities that are gained through conventional training, are perfected, and become almost automatic through experience.
STRESS MANAGEMENT is the personal analysis of the kinds of stress experienced while flying, the application of appropriate stress assessment tools, and other coping mechanisms.

Figure 9-5. These terms are used in AC 60-22 to explain concepts used in ADM training.

change did not occur. A problem is perceived first by the senses, then is distinguished through insight and experience. These same abilities, as well as an objective analysis of all available information, are used to determine the exact nature and severity of the problem.

One critical error that can be made during the decision-making process is incorrectly defining the problem. For example, failure of a landing-gear-extended light to illuminate could indicate that the gear is not down and locked into place or it could mean the bulb is burned out. The actions to be taken in each of these circumstances would be significantly different. Fixating on a problem that does not exist can divert the pilot's attention from important tasks. The pilot's failure to maintain an awareness of the circumstances regarding the flight now becomes the problem. This is why once an initial assumption is made regarding the problem, other sources must be used to verify that the pilot's conclusion is correct.

While on a cross-country flight, you discover that your time en route between two checkpoints is significantly longer than the time you had originally calculated. By noticing this discrepancy, you have recognized a change. Based on your insight, cross-country flying experience, and your knowledge of weather systems, you consider the possibility that you have an increased headwind. You verify that your original calculations are correct and consider factors which may have lengthened the time between checkpoints, such as a climb or deviation off course. To determine if there is a change in the winds aloft forecast and to check recent pilot reports, you contact Flight Watch. After weighing each information source, you conclude that your headwind has increased. To determine the severity of the problem, you calculate your new groundspeed, and reassess fuel requirements.

CHOOSING A COURSE OF ACTION

After the problem has been identified, the pilot must evaluate the need to react to it and determine the actions which may be taken to resolve the situation in the time available. The expected outcome of each possible action should be considered and the risks assessed before the pilot decides on a response to the situation.

You determine your fuel burn if you continue to your destination, and consider other options, such as turning around and landing at a nearby airport that you have passed, diverting off course, or landing prior to your destination at an airport on your route. You must now consider the expected outcome of each possible

action and assess the risks involved. After studying the chart, you conclude that there is an airport which has fueling services within a reasonable distance ahead along your route. You can refuel there and continue to your destination without a significant loss of time.

IMPLEMENTING THE DECISION AND EVALUATING THE OUTCOME

Although a decision may be reached and a course of action implemented, the decision-making process is not complete. It is important to think ahead and determine how the decision could affect other phases of the flight. As the flight progresses, the pilot must continue to evaluate the outcome of the decision to ensure that it is producing the desired result.

To implement your decision, you plot the course changes and calculate a new estimated time of arrival, as well as contact the nearest flight service station to amend your flight plan and check weather conditions at your new destination. As you proceed to the airport, you continue to monitor your groundspeed, aircraft performance, and the weather conditions to ensure that no additional steps need to be taken to guarantee the safety of the flight.

To assist teaching pilots the elements of the decision-making process, a six-step model has been developed using the acronym "DECIDE." The DECIDE model has been used to instruct pilots of varying experience levels, as well as analyze accidents. [Figure 9-6]

DECIDE MODEL

Detect the fact that a change has occurred.
Estimate the need to counter or react to the change.
Choose a desirable outcome for the success of the flight.
Identify actions which could successfully control the change.
Do the necessary action to adapt to the change.
Evaluate the effect of the action.

Figure 9-6. During initial training, the DECIDE model can provide a framework for effective decision making.

RISK MANAGEMENT

During each flight, decisions must be made regarding events which involve interactions between the four **risk elements**—the pilot in command, the aircraft, the environment, and the operation. The decision-making process involves an evaluation of each of these risk ele-

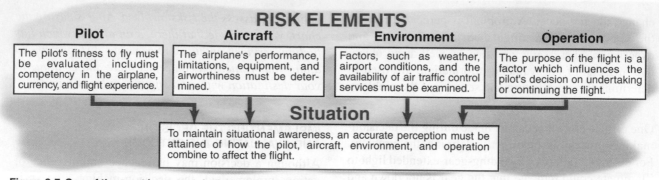

RISK ELEMENTS

Pilot	Aircraft	Environment	Operation
The pilot's fitness to fly must be evaluated including competency in the airplane, currency, and flight experience.	The airplane's performance, limitations, equipment, and airworthiness must be determined.	Factors, such as weather, airport conditions, and the availability of air traffic control services must be examined.	The purpose of the flight is a factor which influences the pilot's decision on undertaking or continuing the flight.

Situation

To maintain situational awareness, an accurate perception must be attained of how the pilot, aircraft, environment, and operation combine to affect the flight.

Figure 9-7. One of the most important decisions that the pilot in command must make is the go/no-go decision. Evaluating each of these risk elements can help the pilot decide whether a flight should be conducted or continued.

ments to achieve an accurate perception of the flight situation. [Figure 9-7]

To reinforce the risk elements and their significance to effective decision making, the instructor can ask the student to identify the risk elements for a flight. The student should also be able to determine whether the risks have been appropriately evaluated in the situation.

A pilot schedules to fly to a business appointment with a client in a nearby city. She is a noninstrument-rated private pilot with no experience in marginal weather conditions, although she did gain some attitude instrument flying experience during her private pilot flight training. She intends to fly in a small four-seat, single-engine airplane with standard communication and navigation equipment. However, the VOR receiver is inoperative. The pilot plans to leave in the morning and return early in the afternoon. When she receives her weather briefing, she is informed that marginal VFR conditions with possible icing in the clouds are forecast for late afternoon. Having been delayed at the office, the pilot departs later than planned. While en route, the pilot encounters low ceilings and restricted visibility and she becomes spatially disoriented due to continued flight by ground reference.

In this case, the pilot did not effectively evaluate the four risk elements when making decisions regarding this flight. When assessing her fitness as a pilot, she overestimated her flying abilities by attempting to fly in marginal VFR conditions. The capability of her airplane was not properly evaluated. The inoperative VOR receiver limits her options if she becomes lost, or is required to navigate with limited visual reference to the ground. In addition, her airplane did not contain sophisticated navigation equipment which may have helped her locate an airport in an emergency situation. The flying environment was less than optimal when she decided to depart despite the threat of marginal conditions. When faced with deteriorating weather, she did not enlist the assistance of **air traffic control (ATC)** or use her instruments as references to turn around. Since she was trying to reach her destination for a business appointment, the operation affected her decision to undertake and continue the flight.

ASSESSING RISK

Examining NTSB reports and other accident research can help students learn to assess risk more effectively. Instructors can point out the phases of flight when accidents are most likely to occur and when risk is the greatest. For example, the majority of accidents occur when approaching or departing airports. [Figure 9-8]

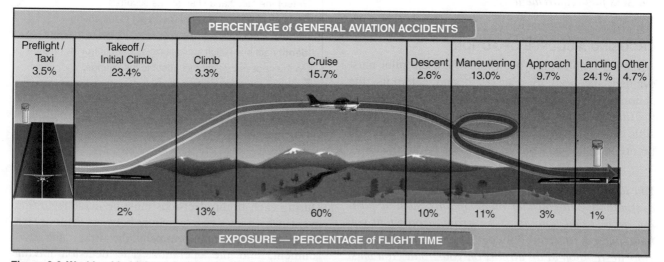

PERCENTAGE of GENERAL AVIATION ACCIDENTS

Preflight / Taxi 3.5%	Takeoff / Initial Climb 23.4%	Climb 3.3%	Cruise 15.7%	Descent 2.6%	Maneuvering 13.0%	Approach 9.7%	Landing 24.1%	Other 4.7%
	2%	13%	60%	10%	11%	3%	1%	

EXPOSURE — PERCENTAGE of FLIGHT TIME

Figure 9-8. Workload is highest during takeoff and landing, which increases the chance of error.

Studies also indicate the types of flight activities that are most likely to result in the most serious accidents. The majority of fatal general aviation accident causes fall under the categories of maneuvering flight, approaches, takeoff/initial climb, and weather. Delving deeper into accident statistics can provide some important details that can help students understand the risks involved with specific flying situations. For example, maneuvering flight is one of the largest single producers of fatal accidents and many of these accidents are attributed to maneuvering during low, slow flight, often during buzzing or unauthorized aerobatics. Fatal accidents which occur during approach often happen at night or in IFR conditions. Takeoff/initial climb accidents frequently are due to the pilot's lack of awareness of the effects of density altitude on aircraft performance or other improper takeoff planning resulting in loss of control or stalls during, or shortly after takeoff. The majority of weather-related accidents occur after attempted VFR flight into IFR conditions.

In addition to discussing these facts, instructors can increase student awareness of these risks by setting positive examples. For instance, ensuring that students obtain weather briefings before every flight develops good habits and emphasizes the importance of the weather check. Instructors should take the time to discuss the conditions, and require the student to arrive at a go/no-go decision. Ignoring a marginal forecast or continuing a flight in poor weather may be sending the message that checking the weather serves no practical purpose. During the flight planning phase, the flight instructor can introduce situations that are different from those planned. The student should be asked to explain the possible consequences of each situation. Even if a flight lesson is canceled based on forecast conditions that never materialize, a lesson in judgment has been accomplished.

FACTORS AFFECTING DECISION MAKING

It is important to point out to students that being familiar with the decision-making process does not ensure that they will have the good judgment to be safe pilots. The ability to make effective decisions as pilot in command depends on a number of factors. Some circumstances, such as the time available to make a decision, may be beyond the pilot's control. However, a pilot can learn to recognize those factors that can be managed, and learn skills to improve decision-making ability and judgment.

PILOT SELF-ASSESSMENT

The pilot in command of an aircraft is directly responsible for, and is the final authority as to, the operation of that aircraft. In order to effectively exercise that responsibility and make effective decisions regarding the outcome of a flight, pilots must have an understanding of their limitations. A pilot's performance during a flight is affected by many factors, such as health, recency of experience, knowledge, skill level, and attitude.

Students must be taught that exercising good judgment begins prior to taking the controls of an aircraft. Often, pilots thoroughly check their aircraft to determine airworthiness, yet do not evaluate their own fitness for flight. Just as a checklist is used when preflighting an aircraft, a personal checklist based on such factors as experience, currency, and comfort level can help determine if a pilot is prepared for a particular flight. Specifying when refresher training should be accomplished, designating weather minimums which may be higher than those listed in Title 14 of the Code of Federal Regulations (14 CFR) part 91, and setting limitations regarding the amount of crosswind for take-offs and landings are examples of elements which may be included on a personal checklist. Instructors set an example by having their own personal checklists and can help students create their own checklists. In addition to a review of personal limitations, pilots should use the I'M SAFE Checklist to further evaluate their fitness for flight. [Figure 9-9]

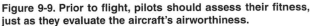

Figure 9-9. Prior to flight, pilots should assess their fitness, just as they evaluate the aircraft's airworthiness.

RECOGNIZING HAZARDOUS ATTITUDES

Being fit to fly depends on more than just a pilot's physical condition and recency of experience. For example, attitude will affect the quality of decisions. **Attitude** can be defined as a personal motivational predisposition to respond to persons, situations, or events in a given manner. Studies have identified five

1. **Anti-Authority:** "Don't tell me."	This attitude is found in people who do not like anyone telling them what to do. In a sense, they are saying, "No one can tell me what to do." They may be resentful of having someone tell them what to do, or may regard rules, regulations, and procedures as silly or unnecessary. However, it is always your prerogative to question authority if you feel it is in error.
2. **Impulsivity:** "Do it quickly."	This is the attitude of people who frequently feel the need to do something, anything, immediately. They do not stop to think about what they are about to do; they do not select the best alternative, and they do the first thing that comes to mind.
3. **Invulnerability:** "It won't happen to me."	Many people feel that accidents happen to others, but never to them. They know accidents can happen, and they know that anyone can be affected. They never really feel or believe that they will be personally involved. Pilots who think this way are more likely to take chances and increase risk.
4. **Macho:** "I can do it."	Pilots who are always trying to prove that they are better than anyone else are thinking, "I can do it –I'll show them." Pilots with this type of attitude will try to prove themselves by taking risks in order to impress others. While this pattern is thought to be a male characteristic, women are equally susceptible.
5. **Resignation:** "What's the use?"	Pilots who think, "What's the use?" do not see themselves as being able to make a great deal of difference in what happens to them. When things go well, the pilot is apt to think that it is good luck. When things go badly, the pilot may feel that someone is out to get me, or attribute it to bad luck. The pilot will leave the action to others, for better or worse. Sometimes, such pilots will even go along with unreasonable requests just to be a "nice guy."

Figure 9-10. Pilots should examine their decisions carefully to ensure that their choices have not been influenced by a hazardous attitude.

hazardous attitudes which can interfere with a pilot's ability to make sound decisions and exercise authority properly. [Figure 9-10]

Hazardous attitudes can lead to poor decision making and actions which involve unnecessary risk. Students must be taught to examine their decisions carefully to ensure that their choices have not been influenced by hazardous attitudes and they must be familiar with positive alternatives to counteract the hazardous attitudes. These substitute attitudes are referred to as antidotes. During a flight operation, it is important to be able to recognize a hazardous attitude, correctly label the thought, and then recall its antidote. [Figure 9-11]

STRESS MANAGEMENT

Everyone is stressed to some degree all the time. A certain amount of stress is good since it keeps a person alert and prevents complacency. However, effects of stress are cumulative and, if not coped with adequately, they eventually add up to an intolerable burden. Performance generally increases with the onset of stress, peaks, and then begins to fall off rapidly as stress levels exceed a person's ability to cope. The ability to make effective decisions during flight can be impaired by stress. Factors, referred to as stressors, can increase a pilot's risk of error in the cockpit. [Figure 9-12]

One way of exploring the subject of stress with a student is to recognize when stress is affecting performance. If a student seems distracted, or has a particularly difficult time accomplishing the tasks of the lesson, the instructor can query the student. Was the student uncomfortable or tired during the flight? Is there some stress in another aspect of the student's life that may be causing a distraction? This may prompt the student to

HAZARDOUS ATTITUDES	ANTIDOTES
Anti-Authority — Although he knows that flying so low to the ground is prohibited by the regulations, he feels that the regulations are too restrictive in some circumstances.	**Follow the rules. They are usually right.**
Impulsivity — As he is buzzing the park, the airplane does not climb as well as Steve had anticipated and without thinking, Steve pulls back hard on the yoke. The airspeed drops and the airplane is close to a stalling attitude as the wing brushes a power line.	**Not so fast. Think first.**
Invulnerability — Steve is not worried about an accident since he has flown this low many times before and he has not had any problems.	**It could happen to me.**
Macho — Steve often brags to his friends about his skills as a pilot and how close to the ground he flies. During a local pleasure flight in his single-engine airplane, he decides to buzz some friends barbecuing at a nearby park.	**Taking chances is foolish.**
Resignation — Although Steve manages to recover, the wing sustains minor damage. Steve thinks to himself, "It's dangerous for the power company to put those lines so close to a park. If somebody finds out about this I'm going to be in trouble, but it seems like no matter what I do, somebody's always going to criticize."	**I'm not helpless. I can make a difference.**

Figure 9-11. Students can be asked to identify hazardous attitudes and the corresponding antidotes when presented with flight scenarios.

Physical Stress—Conditions associated with the environment, such as temperature and humidity extremes, noise, vibration, and lack of oxygen.

Physiological Stress—Physical conditions, such as fatigue, lack of physical fitness, sleep loss, missed meals (leading to low blood sugar levels), and illness.

Psychological Stress—Social or emotional factors, such as a death in the family, a divorce, a sick child, or a demotion at work. This type of stress may also be related to mental workload, such as analyzing a problem, navigating an aircraft, or making decisions.

Figure 9-12. The three types of stressors can affect a pilot's performance.

evaluate how these factors affect performance and judgment. The instructor should also try to determine if there are aspects of pilot training that are causing excessive amounts of stress for the student. For example, if the student consistently makes a decision not to fly, even though weather briefings indicate favorable conditions, it may be due to apprehension regarding the lesson content. Stalls, landings, or an impending solo flight may cause concern for the student. By explaining a specific maneuver in greater detail or offering some additional encouragement, the instructor may be able to alleviate some of the student's stress.

To help students manage the accumulation of life stresses and prevent stress overload, instructors can recommend several techniques. For example, including relaxation time in a busy schedule and maintaining a program of physical fitness can help reduce stress levels. Learning to manage time more effectively can help pilots avoid heavy pressures imposed by getting behind schedule and not meeting deadlines. While these pressures may exist in the workplace, students may also experience the same type of stress regarding their flight training schedule. Instructors can advise students to take assessments of themselves to determine their capabilities and limitations and then set realistic goals. In addition, avoiding stressful situations and encounters can help pilots cope with stress.

USE OF RESOURCES

To make informed decisions during flight operations, students must be made aware of the resources found both inside and outside the cockpit. Since useful tools and sources of information may not always be readily apparent, learning to recognize these resources is an essential part of ADM training. Resources must not only be identified, but students must develop the skills to evaluate whether they have the time to use a particular resource and the impact that its use will have upon the safety of flight. For example, the assistance of ATC may be very useful if a pilot is lost. However, in an emergency situation when action needs be taken quickly, time may not be available to contact ATC immediately. During training, instructors can routinely point out resources to students.

INTERNAL RESOURCES

Internal resources are found in the cockpit during flight. Since some of the most valuable internal resources are ingenuity, knowledge, and skill, pilots can expand cockpit resources immensely by improving their capabilities. This can be accomplished by frequently reviewing flight information publications, such as the CFRs and the AIM, as well as by pursuing additional training.

A thorough understanding of all the equipment and systems in the aircraft is necessary to fully utilize all resources. For example, advanced navigation and autopilot systems are valuable resources. However, if pilots do not fully understand how to use this equipment, or they rely on it so much that they become complacent, it can become a detriment to safe flight. To ensure that students understand the operation of various equipment, instructors must first be familiar with the components of each aircraft in which they instruct.

Checklists are essential cockpit resources for verifying that the aircraft instruments and systems are checked, set, and operating properly, as well as ensuring that the proper procedures are performed if there is a system malfunction or in-flight emergency. Students reluctant to use checklists can be reminded that pilots at all levels of experience refer to checklists, and that the more advanced the aircraft is, the more crucial checklists become. In addition, the POH, which is required to be carried on board the aircraft, is essential for accurate flight planning and for resolving in-flight equipment malfunctions. Other valuable cockpit resources include current aeronautical charts, and publications, such as the *Airport/Facility Directory*.

It should be pointed out to students that passengers can also be a valuable resource. Passengers can help watch for traffic and may be able to provide information in an irregular situation, especially if they are familiar with flying. A strange smell or sound may alert a passenger to a potential problem. The pilot in command should brief passengers before the flight to make sure that they are comfortable voicing any concerns.

EXTERNAL RESOURCES

Possibly the greatest external resources during flight are air traffic controllers and flight service specialists. ATC can help decrease pilot workload by providing traffic advisories, radar vectors, and assistance in emergency situations. Flight service stations can provide updates on weather, answer questions about airport conditions, and may offer direction-finding assistance. The services provided by ATC can be invaluable in enabling pilots to make informed in-flight decisions. Instructors can help students feel comfortable with ATC by encouraging them to take advantage of services, such as flight following and Flight Watch. If students are exposed to ATC as much as possible during training, they will feel confident asking controllers to clarify instructions and be better equipped to use ATC as a resource for assistance in unusual circumstances or emergencies.

Throughout training, students can be asked to identify internal and external resources which can be used in a variety of flight situations. For example, if a discrepancy is found during preflight, what resources can be used to determine its significance? In this case, the student's knowledge of the airplane, the POH, an instructor or another experienced pilot, or an aviation maintenance technician are resources which may help define the problem.

During cross-country training, students may be asked to consider the following situation. On a cross-country flight, you become disoriented. Although you are familiar with the area, you do not recognize any landmarks, and fuel is running low. What resources do you have to assist you? Students should be able to identify their own skills and knowledge, aeronautical charts, ATC, flight service, and navigation equipment as some of the resources that can be used in this situation.

WORKLOAD MANAGEMENT

Effective workload management ensures that essential operations are accomplished by planning, prioritizing, and sequencing tasks to avoid work overload. As experience is gained, a pilot learns to recognize future workload requirements and can prepare for high workload periods during times of low workload. Instructors can teach this skill by prompt-

ing their students to prepare for a high workload. For example, when en route, the student can be asked to explain the actions that will need to be taken during the approach to the airport. The student should be able to describe the procedures for traffic pattern entry and landing preparation. Reviewing the appropriate chart and setting radio frequencies well in advance of when they will be needed helps reduce workload as the flight nears the airport. In addition, the student should listen to ATIS, ASOS, or AWOS, if available, and then monitor the tower frequency or CTAF to get a good idea of what traffic conditions to expect. Checklists should be performed well in advance so there is time to focus on traffic and ATC instructions. These procedures are especially important prior to entering a high-density traffic area, such as Class B airspace.

To manage workload, items should be prioritized. This concept should be emphasized to students and reinforced when training procedures are performed. For example, during a go-around, adding power, gaining airspeed, and properly configuring the airplane are priorities. Informing the tower of the balked landing should be accomplished only after these tasks are completed. Students must understand that priorities change as the situation changes. If fuel quantity is lower than expected on a cross-country flight, the priority can shift from making a scheduled arrival time at the destination, to locating a nearby airport to refuel. In an emergency situation, the first priority is to fly the aircraft and maintain a safe airspeed.

Another important part of managing workload is recognizing a work overload situation. The first effect of high workload is that the pilot begins to work faster. As workload increases, attention cannot be devoted to several tasks at one time, and the pilot may begin to focus on one item. When the pilot becomes task saturated, there is no awareness of inputs from various sources so decisions may be made on incomplete information, and the possibility of error increases. [Figure 9-13]

During a lesson, workload can be gradually increased as the instructor monitors the student's management of tasks. The instructor should ensure that the student has the ability to recognize a work overload situation. When becoming overloaded, the student should stop, think, slow down, and prioritize. It is important that the student understand options that may be available to decrease workload. For example, tasks, such as locating an item on a chart or setting a radio frequency, may be delegated to another pilot or passenger, an autopilot (if available) may be used, or ATC may be enlisted to provide assistance.

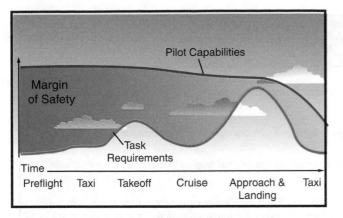

Figure 9-13. Accidents often occur when flying task requirements exceed pilot capabilities. The difference between these two factors is called the margin of safety. Note that in this idealized example, the margin of safety is minimal during the approach and landing. At this point, an emergency or distraction could overtax pilot capabilities, causing an accident.

SITUATIONAL AWARENESS

Situational awareness is the accurate perception of the operational and environmental factors that affect the aircraft, pilot, and passengers during a specific period of time. Maintaining situational awareness requires an understanding of the relative significance of these factors and their future impact on the flight. When situationally aware, the pilot has an overview of the total operation and is not fixated on one perceived significant factor. Some of the elements inside the aircraft to be considered are the status of aircraft systems, pilot, and passengers. In addition, an awareness of the environmental conditions of the flight, such as spatial orientation of the aircraft, and its relationship to terrain, traffic, weather, and airspace must be maintained.

To maintain situational awareness, all of the skills involved in aeronautical decision making are used. For example, an accurate perception of the pilot's fitness can be achieved through self-assessment and recognition of hazardous attitudes. A clear assessment of the status of navigation equipment can be obtained through workload management, and establishing a productive relationship with ATC can be accomplished by effective resource use.

OBSTACLES TO MAINTAINING SITUATIONAL AWARENESS

Fatigue, stress, and work overload can cause the pilot to fixate on a single perceived important item rather than maintaining an overall awareness of the flight situation. A contributing factor in many accidents is a distraction which diverts the pilot's attention from monitoring the instruments or scanning outside the aircraft. Many cockpit distractions begin as a minor problem, such as a gauge that is not reading correctly, but result in accidents as the pilot diverts attention to the perceived problem and neglects to properly control the aircraft.

Complacency presents another obstacle to maintaining situational awareness. When activities become routine, the pilot may have a tendency to relax and not put as much effort into performance. Like fatigue, complacency reduces the pilot's effectiveness in the cockpit. However, complacency is harder to recognize than fatigue, since everything is perceived to be progressing smoothly. For example, cockpit automation can lead to complacency if the pilot assumes that the autopilot is doing its job, and does not crosscheck the instruments or the aircraft's position frequently. If the autopilot fails, the pilot may not be mentally prepared to fly the aircraft manually. Instructors should be especially alert to complacency in students with significant flight experience. For example, a pilot receiving a flight review in a familiar aircraft may be prone to complacency.

By asking about positions of other aircraft in the traffic pattern, engine instrument indications, and the aircraft's location in relationship to references on a chart, the instructor can determine if the student is maintaining situational awareness. The instructor can also attempt to focus the student's attention on an imaginary problem with the communication or navigation equipment. The instructor should point out that situational awareness is not being maintained if the student diverts too much attention away from other tasks, such as controlling the aircraft or scanning for traffic. These are simple exercises that can be done throughout flight training which will help emphasize the importance of maintaining situational awareness.

OPERATIONAL PITFALLS

There are a number of classic behavioral traps into which pilots have been known to fall. Pilots, particularly those with considerable experience, as a rule always try to complete a flight as planned, please passengers, meet schedules, and generally demonstrate that they have the right stuff. The basic drive to demonstrate the right stuff can have an adverse effect on safety, and can impose an unrealistic assessment of piloting skills under stressful conditions. These tendencies ultimately may bring about practices that are dangerous and often illegal, and may lead to a mishap. Students will develop awareness and learn to avoid many of these operational pitfalls through effective ADM training. The scenarios and examples provided by instructors during

Peer Pressure—Poor decision making may be based upon an emotional response to peers, rather than evaluating a situation objectively.

Mind Set—A pilot displays mind set through an inability to recognize and cope with changes in a given situation.

Get-There-Itis—This disposition impairs pilot judgment through a fixation on the original goal or destination, combined with a disregard for any alternative course of action.

Duck-Under Syndrome—A pilot may be tempted to make it into an airport by descending below minimums during an approach. There may be a belief that there is a built-in margin of error in every approach procedure, or a pilot may want to admit that the landing cannot be completed and a missed approach must be initiated.

Scud Running—This occurs when a pilot tries to maintain visual contact with the terrain at low altitudes while instrument conditions exist.

Continuing Visual Flight Rules (VFR) into Instrument Conditions—Spatial disorientation or collision with ground/obstacles may occur when a pilot continues VFR into instrument conditions. This can be even more dangerous if the pilot is not instrument-rated or current.

Getting Behind the Aircraft—This pitfall can be caused by allowing events or the situation to control pilot actions. A constant state of surprise at what happens next may be exhibited when the pilot is getting behind the aircraft.

Loss of Positional or Situational Awareness—In extreme cases, when a pilot gets behind the aircraft, a loss of positional or situational awareness may result. The pilot may not know the aircraft's geographical location, or may be unable to recognize deteriorating circumstances.

Operating Without Adequate Fuel Reserves—Ignoring minimum fuel reserve requirements is generally the result of overconfidence, lack of flight planning, or disregarding applicable regulations.

Descent Below the Minimum En Route Altitude—The duck-under syndrome, as mentioned above, can also occur during the en route portion of an IFR flight.

Flying Outside the Envelope—The assumed high performance capability of a particular aircraft may cause a mistaken belief that it can meet the demands imposed by a pilot's overestimated flying skills.

Neglect of Flight Planning, Preflight Inspections, and Checklists—A pilot may rely on short- and long-term memory, regular flying skills, and familiar routes instead of established procedures and published checklists. This can be particularly true of experienced pilots.

Figure 9-14. All experienced pilots have fallen prey to, or have been tempted by, one or more of these tendencies in their flying careers.

ADM instruction should involve these pitfalls. [Figure 9-14]

EVALUATING STUDENT DECISION MAKING

A student's performance is often evaluated only on a technical level. The instructor determines whether maneuvers are technically accurate and that procedures are performed in the right order. Instructors must learn to evaluate students on a different level. How did the student arrive at a particular decision? What resources were used? Was risk assessed accurately when a go/no-go decision was made? Did the student maintain situational awareness in the traffic pattern? Was workload managed effectively during a cross-country? How does the student handle stress and fatigue?

Instructors should continually evaluate student decision-making ability and offer suggestions for improvement. It is not always necessary to present complex situations which require detailed analysis. By allowing students to make decisions about typical issues that arise throughout the course of training, such as their fitness to fly, weather conditions, and equipment problems, instructors can address effective decision making and allow students to develop judgment skills. For example, when a discrepancy is found during preflight inspection, the student should be allowed to initially determine the action to be taken. Then the effectiveness of the student's choice and other options that may be available can be discussed. Opportunities for improving decision-making abilities occur often during training. If the tower offers the student a runway that requires landing with a tailwind in order to expedite traffic, the student can be directed to assess the risks involved and asked to present alternative actions to be taken. Perhaps the most frequent choice that has to be made during flight training is the go/no-go decision based on weather. While the final choice to fly lies with the instructor, students can be required to assess the weather prior to each flight and make a go/no-go determination.

In addition, instructors can create lessons that are specifically designed to test whether students are applying ADM skills. Planning a flight lesson in which the student is presented with simulated emergencies, a heavy workload, or other operational problems can be valuable in assessing the student's judgment and decision-making skills. During the flight, performance can be evaluated on how effectively the student managed workload, or handled stress. While debriefing the student after the flight, the instructor can suggest ways that problems may have been solved more effectively, how tasks might have been prioritized differently, or other resources that could have been used to improve the situation.

Chapter 10

Planning Instructional Activity

This chapter is oriented to the beginning instructor who may be instructing independently outside of a formal training organization such as a pilot school. Independent instructors who learn to plan instructional activity effectively can provide high-quality training on an individual basis.

Any instructional activity must be well planned and organized if it is to proceed in an effective manner. Much of the basic planning necessary for the flight and ground instructor is provided by the knowledge and proficiency requirements published in Title 14 of the Code of Federal Regulations (14 CFR), approved school syllabi, and the various texts, manuals, and training courses available. This chapter reviews the planning required by the professional aviation instructor as it relates to four key topics—course of training, blocks of learning, training syllabus, and lesson plans.

COURSE OF TRAINING

In education, a **course of training** may be defined as a complete series of studies leading to attainment of a specific goal. The goal might be a certificate of completion, graduation, or an academic degree. For example, a student pilot may enroll in a private pilot certificate course, and upon completion of all course requirements, be awarded a graduation certificate. A course of training also may be limited to something like the additional training required for operating high-performance airplanes.

Other terms closely associated with a course of training include curriculum, syllabus, and training course outline. In many cases, these terms are used interchangeably, but there are important differences.

A **curriculum** may be defined as a set of courses in an area of specialization offered by an educational institution. A curriculum for a pilot school usually includes courses for the various pilot certificates and ratings. A syllabus is a summary or outline of a course of study. In aviation, the term "training syllabus" is commonly used. In this context, a **training syllabus** is a step-by-step, building block progression of learning with provisions for regular review and evaluations at prescribed stages of learning. The syllabus defines the unit of training, states by objective what the student is expected to accomplish during the unit of training, shows an organized plan for instruction, and dictates the evaluation process for either the unit or stages of learning. And, finally, a **training course outline**, within a curriculum, may be described as the content of a particular course. It normally includes statements of objectives, descriptions of teaching aids, definitions of evaluating criteria, and indications of desired outcome.

OBJECTIVES AND STANDARDS

Before any important instruction can begin, a determination of objectives and standards is necessary. Considerable theory regarding objectives and standards has been included in previous chapters. The theory described performance-based objectives as they relate to development of individual lessons and test items. The desired level of learning should also be incorporated into the objectives. In addition, level-of-learning objectives may apply to one or more of the three domains of learning—cognitive (knowledge), affective (attitudes, beliefs, and values), and psychomotor (physical skills). Normally, aviation training aspires to a level-of-learning at the application level or higher.

Standards are closely tied to objectives, since they include a description of the desired knowledge, behavior, or skill stated in specific terms, along with conditions and criteria. When a student is able to perform according to well-defined standards, evidence of learning is apparent. Comprehensive examples of the desired learning outcomes, or behaviors, should be included in the standards. As indicated in Chapter 1, standards for the level-of-learning in the cognitive and psychomotor domains are easily established. However, writing standards to evaluate a student's level-of-learning or overt behavior in the affective domain (attitudes, beliefs, and values) is more difficult.

The overall objective of an aviation training course is usually well established, and the general standards are included in various rules and related publications. For example, eligibility, knowledge, proficiency, and experience requirements for pilots and maintenance students are stipulated in the regulations, and the standards are published in the applicable practical test standards (PTS) or Oral and Practical Tests (O&P). It should be noted, though, that the PTS and O & P standards are limited to the most critical job tasks. Certification tests do not represent an entire training syllabus.

A broad, overall objective of any pilot training course is to qualify the student to be a competent, efficient, safe pilot for the operation of specific aircraft types under stated conditions. The established criteria or standards to determine whether the training has been adequate are the passing of knowledge and practical tests required by 14 CFR for the issuance of pilot certificates. Similar objectives and standards are established for aviation maintenance technician (AMT) students. Professional instructors should not limit their objectives to meeting only the published requirements for pilot or AMT certification. Instructional objectives should also extend beyond those listed in official publications. Successful instructors teach their students not only how, but also why and when. Ultimately, this leads to sound judgment and decision-making skills.

BLOCKS OF LEARNING

After the overall training objectives have been established, the next step is the identification of the blocks of learning which constitute the necessary parts of the total objective. Just as in building a pyramid, some blocks are submerged in the structure and never appear on the surface, but each is an integral and necessary part of the structure. Stated another way, the various blocks are not isolated subjects but essential parts of the whole. During the process of identifying the blocks of learning to be assembled for the proposed training activity, the planner must also examine each carefully to see that it is truly an integral part of the structure. Extraneous blocks of instruction are expensive frills, especially in flight instruction, and detract from, rather than assist in, the completion of the final objective.

While determining the overall training objectives is a necessary first step in the planning process, early identification of the foundation blocks of learning is also essential. Training for any such complicated and involved task as piloting or maintaining an aircraft requires the development and assembly of many segments or blocks of learning in their proper relationships. In this way, a student can master the segments or blocks individually and can progressively combine these with other related segments until their sum meets the overall training objectives.

The blocks of learning identified during the planning and management of a training activity should be fairly consistent in scope. They should represent units of learning which can be measured and evaluated—not a sequence of periods of instruction. For example, the flight training of a private pilot might be divided into the following major blocks: achievement of the knowledge and skills necessary for solo, the knowledge and skills necessary for solo cross-country flight, and the knowledge and skills appropriate for obtaining a private pilot certificate. [Figure 10-1]

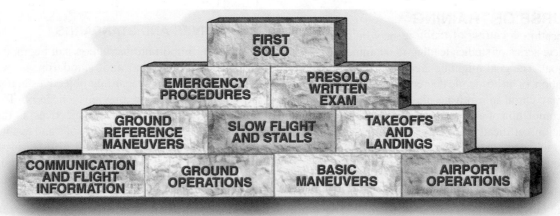

Figure 10-1. The presolo stage, or phase, of private pilot training is comprised of several basic building blocks. These blocks of learning, which should include coordinated ground and flight training, lead up to the first solo.

Use of the building block approach provides the student with a boost in self-confidence. This normally occurs each time a block is completed. Otherwise an overall goal, such as earning a private pilot certificate, may seem unobtainable. If the larger blocks are broken down into smaller blocks of instruction, each on its own is more manageable.

TRAINING SYLLABUS

There are a number of valid reasons why all aviation instructors should use a training syllabus. As technology advances, training requirements become more demanding. At the same time, new, and often more complicated rules continue to be proposed and implemented. In addition, the rules for instruction in other than an approved flight school are still quite specific about the type and duration of training. These factors, along with the continuing growth of aviation, add to the complexity of aviation training and certification. Instructors need a practical guide to help them make sure the training is accomplished in a logical sequence and that all of the requirements are completed and properly documented. A well organized, comprehensive syllabus can fulfill these needs.

SYLLABUS FORMAT AND CONTENT

The format and organization of the syllabus may vary, but it always should be in the form of an abstract or digest of the course of training. It should contain blocks of learning to be completed in the most efficient order.

Since a syllabus is intended to be a summary of a course of training, it should be fairly brief, yet comprehensive enough to cover essential information. This information is usually presented in an outline format with lesson-by-lesson coverage. Some syllabi include tables to show recommended training time for each lesson, as well as the overall minimum time requirements. [Figure 10-2]

While many instructors may develop their own training syllabi, there are many well-designed commercial products that may be used. These are found in various training manuals, approved school syllabi, and other publications available from industry.

Syllabi developed for approved flight schools contain specific information that is outlined in 14 CFR parts 141 and 147. In contrast, syllabi designed for training in other than approved schools may not provide certain details such as enrollment prerequisites, planned completion times, and descriptions of checks and tests to measure student accomplishments for each stage of training.

Since effective training relies on organized blocks of learning, all syllabi should stress well-defined objec-

STAGE I
GROUND LESSON 2

LESSON OBJECTIVES:
The objective of this lesson is for the student to learn important safety of flight considerations and become thoroughly familiar with airports, including marking and lighting aids. The student also will learn the significance of airspace divisions and how to use the radio for communications. In addition, the student will understand the capabilities and use of radar and other ATC services.

Content:
Introduce:
Section A—"Safety of Flight"
— Visual Scanning
— Collision Avoidance Precautions
— Blind Spots and Aircraft Design
— Right-of-Way Rules
— Minimum Safe Altitudes
— VFR Cruising Altitudes
— Special Safety Considerations
Section B—"Airports"
— Controlled and Uncontrolled Airports
— Runway and Taxiway Markings
— Airport Signs
— Wind Direction Indicators
— Segmented Circle
— Noise Abatement Procedures
— Airport Lighting
Section C—"Airspace"
— Cloud Clearance and Visibility
— Special Use and Other Airspace Areas
Section D—"Radio Communications"
— VHF Communications Equipment
— Coordinated Universal Time
— Radio Procedures
— Common Traffic Advisory Frequency
— Flight Service Stations
Section E—"Radar and ATC Services"
— Radar
— Transponder
— FAA Radar Systems

Completion Standards:
The student will complete Private Pilot Exercises 2A, 2B, 2C, 2D, and 2E with a minimum passing score of 80%, and the instructor will review each incorrect response to ensure understanding before the student progresses to Ground Lesson 3.

Figure 10-2. This excerpt of a ground lesson shows a unit of ground instruction. In this example, neither the time nor the number of ground training periods to be devoted to the lesson is specified. The lesson should include three key parts—the objective, the content, and the completion standards.

tives and standards for each lesson. Appropriate objectives and standards should be established for the overall course, the separate ground and flight segments, and for each stage of training. Other details may be added to a syllabus in order to explain how to use it and describe the pertinent training and reference materials. Examples of the training and reference materials include textbooks, video, compact disks, exams, briefings and instructional guides.

HOW TO USE A TRAINING SYLLABUS

Any practical training syllabus must be flexible, and should be used primarily as a guide. When necessary, the order of training can and should be altered to suit the progress of the student and the demands of special circumstances. For example, previous experience or different rates of learning often will require some alteration or repetition to fit individual students. The syllabus also should be flexible enough so it can be adapted to weather variations, aircraft availability, and scheduling changes without disrupting the teaching process or completely suspending training.

In departing from the order prescribed by the syllabus, however, it is the responsibility of the instructor to consider how the relationships of the blocks of learning are affected. It is often preferable to skip to a completely different part of the syllabus when the conduct of a scheduled lesson is impossible, rather than proceeding to the next block, which may be predicated completely on skills to be developed during the lesson which is being postponed.

Each approved training course provided by a certificated pilot school should be conducted in accordance with a training syllabus specifically approved by the Federal Aviation Administration (FAA). At certificated schools, the syllabus is a key part of the training course outline. The instructional facilities, airport, aircraft, and instructor personnel must be able to support the course of training specified in the syllabus. Compliance with the appropriate, approved syllabus is a condition for graduation from such courses. Therefore, effective use of a syllabus requires that it be referred to throughout the entire course of training. Both the instructor and the student should have a copy of the approved syllabus. However, as previously mentioned, a syllabus should not be adhered to so stringently that it becomes inflexible or unchangeable. It must be flexible enough to adapt to special needs of individual students.

Ground training lessons concentrate on the cognitive domain of learning. A typical lesson might include several knowledge areas. Many of these knowledge areas are directly or indirectly concerned with safety, aeronautical decision making, and judgment. These subjects tend to be closely associated with the affective domain of learning. Thus, instructors who find a way to stress safety, ADM, and judgment, along with the traditional aviation subjects, can favorably influence a student's attitude, beliefs, and values.

Flight training lessons also include knowledge areas, but they generally emphasize the psychomotor domain of learning. In addition, the affective domain of learning is also important in flight training. A student's attitude, especially toward flight safety, ADM, and judgment, should be a major concern of the instructor. [Figure 10-3]

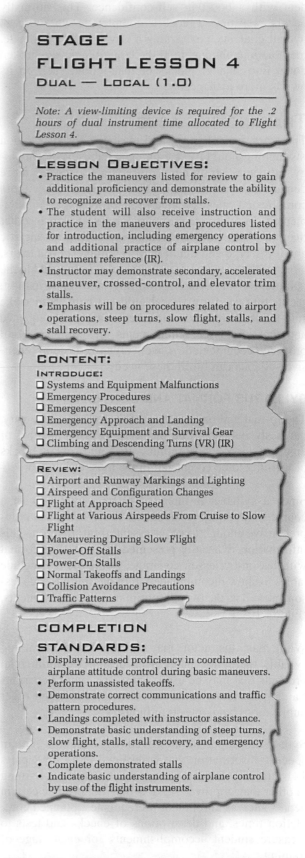

STAGE I

FLIGHT LESSON 4

DUAL — LOCAL (1.0)

Note: A view-limiting device is required for the .2 hours of dual instrument time allocated to Flight Lesson 4.

LESSON OBJECTIVES:
- Practice the maneuvers listed for review to gain additional proficiency and demonstrate the ability to recognize and recover from stalls.
- The student will also receive instruction and practice in the maneuvers and procedures listed for introduction, including emergency operations and additional practice of airplane control by instrument reference (IR).
- Instructor may demonstrate secondary, accelerated maneuver, crossed-control, and elevator trim stalls.
- Emphasis will be on procedures related to airport operations, steep turns, slow flight, stalls, and stall recovery.

CONTENT:

INTRODUCE:
- ☐ Systems and Equipment Malfunctions
- ☐ Emergency Procedures
- ☐ Emergency Descent
- ☐ Emergency Approach and Landing
- ☐ Emergency Equipment and Survival Gear
- ☐ Climbing and Descending Turns (VR) (IR)

REVIEW:
- ☐ Airport and Runway Markings and Lighting
- ☐ Airspeed and Configuration Changes
- ☐ Flight at Approach Speed
- ☐ Flight at Various Airspeeds From Cruise to Slow Flight
- ☐ Maneuvering During Slow Flight
- ☐ Power-Off Stalls
- ☐ Power-On Stalls
- ☐ Normal Takeoffs and Landings
- ☐ Collision Avoidance Precautions
- ☐ Traffic Patterns

COMPLETION STANDARDS:
- Display increased proficiency in coordinated airplane attitude control during basic maneuvers.
- Perform unassisted takeoffs.
- Demonstrate correct communications and traffic pattern procedures.
- Landings completed with instructor assistance.
- Demonstrate basic understanding of steep turns, slow flight, stalls, stall recovery, and emergency operations.
- Complete demonstrated stalls
- Indicate basic understanding of airplane control by use of the flight instruments.

Figure 10-3. A flight training lesson, like a ground training lesson, should include an objective, content, and completion standards. More than one objective could, and often does, apply to a single flight lesson.

Individual flight lessons are much like ground lessons. Organization and format are similar. The lesson shown in figure 10-3 is an example showing the main elements.

A syllabus should include special emphasis items that have been determined to be cause factors in aircraft accidents or incidents. For example, the instructor should emphasize collision and wake turbulence avoidance procedures throughout a student's flight training.

A syllabus lesson may include several other items that add to or clarify the objective, content, or standards. A lesson may specify the recommended class time, reference or study materials, recommended sequence of training, and study assignment for the next lesson. Both ground and flight lessons may have explanatory information notes added to specific lessons. [Figure 10-4]

TYPICAL SYLLABUS NOTES

- Students should read Chapter 1 of the textbook prior to Ground Lesson 1.

- All preflight duties and procedures will be performed and evaluated prior to each flight. Therefore, they will not appear in the content outlines.

- The notation VR or IR is used to indicate maneuvers which should be performed by both visual references and instrument references during the conduct of integrated flight instruction.

- A view-limiting device is required for the .2 hours of dual instrument time allocated to Flight Lesson 4.

- The demonstrated stalls are not a proficiency requirement for private pilot certification. The purpose of the demonstrations is to help the student learn how to recognize, prevent, and if necessary, recover before the stall develops into a spin. These stalls should not be practiced without a qualified flight instructor. In addition, some stalls may be prohibited in some airplanes.

Figure 10-4. Information in the form of notes may be added to individual ground or flight lessons in a syllabus when they are necessary.

While a syllabus is designed to provide a road map showing how to accomplish the overall objective of a course of training, it may be useful for other purposes. As already mentioned, it can be used as a checklist to ensure that required training has successfully been completed. Thus, a syllabus can be an effective tool for record keeping. Enhanced syllabi, which also are designed for record keeping, can be very beneficial to the independent instructor.

This record-keeping function is usually facilitated by boxes or blank spaces adjacent to the knowledge areas, procedures, or maneuvers in a flight lesson. Most syllabi introduce each procedure or maneuver in one flight lesson and review them in subsequent lessons. Some syllabi also include provisions for grading student performance and recording both ground and flight training time. Accurate record keeping is necessary to keep both the student and the instructor informed on the status of training. These records also serve as a basis for endorsements and recommendations for knowledge and practical tests.

Another benefit of using a syllabus is that it helps in development of lesson plans. A well constructed syllabus already contains much of the essential information that is required in a lesson plan, including objectives, content, and completion standards.

LESSON PLANS

A **lesson plan** is an organized outline for a single instructional period. It is a necessary guide for the instructor in that it tells what to do, in what order to do it, and what procedure to use in teaching the material of a lesson. Lesson plans should be prepared for each training period and be developed to show specific knowledge and/or skills to be taught.

A mental outline of a lesson is not a lesson plan. A lesson plan should be put into writing. Another instructor should be able to take the lesson plan and know what to do in conducting the same period of instruction. When putting it in writing, the lesson plan can be analyzed from the standpoint of adequacy and completeness.

PURPOSE OF THE LESSON PLAN

Lesson plans are designed to assure that each student receives the best possible instruction under the existing conditions. Lesson plans help instructors keep a constant check on their own activity, as well as that of their students. The development of lesson plans by instructors signifies, in effect, that they have taught the lessons to themselves prior to attempting to teach the lessons to students. An adequate lesson plan, when properly used, should:

- Assure a wise selection of material and the elimination of unimportant details.

- Make certain that due consideration is given to each part of the lesson.

- Aid the instructor in presenting the material in a suitable sequence for efficient learning.

- Provide an outline of the teaching procedure to be used.

- Serve as a means of relating the lesson to the objectives of the course of training.

- Give the inexperienced instructor confidence.

- Promote uniformity of instruction regardless of the instructor or the date on which the lesson is given.

CHARACTERISTICS OF A WELL-PLANNED LESSON

The quality of planning affects the quality of results. Successful professionals understand the price of excellence is hard work and thorough preparation. The effective instructor realizes that the time and energy spent in planning and preparing each lesson is well worth the effort in the long run.

A complete cycle of planning usually includes several steps. After the objective is determined, the instructor must research the subject as it is defined by the objective. Once the research is complete, the instructor must determine the method of instruction and identify a useful lesson planning format. Other steps, such as deciding how to organize the lesson and selecting suitable support material also must be accomplished. The final steps include assembling training aids and writing the lesson plan outline. One technique for writing the lesson plan outline is to prepare the beginning and ending first. Then, complete the outline and revise as required. A lesson plan should be a working document that can and should be revised as changes occur or are needed. The following are some of the important characteristics that should be reflected in all well-planned lessons.

- **Unity**—Each lesson should be a unified segment of instruction. A lesson is concerned with certain limited objectives, which are stated in terms of desired student learning outcomes. All teaching procedures and materials should be selected to attain these objectives.

- **Content**—Each lesson should contain new material. However, the new facts, principles, procedures, or skills should be related to the lesson previously presented. A short review of earlier lessons is usually necessary, particularly in flight training.

- **Scope**—Each lesson should be reasonable in scope. A person can master only a few principles or skills at a time, the number depending on complexity. Presenting too much material in a lesson results in confusion; presenting too little material results in inefficiency.

- **Practicality**—Each lesson should be planned in terms of the conditions under which the training is to be conducted. Lesson plans conducted in an airplane or ground trainer will differ from those conducted in a classroom. Also, the kinds and quantities of instructional aids available have a great influence on lesson planning and instructional procedures.

- **Flexibility**—Although the lesson plan provides an outline and sequence for the training to be conducted, a degree of flexibility should be incorporated. For example, the outline of content may include blank spaces for add-on material, if required.

- **Relation to Course of Training**—Each lesson should be planned and taught so that its relation to the course objectives are clear to each student. For example, a lesson on short-field takeoffs and landings should be related to both the certification and safety objectives of the course of training.

- **Instructional Steps**—Every lesson, when adequately developed, falls logically into the four steps of the teaching process— preparation, presentation, application, and review and evaluation.

HOW TO USE A LESSON PLAN PROPERLY

- **Be Familiar with the Lesson Plan**—The instructor should study each step of the plan and should be thoroughly familiar with as much information related to the subject as possible.

- **Use the Lesson Plan as a Guide**—The lesson plan is an outline for conducting an instructional period. It assures that pertinent materials are at hand and that the presentation is accomplished with order and unity. Having a plan prevents the instructor from getting off the track, omitting essential points, and introducing irrelevant material. Students have a right to expect an instructor to give the same attention to teaching that they give to learning. The most certain means of achieving teaching success is to have a carefully thought-out lesson plan.

- **Adapt the Lesson Plan to the Class or Student**—In teaching a ground school period, the instructor may find that the procedures outlined in the lesson plan are not leading to the desired results. In this situation, the instructor should change the approach. There is no certain way of predicting the reactions of different groups of students. An approach that has been successful with one group may not be equally successful with another.

A lesson plan for an instructional flight period should be appropriate to the background, flight experience, and ability of the particular student. A lesson plan may have to be modified considerably during flight, due to deficiencies in the student's knowledge or poor mastery of elements essential to the effective completion of the lesson. In some cases, the entire lesson plan may have to be abandoned in favor of review.

- **Revise the Lesson Plan Periodically**—After a lesson plan has been prepared for a training period, a continuous revision may be necessary. This is true for a number of reasons, including availability or nonavailability of instructional aids, changes in regulations, new manuals and textbooks, and changes in the state-of-the art among others.

LESSON PLAN FORMATS

The format and style of a lesson plan depends on several factors. Certainly the subject matter has a lot to do with how a lesson is presented and what teaching method is used. Individual lesson plans may be quite simple for one-on-one training, or they may be elaborate and complicated for large, structured classroom lessons. Preferably, each lesson should have somewhat limited objectives that are achievable within a reasonable period of time. This principle should apply to both ground and flight training. However, as previously noted, aviation training is not simple. It involves all three domains of learning, and the objectives usually include the higher levels of learning, at least at the application level.

In spite of need for varied subject coverage, diverse teaching methods, and relatively high level learning objectives, most aviation lesson plans have the common characteristics already discussed. They all should include objectives, content to support the objectives, and completion standards. Various authorities often divide the main headings into several subheadings, and terminology, even for the main headings, varies extensively. For example, completion standards may be called assessment, review and feedback, performance evaluation, or some other related term.

Commercially-developed lesson plans are acceptable for most training situations, including use by flight instructor applicants during their practical tests. However, all instructors should recognize that even well-designed preprinted lesson plans may need to be modified. Therefore, instructors are encouraged to use creativity when adapting preprinted lesson plans or when developing their own lesson plans for specific students or training circumstances.

As indicated by much of this discussion, the main concern in developing a lesson plan is the student. With this in mind, it is apparent that one format does not work well for all students, or for all training situations. Because of the broad range of aviation training requirements, a variety of lesson plans and lesson plan formats is recommended. Examples of various lesson plans and lesson plan formats are included in the following pages.

LESSON PLAN

Introduction (3 minutes)

ATTENTION:

Relate aircraft accident in which a multi-engine airplane ran off the end of the runway. This could have been avoided by correctly computing the landing distance. Relate similar personal experience of the same type of mishap.

MOTIVATION:

Tell students how landing distance can affect them (any aircraft, plus future application).

OVERVIEW:

Explain what will be learned. Explain how the lesson will proceed. Define landing distance and explain the normal landing distance chart. Then, demonstrate how to solve for landing distance. The students will practice the procedure: at least once with supervision and at least once with as little help as possible. Next, the students will be evaluated according to the standards. Finally, the lesson will conclude with questions and answers, followed by a brief summary.

Body (29 minutes)

EXPLANATION DEMONSTRATION: (8 minutes)

Define landing distance. Explain the normal landing distance chart to include the scale and interpolation. Ensure students can see demonstration and encourage questions. Demonstrate the procedure using °C with a headwind and °F with a tailwind. Show the normal landing distance chart with given data in the following order:
1. temperature
2. pressure altitude
3. gross weight
4. headwind-tailwind component
5. read ground roll distance from graph

PERFORMANCE SUPERVISION: (15 minutes)

Review standards. Hand out chart and practice problems. Remind students to use a pencil, to make small tick marks, and to work as accurately as possible. Explain that they should follow the procedure on the chart to work the practice problems. Encourage students to ask questions. Check progress of each student continually so they develop skill proficiency within acceptable standards. Reteach any area(s) of difficulty to the class as they go along.

EVALUATION: (6 minutes)

Review procedure again from the chart. Reemphasize standards of acceptable performance including time available. Prepare area for evaluation by removing the task step chart and practice problem sheets, and by handing out the evaluation problems. Ask students to work the three problems according to conditions and standards specified. Terminate evaluation after 6 minutes. Evaluate each student's performance and tactfully reveal results. Record results for use in reteaching any area(s) of difficulty in the summary.

Conclusion (3 minutes)

SUMMARY:

Review lessons with emphasis on any weak area(s).

REMOTIVATION:

Remind students that landing distance will be an important consideration in any aircraft they fly.

CLOSURE:

Advise students that this lesson will be used as a starting point for the next lesson. Assign study materials for the next lesson.

This is an example of the lesson plan designed for a traditional ground school in a classroom environment.

Flight 6

Student:Judy Smith

DUAL-LOCAL

(7 to 10 knot crosswind conditions required)

SEQUENCE:

1. Preflight Orientation
2. Flight
3. Postflight Evaluation

LESSON OBJECTIVE:

During the lesson, the student will review crosswind landing techniques in actual crosswind conditions and attempt to increase understanding and proficiency during their execution. The principle of a stabilized landing approach will be emphasized.

LESSON REVIEW:

1. Slips
2. Crosswind Landings

COMPLETION STANDARDS:

The student will demonstrate an understanding of how the slip is used to perform crosswind landings. In addition, the student will demonstrate safe crosswind landings in light crosswind conditions.

NOTES: Emphasize that the runway, airplane path, and longitudinal axis of airplane must be aligned at touchdown. Have the student establish a slip early on the final approach rather than crabbing and establishing slip just prior to touchdown. This should allow the student to concentrate on keeping the upwind wing low while maintaining runway alignment during the flare.

In this example, the lesson plan is specifically intended to help a student who is having difficulty with crosswind approaches and landings.

GROUND LESSON 8 — PCATD

OBJECTIVE

• Review of VOR concepts, intercepts, and tracks.

EMPHASIS

• Situational awareness; requires pilot constantly asking: Where am I? Where am I going? What am I going to do next?
• VOR utilization

SET-UP

• Choose an unfamiliar environment in which to fly (from the database map).
• Set airplane location off of a line between 2 NAVAID(s) about 40 miles apart (save as file for future use); configuration can be cruise flight or normal maneuvering flight regime.
• Utilize cockpit instrument check to set frequencies.
• Review terminology: bearing vs. radial, tracking inbound vs. outbound.

EXERCISES and MANEUVERS

• Determine position by orientation of TO/FROM and CDI centering; have student identify position on chart (paper) before looking at map screen, verify on map screen; discuss errors.
• Re-position airplane on the map screen, determine and note changes in CDI centering.
• Fly direct to selected NAVAID(s).
• Intercept a dictated radial:
    Tune/identify NAVAID(s).
    Determine location with respect to bearing by turning to the heading of course dictated; note on which side of airplane is desired course.
    Determine intercept angle and turn to intercept heading.
    Demonstrate bracketing techniques.

COMPLETION STANDARDS

• Correctly determine location and orientation TO/FROM NAVAID(s).
• Correctly determine appropriate intercept angle and heading.
• Recognize that the ability to track is heavily dependent on accurate maintenance of heading.
• Ability to visualize position.

This example lesson plan may be used for ground training in a personal computer-based aviation training device (PCATD) or a flight training device (FTD).

OBJECTIVE

- To familiarize the student with the stall warnings and handling characteristics of the airplane as it approaches a stall. To develop the student's skill in recognition and recovery from stalls.

CONTENT

- Configuration of airplane for power-on and power-off stalls.
- Observation of airplane attitude, stall warnings, and handling characteristics as it approaches a stall.
- Control of airplane attitude, altitude, and heading.
- Initiation of stall recovery procedures.

SCHEDULE

- Preflight Discussion   :10
- Instructor Demonstrations   :25
- Student Practice   :45
- Postflight Critique   :10

EQUIPMENT

- Chalkboard or notebook for preflight discussion.

INSTRUCTOR'S ACTIONS

- Preflight — Discuss lesson objective.
- Inflight — Demonstrate elements. Demonstrate power-on and power-off stalls and recovery procedures. Coach student practice.
- Postflight — Critique student performance and assign study material.

STUDENT'S ACTIONS

- Preflight — Discuss lesson objective and resolve questions.
- Inflight — Review previous maneuvers including slow flight. Perform each new maneuver as directed.
- Postflight — Ask pertinent questions.

COMPLETION STANDARDS

- Student should demonstrate competency in controlling the airplane at airspeeds approaching a stall. Student should recognize and take prompt corrective action to recover from power-on and power-off stalls.

This is a typical lesson plan for flight training which emphasizes stall recognition and recovery procedures.

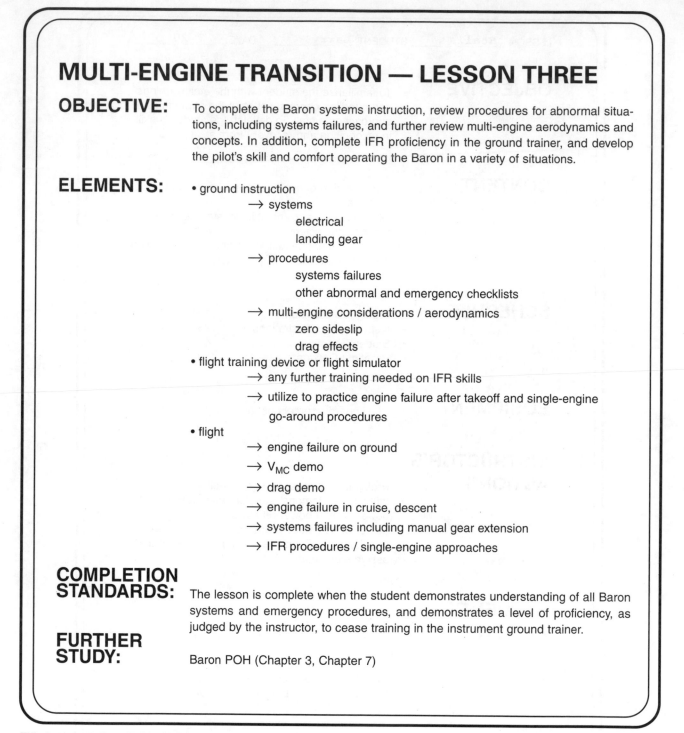

MULTI-ENGINE TRANSITION — LESSON THREE

OBJECTIVE: To complete the Baron systems instruction, review procedures for abnormal situations, including systems failures, and further review multi-engine aerodynamics and concepts. In addition, complete IFR proficiency in the ground trainer, and develop the pilot's skill and comfort operating the Baron in a variety of situations.

ELEMENTS:
- ground instruction
  → systems
    - electrical
    - landing gear
  → procedures
    - systems failures
    - other abnormal and emergency checklists
  → multi-engine considerations / aerodynamics
    - zero sideslip
    - drag effects
- flight training device or flight simulator
  → any further training needed on IFR skills
  → utilize to practice engine failure after takeoff and single-engine go-around procedures
- flight
  → engine failure on ground
  → V$_{MC}$ demo
  → drag demo
  → engine failure in cruise, descent
  → systems failures including manual gear extension
  → IFR procedures / single-engine approaches

COMPLETION STANDARDS: The lesson is complete when the student demonstrates understanding of all Baron systems and emergency procedures, and demonstrates a level of proficiency, as judged by the instructor, to cease training in the instrument ground trainer.

FURTHER STUDY: Baron POH (Chapter 3, Chapter 7)

This is a specialized flight training lesson plan for multi-engine transition.

LESSON PLAN
AVIATION MAINTENANCE TRAINING

INSTRUCTOR: William Brown

METHOD OF INSTRUCTION: Lecture, Audio Visuals, and Demonstration

TITLE: Flight line, Hangar, and Shop Safety

OBJECTIVE No 1: Recognize and neutralize or avoid (as appropriate) safety hazards that may be found in flight line, hangar, and maintenance shop areas.

OBJECTIVE No 2: Consistently apply safety practices on forming various aircraft maintenance functions.

MATERIALS YOU PLAN TO USE:

Visuals: Videos, overheads, and photographs showing safe and unsafe practices/conditions and their consequences.

Tools/Equipment: Power and hand tools, aircraft and aircraft systems, parts, and appliances, test and inspection tools, protective clothing and equipment, fire extinguishers, and chemicals commonly used in performing aircraft maintenance.

References: Material Safety Data Sheets (MSDS), aircraft maintenance manuals, government and industry published safety data, and equipment manufacturer's instructions.

PRESENTATION:

Topics/Steps: Personal Safey
Key Points:
1. Safety related terms.
2. General safety practices.
3. Causes of accidents.
4. Steps to be followed after an accident.
5. Accident report completion.

Flight Line, Shop, and Hangar Safety
Key Points:
1. Recognizing and identifying safety color codes and signs and their correct application.
2. Performing a safety inspection of flight line, hangar, and shop areas.
3. Identifying hazardous parts of various power tools.
4. Rules for safe use of hand and power tools and shop equipment.
5. Demonstrate proper use of power tools and shop equipment.

Chemical Safety
Key Points:
1. Using hazardous materials.
2. Using MSDS and manufacturer's instructions.

Fire Safety
Key Points:
1. Classes of fire.
2. Types of fire extinguishers and their inspection.
3. Matching fire extinguishing agents to classes of fires.
4. Proper techniques for using fire extinguishers.

PRACTICE: Identifying flight line, shop, and hangar safety hazards.
Safe use of hand and power tools, and flight line, shop, and hangar equipment.

ASSESSMENT: Written test covering category key points. Practical test covering practice items.

In this example, an aviation maintenance training lesson plan emphasizes safety.

Chapter 11

Professional Development

Aviation is changing rapidly and aviation instructors must continue to develop their knowledge and skills in order to teach successfully in this environment. This chapter addresses the topic of how instructors can grow and develop as professionals and as safety advocates, and also suggests some sources of information to assist in this development.

GROWTH AND DEVELOPMENT

The aviation instructor is usually well respected by other technicians and pilots because instructors must meet additional training requirements in order to be certified. Instructors have had to undergo comprehensive evaluations and a practical test to obtain a flight instructor certificate. Title 14 of the Code of Federal Regulations (14 CFR) part 147 requires all instructors teaching maintenance subjects to hold an FAA certificate as an aircraft maintenance technician.

The presumption of detailed knowledge is true because, in most cases, an instructor must know the aviation subject area to a much greater depth in order to teach the subject. The most knowledgeable people in any subject area are the ones who are teaching that subject. With the aviation field constantly changing, it is incumbent on the instructor to continually keep up with current information. Because instructors are regarded as authorities, they are in a unique position to influence education in the aviation field.

THE INSTRUCTOR AS A SAFETY ADVOCATE

In Chapter 8, the instructor is portrayed as the person the student will emulate. This is especially true con-

cerning safety. The instructor who violates accepted safety procedures will adversely affect the safety practices of the students who observe such unsafe acts. One of the most productive actions a flight or maintenance instructor can take to enhance aviation safety is to consistently emphasize safety by example. Another way to further safety is to actively participate in the FAA Aviation Safety Program. The program's objective is to improve safety in general aviation by improving attitudes, increasing knowledge and proficiency through education, and reducing environmental hazards. The Flight Standards District Office (FSDO) **Safety Program Manager** is involved in all areas of safety within the district. The Aviation Safety Program has several features that the instructor can use to promote safety. The aviation instructor who is actively involved in the Aviation Safety Program will be a more capable and professional instructor.

AVIATION SAFETY COUNSELORS

Aviation Safety Counselors are well known and highly respected members of the aviation community who are selected by the Safety Program Manager with the concurrence of the manager of the FSDO. They generally are pilots, flight instructors, or aviation maintenance technicians; however, this is not a prerequisite for selection. Counselors are volunteers who are willing to devote time, energy, and thought toward the objective of solving aviation safety problems in their community. They assist the FAA in the promotion of safety by organizing and participating in safety programs, and helping to correct conditions that are hazardous to aircraft and aviation personnel. FAA-M-8740.3, *Aviation*

Safety Counselor Manual, outlines some of the specific activities of the Aviation Safety Counselor, and provides guidelines for performing those activities. Some of the activities of the Aviation Safety Counselor, as outlined in the manual, are listed below.

- Counseling individuals who may have exhibited potentially unsafe acts.

- Assisting pilots, aircraft owners, and aircraft maintenance technicians on matters pertaining to proper maintenance of aircraft and avionics equipment.

- Counseling individuals following incidents requiring flight assistance from Air Traffic Control (ATC) personnel.

- Assisting the FAA in transmitting safety information to pilots, aircraft owners, maintenance facilities, and technicians.

- Conducting proficiency flights (when appropriately rated).

- Providing information and assistance to the FAA in establishing local airport safety committees.

- Notifying the appropriate authorities of the need for corrective action when hazardous conditions affecting safe flight or ground operations are observed.

- Organizing and participating in safety meetings, workshops, and seminars.

CONTINUING EDUCATION

Part of being a professional aviation instructor is being knowledgeable on the subjects of aviation and instructing. Instructors need to continually update their knowledge and skills. This effort to improve aviation knowledge and skills can range from simply reading an article in a technical publication to taking courses at a technical school or college. There are many different sources of information the aviation instructor can use in order to further aviation knowledge. [Figure 11-1]

CONTINUING EDUCATION SOURCES

- **Government**
  - **Educational/Training Institutions**
    - **Commercial Enterprises**
      - **Industry Organizations**

Figure 11-1. The aviation instructor has many sources to use for continuing education.

GOVERNMENT

One of the first educational sources for the instructor is the FAA and other governmental agencies. The FAA either sponsors or collaborates in sponsoring seminars and workshops that are available to the public in the furtherance of knowledge of aviation. Some examples would be safety seminars conducted around the country by the FAA in conjunction with industry. These seminars, although directed at pilots, can be a useful source of knowledge for aviation instructors.

The FAA is a source of many documents which can be used to further an instructor's knowledge. Many of these are published as advisory circulars and are available by mail.

The requirements for a flight instructor's participation in the Proficiency Award Program were outlined in Chapter 8. Participation in this program is a good way for a flight instructor to improve proficiency and to serve as an example to students. Another way is to work toward the Gold Seal Flight Instructor Certificate. Accomplishing the requirements of the certificate is evidence that the instructor has performed at a very high level as a flight instructor. See AC 61-65, *Certification: Pilots and Flight Instructors*, for a list of requirements for earning this certificate.

Similarly, the Aviation Maintenance Awards Program affords the aviation maintenance instructor the opportunity for increased education through attendance at FAA or industry maintenance training seminars. Details for the awarding of bronze through diamond pins can be found in AC 65-25, *Aviation Maintenance Technician Awards Program*.

The FAA approves the sponsors who conduct Flight Instructor Refresher Clinics (FIRCs) in accordance with AC 61-83. *Nationally Scheduled FAA-Approved Industry-Conducted Flight Instructor Refresher Clinics (FIRC)*. These courses are available for flight instructors to complete the training requirements for renewal of flight instructor certificates.

The FAA co-sponsors Inspection Authorization (IA) seminars. These seminars are open to all maintenance technicians, and are a good source of additional training and education for maintenance instructors.

EDUCATIONAL/TRAINING INSTITUTIONS

Professional aviation instructors can further increase their knowledge and skill in aviation specialties through FAA programs and seminars. They can also increase their professional knowledge and skills through post-secondary schools. These range from local community colleges to technical schools and universities. These schools may offer complete degree programs in aviation subjects as well as single-subject courses of benefit to instructors.

COMMERCIAL ORGANIZATIONS

Commercial organizations are another important source of education/training for the aviation instructor. Some may be publishers of training materials while others may provide complete ground and flight training programs for professional pilots and instructors. These companies often provide a wide variety of study programs including videos, computer-based training, and printed publications. Many offer training that can be attended either at the home base of the company or in traveling classes/seminars so instructors can more easily attend.

There are numerous organizations around the country that offer courses of training for aviation instructors. These are generally courses that are available to all pilots and technicians, but are especially useful for instructors to improve their abilities. Examples of such courses include workshops for maintenance technicians to enhance their skills in subjects such as composites, sheet metal fabrication, and fabric covering. For pilots there are courses in mountain flying, spin training, and tailwheel qualification. Flight instructors also may increase their aviation knowledge and experience by adding additional category and class ratings to their certificates.

INDUSTRY ORGANIZATIONS

Other significant sources of ongoing education for aviation instructors are the myriad of aviation organizations. These organizations not only provide educational articles in their publications, but also present training programs or co-sponsor such programs.

Many industry organizations have local affiliated chapters that make it easy to meet other pilots, technicians, and instructors. These meetings frequently include presentations by industry experts, as well as formal training sessions. Some aviation industry organizations conduct their own training sessions on areas such as flight instructor refresher clinics and Inspection Authorization (IA) seminars. Properly organized safety symposiums and training clinics are valuable sources of refresher training. They also are an excellent opportunity to exchange information with other instructors.

SOURCES OF MATERIAL

An aviation instructor should maintain access to current flight publications or maintenance publications. For the flight instructor, this includes current copies of regulations pertinent to pilot qualification and certification, *Aeronautical Information Manual* (AIM),

appropriate *Practical Test Standards* (PTS), and pilot training manuals. The aviation maintenance instructor should have copies of applicable regulations, current knowledge and practical test standards, and maintenance training manuals. Aviation instructors must be completely familiar with current certification and rating requirements in order to provide competent instruction. AC 00-2 *Advisory Circular Checklist*, is a listing of all current advisory circulars and other FAA publications sold by the Superintendent of Documents, U.S. Government Printing Office (GPO). Many of the advisory circulars should be considered by the aviation instructor for inclusion in a personal reference library. This checklist can be obtained from U.S. Government Bookstores or from the U.S. Government Printing Office.

In addition to government publications, a number of excellent handbooks and other reference materials are available from commercial publishers. Aviation periodicals and technical journals from the aviation industry are other sources of valuable information for instructors. Many public and institutional libraries have excellent resource material on educational psychology, teaching methods, testing, and other aviation-related subjects.

The aviation instructor has two reasons to maintain a source of current information and publications. First the instructor needs a steady supply of fresh material to make instruction interesting and up-to-date. Second, instructors should keep themselves well informed by maintaining familiarity with what is being written in current aviation publications. Most of these publications are in printed form, but increasingly, information is available through electronic means. [Figure 11-2]

Figure 11-2. Aviation instructors can improve their knowledge by becoming familiar with information on the Internet.

PRINTED MATERIAL

Printed materials have the advantage of portability. In aviation, documentation in the form of flight publications or maintenance data must be immediately available for referral while flying or conducting maintenance. Printed material makes this possible, but hard copy can also be a disadvantage, taking up space for storage and often becoming tedious to keep current. While most periodicals are still available in hard copy, some are starting to be available partially or totally in electronic form. Most FAA regulations, standards, and guides are available either in electronic form or as hard copy.

Non-FAA publications are available through the GPO and from the National Technical Information Service (NTIS). Publications not printed by the U.S. Government Printing Office are available from the many publishers and suppliers of books. Commercial publishers usually provide catalogues and toll-free numbers or web sites for ordering their products.

ELECTRONIC SOURCES

Access to the Internet via personal computers has opened up a vast storehouse of information for the aviation instructor. In the past, aviation instructors had limited access to information, but the personal computer has greatly expanded sources of aviation information. This section will list some sources of information on the **Internet**. In the following discussion, several **sites** for accessing FAA materials are explored, and some non-FAA sites are included. Once instructors begin to **navigate** the Internet, they will find sites which provide the information they use most frequently. [Figure 11-3]

Figure 11-3. Aviation instructors can improve their knowledge by becoming comfortable navigating the Web.

Obviously, some FAA publications are more important to the aviation instructor than others. Many of the publications of interest to the aviation instructor can be accessed through the FAA Flight Standards Service

Aviation Information (AV-INFO) Web Site (http://av-info.faa.gov). These publications can be accessed by clicking on the button marked Regulatory Support Division (AFS-600). At the AFS-600 site, selecting "Publications: Training, Testing, and Technical" accesses Airman Knowledge Test Question Banks, Knowledge Test Guides, Practical Test Standards, and select Advisory Circulars.

From the AV-INFO Web Site, aviation instructors have access to the National Transportation Safety Board, Airworthiness Directives, Listings of FAA Certificated Maintenance and Pilot schools, and FAA forms. Once the instructor has located a site of interest, the site can be saved by clicking on the **Bookmark** option (or other designation such as "Favorite") provided by the **web browser** used. This allows the instructor to return to the site without going through multiple **links**.

The FAA home page can also be reached through the AV-INFO Web Site. After opening the FAA home page, one of the fastest ways to view a variety of FAA materials is to select an option from the prominent pull-down list. Once an area of interest has been selected, the instructor can click on the "GO!" button to link to various FAA sites. For example, an instructor can select "Publications" from the list to locate all FAA publications available from the Department of Transportation (DOT), U.S. Government Printing Office (GPO), National Technical Information Service (NTIS), and the Federal Depository Libraries.

FAA web sites are not the only source of aviation or education-related information on the Internet. The aviation instructor can access a myriad of aviation-related publications at other governmental or non-governmental web sites. An easy way to reach some of these sites is through the AV-INFO Web Site by clicking on the button marked "Public Aviation Sites." Others can be accessed via published web addresses or by using the search function of the web browser. Conducting a search on the word "aviation" gives the aviation instructor access to literally thousands of related web sites.

Keep in mind that most sites on the Internet are updated periodically. In addition, new sites are added and old sites are discontinued on a regular basis. The aviation instructor can become more adept at obtaining information by entering and navigating around the Internet to become informed about the contents and how to best locate desired information. The more familiar aviation instructors become with the Internet, the better they will be able to adapt to any changes that may occur.

Professional aviation instructors must continue to expand their knowledge and skills in order to be competent instructors. The field of aviation is advancing, and the instructor also must advance. Instructors can best do this by taking advantage of the wide variety of materials available from the FAA, other governmental agencies, commercial publishers and vendors, and from industry trade groups. These materials are available at training sessions and seminars, from printed books, papers, magazines, and from the Internet and other electronic sources. Instructors who commit to continuing education will be able to provide the highest quality instruction to their students.

APPENDIX A—SAMPLE TEST ITEMS

There are four types of test items in common use today. They are multiple-choice, matching, true-false, and supply-type. The most used type is the multiple-choice test item in one of several forms. Listed below are examples of some of the more widely used forms.

MULTIPLE-CHOICE TEST ITEMS

Multiple-choice test items consist of a stem or question and three or more alternative answers with the correct answer sometimes called the keyed response and the incorrect answers called distractors. Detailed information on the writing of stems and alternatives can be found in Chapter 6.

Stem Presented as a Question. This form is generally better than the incomplete stem because it is simpler and more natural.

Who is primarily responsible for maintaining an aircraft in an airworthy condition?

    A.   Pilot in command or operator.
    B.   Owner or operator of the aircraft.
    C.   The lead mechanic responsible for that aircraft.

Stem as an Incomplete Statement. When using this form, care must be exercised to avoid ambiguity, giving clues, and using unnecessarily complex or unrelated alternatives.

VFR cruising altitudes are required to be maintained when flying

    A.   at 3,000 feet or more AGL, based on true course.
    B.   more than 3,000 feet AGL, based on magnetic course.
    C.   at 3,000 feet or more above MSL, based on magnetic heading.

Stem Supplemented by an Illustration. This form is useful for measuring the ability to read instruments, or identify objects.

(Refer to figure 1.) The acute angle A is the angle of

    A.   attack.
    B.   dihedral.
    C.   incidence.

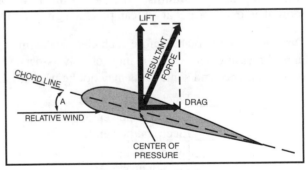

FIGURE 1.—Lift Vector.

Multiple Response is Required. This form is a variation of the previous forms in that it contains more than one correct answer, and students are instructed to select all correct answers.

Which of the following statements is/are generally true regarding the charging of several aircraft batteries together?

    1.   Batteries of different voltage (but similar capacities) can be connected in series with each other across the charger, and charged using the constant current method.
    2.   Batteries of different ampere-hour capacity and same voltage can be connected in parallel with each other across the charger, and charged using the constant voltage method.
    3.   Batteries of the same voltage and same ampere-hour capacity must be connected in series with each other across the charger, and charged using the constant current method.

    A.   3.
    B.   1 and 2.
    C.   2 and 3.

Negative Variety Type. This form is not suggested but, if used, always emphasize the negative word.

Which of the following is **NOT** considered a method of heat transfer?

> A.   Diffusion.
> B.   Conduction.
> C.   Convection.

Association Type. This form is useful if a limited number of associations are to be made.

Which aircraft has the right-of-way over the other aircraft listed?

> A.   Airship.
> B.   Gyroplane.
> C.   Aircraft towing other aircraft.

Definition Type. This form is used to determine knowledge of a specific definition.

Aspect ratio of a wing is defined as the ratio of the

> A.   wingspan to the wing root.
> B.   wingspan to the mean chord.
> C.   square of the chord to the wingspan.

MATCHING TEST ITEMS

Matching test items are used to test a student's ability to recognize relationships and to make associations between terms, parts, words, phrases, clauses, or symbols in one column with related alternatives in another column. When using this form of test item, it is a good practice to provide alternatives in the response column that are used more than once, or not at all, to preclude guessing by elimination. Matching test items may have either an equal or unequal number of selections in each column.

Matching-Equal Columns. When using this form, providing for some items in the response column to be used more than once, or not at all, can preclude guessing by elimination.

Directions: In the blank before each electrical term in the left-hand column, write the letter corresponding to the unit of measurement which is most closely associated with that term. Each unit of measurement may be used more than once and some units may not be used at all.

1. ____ Electromotive force	a. Watt
2. ____ Electrical power, apparent	b. Volt
3. ____ Electrical power, true	c. Ampere
4. ____ Resistance	d. Coulomb
5. ____ Capacitance	e. Ohm
6. ____ Inductance	f. VAR
7. ____ Current	g. Farad
8. ____ Impedance	h. Henry

Matching-Unequal Columns. Generally preferable to equal columns.

Directions: In the blank before each phrase in the left-hand column, write the letter(s) corresponding to the type(s) of drag which is/are most closely associated with that phrase. Each type of drag may be used more than once, and some types may not be used at all.

1. ____ Occurs when varied currents over an airplane meet and interact.	a. Form drag b. Induced drag
2. ____ Results from the turbulent wake caused by the separation of airflow from the surface of a structure.	c. Skin friction drag d. Static drag
3. ____ Caused by the roughness of the airplane's surfaces.	e. Interference drag
4. ____ Generated by the airflow circulation around the airfoil as it creates lift.	f. Rolling drag g. Sliding drag

TRUE-FALSE TEST ITEMS

A True-False test item requires the student to determine whether a statement is true or false. The chief disadvantage of this type is the opportunity for successful guessing.

Directions: Circle the correct response to the following statements.

1. True or False. To operate within Class B airspace, the aircraft must have two-way radio communication capability and a Mode C transponder.

2. True or False. An aviation maintenance technician must hold an Inspection Authorization to legally conduct annual inspections on small aircraft.

SUPPLY-TYPE TEST ITEMS

The aviation instructor is able to determine the students' level of generalized knowledge of a subject through the use of supply-type questions. Short-answer essay test items are the most common.

1. Describe the position of the elevator and ailerons when taxiing a tricycle-gear airplane into a right quartering headwind. _____

_____

_____

2. What conditions are used in determining the published value of V_{MC}? _____

_____

APPENDIX B—INSTRUCTOR ENDORSEMENTS

14 CFR section 61.189 requires that instructors sign the logbook of each person they have given ground or flight training. AC 61-65 contains suggested endorsements, and this appendix reprints several of the more commonly used endorsements. All of these examples contain the essential elements, but it is not necessary for endorsements to be worded exactly as those in the AC. For example, changes to regulatory requirements may affect the wording or the instructor may customize the endorsement for any special circumstances of the student.

STUDENT PILOT ENDORSEMENTS

Pre-solo aeronautical knowledge: §61.87(b)

I certify that (First name, MI, Last name) has satisfactorily completed the pre-solo knowledge exam of §61.87(b) for the (make and model aircraft). S/S [date] J.J. Jones 987654321 CFI Exp. 12-31-00

Pre-solo flight training at night: §61.87(c) and (m)

I certify that (First name, MI, Last name) has received the required pre-solo training in a (make and model aircraft). I have determined that he/she has demonstrated the proficiency of §61.87(m), and is proficient to make solo flights at night in a (make and model aircraft). S/S [date] J.J. Jones 987654321 CFI Exp. 12-31-00

Solo flight (each additional 90-day period): §61.87(n)

I certify that (First name, MI, Last name) has received the required training to qualify for solo flying. I have determined he/she meets the applicable requirements of §61.87(n), and is proficient to make solo flights in a (make and model aircraft). S/S [date] J.J. Jones 987654321 CFI Exp. 12-31-00

Initial solo cross-country flight: §61.93(c)(1)

I certify that (First name, MI, Last name) has received the required solo cross-country training. I find he/she has met the applicable requirements of §61.93, and is proficient to make solo cross-country flights in a (make and model aircraft). S/S [date] J.J. Jones 987654321 CFI Exp. 12-31-00

Solo cross-country flight: §61.93(c)(2)

I have reviewed the cross-country planning of (First name, MI, Last name), I find the planning and preparation to be correct to make the solo flight from (location) to (destination) via (route of flight) with landings at (name the airports) in a (make and model aircraft) on (date). May list any appropriate conditions or limitations. S/S [date] J.J. Jones 987654321 CFI Exp. 12-31-00

Solo flight in Class B airspace: §61.95(a)

I certify that (First name, MI, Last name) has received the required training of §61.95(a). I have determined he/she is proficient to conduct solo flights in (name of Class B) airspace. May list any applicable conditions or limitations. S/S [date] J.J. Jones 987654321 CFI Exp. 12-31-00

Solo flight to, from, or at an airport located in Class B airspace: §§61.95(b) and 91.131(b)(1)

I certify that (First name, MI, Last name) has received the required training of §61.95(b)(1). I have determined that he/she is proficient to conduct solo flight operations at (name of airport). May list any applicable conditions or limitations. S/S [date] J.J. Jones 987654321 CFI Exp. 12-31-00

PRIVATE PILOT ENDORSEMENTS

Aeronautical knowledge test: §§61.35(a)(1), 61.103(d), and 61.105

I certify that (First name, MI, Last name) has received the required training of §61.105. I have determined he/she is prepared for the (name the knowledge test). S/S [date] JJ Jones 987654321 CFI Exp. 12-31-00

Flight proficiency/practical test: §§61.103(f), 61.107(b), and 61.109

I certify that (First name, MI, Last name) has received the required training of §§61.107 and 61.109. I determined he/she is prepared for the (name the practical test). S/S [date] J.J. Jones 987654321 CFI Exp. 12-31-00

FLIGHT INSTRUCTOR ENDORSEMENTS

Spin training: §61.183(i)(1)

I certify that (First name, MI, Last name) has received the required training of §61.183(i). I have determined that he/she is competent and proficient on instructional skills for training stall awareness, spin entry, spins, and spin recovery procedures. S/S [date] J.J. Jones 987654321 CFI Exp. 12-31-00

ADDITIONAL ENDORSEMENTS

Completion of a flight review: §61.56(a) and (c)

I certify that (First name, MI, Last name), (pilot certificate) (certificate number) has satisfactorily completed a flight review of §61.56(a) on (date). S/S [date] J.J. Jones 987654321 CFI Exp. 12-31-00

Completion of an instrument proficiency check: §61.57(d)

I certify that (First name, MI, Last name), (pilot certificate) (certificate number) has satisfactorily completed the instrument proficiency check of §61.57(d) in a (list make and model of aircraft) on (date). S/S [date] J.J. Jones 987654321 CFI Exp. 12-31-00

Re-testing after failure of a knowledge or practical test (pilot): §61.49

I certify that (First name, MI, Last name) has received the additional (flight and/or ground) training as required by §61.49. I have determined that he/she is prepared for the (name the knowledge/practical test). S/S [date] J.J. Jones 987654321 CFI Exp. 12-31-00

Re-testing after failure of a knowledge or oral and practical test (mechanic): §65.19

I have given Mr./Ms. (First name, MI, Last name) additional instruction in each subject area shown to be deficient and consider the applicant competent to pass the test.

Last name _____   First name _____
Cert. No. _____   Type/Rating(s) _____
Signature _____   Date _____

Completion of a phase of an FAA-sponsored pilot proficiency award program (WINGS): §61.56(e)

I certify that (First name, MI, Last name), (pilot certificate) (certificate number) has satisfactorily completed Phase No.___of a WINGS program on (date). S/S [date] J.J. Jones 987654321 CFI Exp. 12-31-00

REFERENCES

Ashcraft, M.H., 1994: *Human Memory and Cognition.* New York, NY. Harper Collins.

Bloom, B.S. (Ed.), 1956: *Taxonomy of Educational Objectives: The Classification of Educational Goals, Handbook I: Cognitive Domain.* New York, NY. David McKay.

Bloom, B.S., and others, 1971: *Handbook on Formative and Summative Evaluation of Student Learning.* New York, NY. McGraw-Hill

Brookfield, S.D., 1986: *Understanding and Facilitating Adult Learning.* San Francisco, CA. Jossey-Bass.

Claxton, C.S., & Murrell, P.H., 1987: *Learning Styles: Implications for Improving Instructional Practices.* ASHE-ERIC Higher Education Report No. 4, Association for the Study of Higher Education.

Council of Aviation Accreditation, 1995: *Accreditation Standards Manual.* Auburn, AL. Council of Aviation Accreditation.

Davis, J.R., 1993: *Better Teaching, More Learning: Strategies for Success in Postsecondary Settings.* Phoenix, AZ. Oryx Press.

Dick, W., & Carey, L., 1996: *The Systematic Design of Instruction.* New York, NY. Harper Collins.

Driscoll, M.P., 1994: *Psychology of Learning for Instruction.* Boston, MA. Allyn & Bacon.

Duncan, P.A., 1998, 1999: *Surfing the Aviation Web, Parts 1, 2, and 3; FAA Aviation News, Nov/Dec, Jan/Feb, Mar.* U.S. Department of Transportation, Federal Aviation Administration, Washington, DC.

ERIC (Educational Resources Information Center), 1992-1997: *ERIC Digests.* U.S. Department of Education, Office of Educational Research and Improvement, Washington, DC.

FAA, 1991: *Aeronautical Decision Making, AC 60-22.* U.S. Department of Transportation, Federal Aviation Administration, Washington, DC.

FAA, 1999: *Certification: Pilots and Flight Instructors, AC 61-65.* U.S. Department of Transportation, Federal Aviation Administration, Washington, DC.

FAA, 1991: *Stall and Spin Awareness Training, AC 61-67.* U.S. Department of Transportation, Federal Aviation Administration, Washington, DC.

FAA, 1995: *Nationally Scheduled FAA-Approved, Industry-Conducted Flight Instructor Refresher Clinics, AC 61-83.* U.S. Department of Transportation, Federal Aviation Administration, Washington, DC.

FAA, 1991: *Pilot Certificates: Aircraft Type Ratings, AC 61-89.* U.S. Department of Transportation, Federal Aviation Administration, Washington, DC.

FAA, 1996: *Pilot Proficiency Award Program, AC 61-91.* U.S. Department of Transportation, Federal Aviation Administration, Washington, DC.

FAA, 1991: *Currency and Additional Qualification Requirements for Certificated Pilots, AC 61-98.* U.S. Department of Transportation, Federal Aviation Administration, Washington, DC.

FAA, 1989: *Announcement of Availability: Industry-Developed Transition Training Guidelines for High Performance Aircraft, AC 61-103.* U.S. Department of Transportation, Federal Aviation Administration, Washington, DC.

FAA, 1991: *Operations of Aircraft at Altitudes Above 25,000 Feet MSL and/or MACH Numbers (Mmo) Greater than .75, AC 61-107.* U.S. Department of Transportation, Federal Aviation Administration, Washington, DC.

FAA, 1993: *Aviation Maintenance Technician Awards Program, AC 65-25.* U.S. Department of Transportation, Federal Aviation Administration, Washington, DC.

FAA, 1995: *Crew Resource Management Training, AC 120-51.* U.S. Department of Transportation, Federal Aviation Administration, Washington, DC.

FAA, 1987: *Aeronautical Decision Making for Students and Private Pilots.* DOT/FAA/PM-86/41. National Technical Information Service, Springfield, VA.

FAA, 1988: *Aeronautical Decision Making for Commercial Pilots.* DOT/FAA/PM-86/42. National Technical Information Service, Springfield, VA.

FAA, 1987: *Aeronautical Decision Making for Instrument Pilots.* DOT/FAA/PM-86/43. National Technical Information Service, Springfield, VA.

FAA, 1987: *Aeronautical Decision Making for Instructor Pilots.* DOT/FAA/PM-86/44. National Technical Information Service, Springfield, VA.

FAA, 1987: *Aeronautical Decision Making for Helicopter Pilots*. DOT/FAA/PM-86/45. National Technical Information Service, Springfield, VA.

FAA, 1989: *Aeronautical Decision Making/Cockpit Resource Management*. DOT/FAA/PM-86/46. National Technical Information Service, Springfield, VA.

FAA, 1995: *Private Pilot Practical Test Standards*. FAA-S-8081-14. U.S. Department of Transportation, Federal Aviation Administration, Washington, DC.

FAA, 1995: *Aviation Safety Program Managers Handbook*. FAA-H-8740.1. U.S. Department of Transportation, Federal Aviation Administration, Washington, DC.

FAA, 1996: *Aviation Safety Counselor Manual*. FAA-M-8740.3. U.S. Department of Transportation, Federal Aviation Administration, Washington, DC.

Gagne, R.M., & Briggs, L.J., 1974: *Principles of Instructional Design*. New York, NY. Holt, Reinhart and Winston.

Garland, Daniel J., Will, John A., & Hopkins, V. David, 1999: *Handbook of Aviation Human Factors*. Mahwak, NJ. Lawrence Erlbaum Associates.

Gredler, M.E., 1997: *Learning and Instruction: Theory into Practice*. Upper Saddle River, NJ. Prentice-Hall.

Hawkins, F.H., 1987: *Human Factors in Flight*. Brookfield, VT. Ashgate.

Hunt, G.J.F. (Ed.), 1997: *Designing Instruction for Human Factors Training*. Brookfield, VT. Ashgate.

Jacobs, L.C., & Chase, C.I., 1992: *Developing and Using Tests Effectively*. San Francisco, CA. Jossey-Bass.

Jeppesen Sanderson, 1990-1999: *CFI Renewal Program, Volumes 1 through 6*. Englewood, CO. Jeppesen Sanderson.

Johnston, N., Fuller, R., & McDonald, N. (Eds.), 1995: *Aviation Psychology: Training and Selection*. Brookfield, VT. Ashgate.

Kemp, J.E., 1985: *The Instructional Design Process*. New York, NY. Harper & Row.

Krathwohl, D.R., and others, 1964: *Taxonomy of Educational Objectives: The Classification of Educational Goals, Handbook II: Affective Domain*. New York, NY. David McKay

Mager, R.F., 1988: *Making Instruction Work*. Belmont, CA. David S. Lake Publishers

Mager, R.F., 1984: *Preparing Instructional Objectives*. Belmont, CA. David S. Lake Publishers

Mazur, J.E., 1998: *Learning and Behavior*. (4th ed.) Upper Saddle River, NJ. Prentice-Hall.

Meyers, C., & Jones, T.B., 1993: *Promoting Active Learning*. San Francisco, CA. Jossey-Bass.

Rothwell, W.J., & Kazanas, H.F., 1992: *Mastering the Instructional Design Process: A Systematic Approach*. San Francisco, CA. Jossey-Bass.

Sarasin, L.C., 1998: *Learning Style Perspectives: Impact in the Classroom*. Madison, WI. Atwood.

Taylor, R.L., 1991: *Human Factors, Volume 6*. Greenwich, CT. Belvoir Publications.

Telfer, R.A. (Ed.), 1993: *Aviation Instruction and Training*. Brookfield, VT. Ashgate.

Telfer, R.A. & Biggs, J.,1988: *The Psychology of Flight Training*. Ames, IA. Iowa State University Press

Telfer, R.A., & Moore, P.J. (Eds.), 1997: *Aviation Training; Learners, Instruction and Organization*. Brookfield, VT. Ashgate.

Thorndike, R.L., (Ed.), 1971: *Educational Measurement, 2d Edition*. Washington, DC. American Council on Education.

Trollip, S.R., & Jensen, R.S., 1991: *Human Factors for General Aviation*. Englewood, CO. Jeppesen Sanderson.

USAF, 1994: *Guidebook for Air Force Instructors, AF Manual 36-2236*. Department of Defense, United States Air Force, Washington, DC.

Wickens, C.D., 1992: *Engineering Psychology and Human Performance*. New York, NY. Harper Collins.

Wiener, E.L. & Nagel, D.C., 1988: *Human Factors in Aviation*. San Diego, CA. Academic Press.

GLOSSARY

ABSTRACTIONS—Words that are general rather than specific. *Aircraft* is an abstraction; *airplane* is less abstract; *jet* is more specific; and *jet airliner* is still more specific.

AERONAUTICAL DECISION MAKING (ADM)—A systematic approach to the mental process used by aircraft pilots to consistently determine the best course of action in response to a given set of circumstances.

AFFECTIVE DOMAIN—A grouping of levels of learning associated with a person's attitudes, personal beliefs, and values which range from receiving through responding, valuing, and organization to characterization.

AIR TRAFFIC CONTROL (ATC)—A service provided by the FAA to promote the safe, orderly, and expeditious flow of air traffic.

AIRCRAFT CHECKOUTS—An instructional program designed to familiarize and qualify a pilot to act as pilot in command of a particular aircraft type.

ANXIETY—Mental discomfort that arises from the fear of anything, real or imagined. May have a potent effect on actions and the ability to learn from perceptions.

APPLICATION—A basic level of learning where the student puts something to use that has been learned and understood.

APPLICATION STEP—The third step of the teaching process, where the student performs the procedure or demonstrates the knowledge required in the lesson. In the telling-and-doing technique of flight instruction, this step consists of the student doing the procedure while explaining it.

AREAS OF OPERATION—Phases of the practical test arranged in a logical sequence within the PTS.

ATTITUDE—A personal motivational predisposition to respond to persons, situations, or events in a given manner that can, nevertheless, be changed or modified through training as a sort of mental shortcut to decision making.

ATTITUDE MANAGEMENT—The ability to recognize ones own hazardous attitudes in oneself and the willingness to modify them as necessary through the application of an appropriate antidote thought.

AVIATION SAFETY COUNSELORS—Volunteers within the aviation community who share their technical expertise and professional knowledge as a part of the FAA Aviation Safety Program.

BASIC NEED—A perception factor that describes a person's ability to maintain and enhance the organized self.

BEHAVIORISM—Theory of learning that stresses the importance of having a particular form of behavior reinforced by someone, other than the student, to shape or control what is learned.

BOOKMARK—A means of saving addresses on the World Wide Web (WWW) for easy future access. Usually done by selecting a button on the web browser screen, it saves the current web address so it does not have to be input again in a lengthy series of characters.

BRANCHING—A programming technique which allows users of interactive video, multimedia courseware, or online training to choose from several courses of action in moving from one sequence to another.

BRIEFING—An oral presentation where the speaker presents a concise array of facts without inclusion of extensive supporting material.

BUILDING BLOCK CONCEPT—Concept of learning that new knowledge and skills are best based on a solid foundation of previous experience and/or old learning. As knowledge and skills increase, the base expands supporting further learning.

COGNITIVE DOMAIN—A grouping of levels of learning associated with mental activity which range from knowledge through comprehension, application, analysis, and synthesis to evaluation.

COMPACT DISK (CD)—A small plastic optical disk which contains recorded music or computer data. Also, a popular foremat for storing information digitally. The major advantage of a CD is its capability to store enormous amounts of information.

COMPREHENSIVENESS—Is the degree to which a test measures the overall objective.

COMPUTER-ASSISTED INSTRUCTION—Synonymous with computer-based training or instruction emphasizing the point that the instructor is responsible for the class and uses the computer to assist in the instruction.

COMPUTER-BASED TRAINING (CBT)—The use of the computer as a training device. CBT is sometimes called computer-based instruction (CBI); the terms and acronyms are synonymous and may be used interchangeably.

CONDITIONS—The second part of a performance-based objective which describes the framework under which the skill or behavior will be demonstrated.

CONFUSION BETWEEN THE SYMBOL AND THE SYMBOLIZED OBJECT—Results when a word is confused with what it is meant to represent. Words and symbols create confusion when they mean different things to different people.

COOPERATIVE OR GROUP LEARNING—An instructional strategy which organizes students into small groups so that they can work together to maximize their own and each other's learning.

CORRELATION—A basic level of learning where the student can associate what has been learned, understood, and applied with previous or subsequent learning.

COURSE OF TRAINING—A complete series of studies leading to attainment of a specific goal, such as a certificate of completion, graduation, or an academic degree.

CREW RESOURCE MANAGEMENT (CRM)—The application of team management concepts in the flight deck environment. It was initially known as cockpit resource management, but as CRM programs evolved to include cabin crews, maintenance personnel and others, the phrase crew resource management has been adopted. This includes single pilots, as in most general aviation aircaft. Pilots of small aircraft, as well as crews of larger aircraft, must make effective use of all available resources; human resources, hardware, and information. A current definition includes all groups routinely working with the cockpit crew who are involved in decisions required to operate a flight safely. These groups include, but are not limited to: pilots, dispatchers, cabin crewmembers, maintenance personnel, and air traffic controllers. CRM is one way of addressing the challenge of optimizing the human/machine interface and accompanying interpersonal activities.

CRITERIA—The third part of a performance-based objective which describes the standards which will be used to measure the accomplishment of the objective.

CRITERION-REFERENCED TESTING—System of testing where students are graded against a carefully written, measurable standard or criterion rather than against each other.

CURRICULUM—May be defined as a set of courses in an area of specialization offered by an educational institution. A curriculum for a pilot school usually includes courses for the various pilot certificates and ratings.

CUT-AWAY—Model of an object that is built in sections so it can be taken apart to reveal the inner structure.

DEFENSE MECHANISMS—Subconscious ego-protecting reactions to unpleasant situations.

DEMONSTRATION-PERFORMANCE METHOD—An educational presentation where an instructor first shows the student the correct way to perform an activity and then has the student attempt the same activity.

DESCRIPTION OF THE SKILL OR BEHAVIOR—The first part of a performance-based objective which explains the desired outcome of instruction in concrete terms that can be measured.

DETERMINERS—In test items, words which give a clue to the answer. Words such as "always" and "never" are determiners in true-false questions. Since absolutes are rare, such words usually make the statement false.

DIRECT QUESTION—A question used for follow-up purposes, but directed at a specific individual.

DISCRIMINATION—Is the degree to which a test distinguishes the differences between students.

DISTRACTORS—Incorrect responses to a multiple-choice test item.

DISUSE—A theory of forgetting that suggests a person forgets those things which are not used.

EFFECT—A principle of learning that learning is strengthened when accompanied by a pleasant or satisfying feeling, and that learning is weakened when associated with an unpleasant feeling.

ELEMENT OF THREAT—A perception factor that describes how a person is unlikely to easily comprehend an event if that person is feeling threatened since most of a person's effort is focused on whatever is threatening them.

EXERCISE—A principle of learning that those things most often repeated are best remembered.

FLIGHT REVIEW—An industry-managed, FAA monitored currency program designed to assess and update a pilot's knowledge and skills.

FLIGHT TRAINING DEVICES (FTD)—A full-size replica of the instruments, equipment, panels, and controls of an aircraft, or set of aircraft, in an open flight deck area or in an enclosed cockpit. A force (motion) cueing system or visual system is not required.

FOLLOW-UP QUESTION—In the guided discussion method, a question used by an instructor to get the discussion back on track or to get the students to explain something more thoroughly.

FORMAL LECTURE—An oral presentation where the purpose is to inform, persuade, or entertain with little or no verbal participation by the listeners.

GOALS AND VALUES—A perception factor that describes how a person's perception of an event depends on beliefs. Motivation toward learning is affected by how much value a person puts on education. Instructors who have some idea of the goals and values of their students will be more successful in teaching them.

GUIDED DISCUSSION METHOD—An educational presentation typically used in the classroom where the topic to be covered by a group is introduced and the instructor participates only as necessary to keep the group focused on the subject.

HEADWORK—Is required to accomplish a conscious, rational thought process when making decisions. Good decision making involves risk identification and assessment, information processing, and problem solving.

HIERARCHY OF HUMAN NEEDS—A listing by Abraham Maslow of needs from the most basic to the most fulfilling. These range from physical through safety, social, and ego to self-fulfillment.

HUMAN FACTORS—A multidisciplinary field devoted to optimizing human performance and reducing human error. It incorporates the methods and principles of the behavioral and social sciences, engineering, and physiology. It may be described as the applied science which studies people working together in concert with machines. Human factors involve variables that influence individual performance, as well as team or crew performance.

ILLUSTRATED TALK—An oral presentation where the speaker relies heavily on visual aids to convey ideas to the listeners.

INSIGHT—The grouping of perceptions into meaningful wholes. Creating insight is one of the instructor's major responsibilities.

INSTRUCTIONAL AIDS—Devices that assist an instructor in the teaching-learning process. They are supplementary training devices and are not self-supporting.

INSTRUMENT PROFICIENCY CHECK—An evaluation ride based on the instrument rating practical test standard which is required to regain instrument flying privileges when the privileges have expired due to lack of currency.

INTEGRATED FLIGHT INSTRUCTION—A technique of flight instruction where students are taught to perform flight maneuvers by reference to both the flight instruments and to outside visual references from the time the maneuver is first introduced. Handling of the controls is the same regardless of whether flight instruments or outside references are being used.

INTENSITY—A principle of learning where a dramatic or exciting learning experience is likely to be remembered longer than a boring experience. Students experiencing the real thing will learn more than when they are merely told about the real thing.

INTERACTIVE VIDEO—Software that responds quickly to certain choices and commands by the user. A typical system consists of a compact disk, computer, and video technology.

INTERFERENCE—(1) A theory of forgetting where a person forgets something because a certain experience overshadows it, or the learning of similar things has intervened. (2) Barriers to effective communication that are caused by physiological, environmental, and psychological factors outside the direct control of the instructor. The instructor must take these factors into account in order to communicate effectively.

INTERNET—An electronic network which connects computers around the world.

JUDGMENT—The mental process of recognizing and analyzing all pertinent information in a particular situation, a rational evaluation of alternative actions in response to it, and a timely decision on which action to take.

LACK OF COMMON EXPERIENCE—In communication, a difficulty which arises because words have different meanings for the source and the receiver of information due to their differing backgrounds.

LEAD-OFF QUESTION—In the guided discussion method, a question used by an instructor to open up an area for discussion and get the discussion started.

LEARNING—A change in behavior as a result of experience.

LEARNING PLATEAU—A learning phenomenon where progress appears to cease or slow down for a significant period of time before once again increasing.

LEARNING STYLE—The concept that how a person learns is dependent on that person's background and personality, as well as the instructional methods used.

LECTURE METHOD—An educational presentation usually delivered by an instructor to a group of students with the use of instructional aids and training devices. Lectures are useful for the presentation of new material, summarizing ideas, and showing relationships between theory and practice.

LESSON PLAN—An organized outline for a single instructional period. It is a necessary guide for the instructor in that it tells what to do, in what order to do it, and what procedure to use in teaching the material of a lesson.

LINK—On the Internet, a particular site may have additional locations which can be accessed by merely clicking on words identifying the new site. They are usually identified by a different color type, underlining, or a button (picture or icon) indicating access to a new site.

LONG-TERM MEMORY—The portion of the brain that stores information which has been determined to be of sufficient value to be retained. In order for it to be retained in long-term memory, it must have been processed or coded in the working memory.

MATCHING—A test item consisting of two lists where the student is asked to match alternatives on one list to related alternatives on the second list. The lists may include a combination of words, terms, illustrations, phrases, or sentences.

MOCK-UP—Three-dimensional working model used where the actual object is either unavailable or too expensive to use. Mock-ups may emphasize some elements while eliminating nonessential elements.

MODEL—A copy of a real object which can be life-size, smaller, or larger than the original.

MOTIVATION—A need or desire that causes a person to act. Motivation can be positive or negative, tangible or intangible, subtle or obvious.

MULTIMEDIA—A combination of more than one instructional medium. This format can include audio, text, graphics, animations, and video. Recently, multimedia implies a computer-based presentation.

MULTIPLE-CHOICE—A test item consisting of a question or statement followed by a list of alternative answers or responses.

NAVIGATE—With respect to the Internet, to move between sites on the Internet. Navigation is often accomplished by means of links or connections between sites.

NORM-REFERENCED TESTING —System of testing where students are ranked against the performance of other students.

OBJECTIVITY—Describes singleness of scoring of a test; it does not reflect the biases of the person grading the test.

OVERHEAD QUESTION—In the guided discussion method, a question directed to the entire group in order to stimulate thought and discussion from the entire group. An overhead question may be used by an instructor as the lead-off question.

PERCEPTIONS—The basis of all learning. Perceptions result when a person gives meaning to external stimuli or sensations. Meanings which are derived from perceptions are influenced by an individual's

experience and many other factors.

PERFORMANCE-BASED OBJECTIVES—A statement of purpose for a lesson or instructional period that includes three elements: a description of the skill or behavior desired of the student, a set of conditions under which the measurement will be taken, and a set of criteria describing the standard used to measure accomplishment of the objective.

PERSONAL COMPUTER-BASED AVIATION TRAINING DEVICES (PCATD)—A device which uses software which can be displayed on a personal computer to replicate the instrument panel of an airplane. A PCATD must replicate a type of airplane or family of airplanes and meet the virtual control requirements specified in AC 61-126.

PERSONALITY—The embodiment of personal traits and characteristics of an individual that are set at a very early age and are extremely resistant to change.

PHYSICAL ORGANISM—A perception factor that describes a person's ability to sense the world around them.

PILOT ERROR—Means that an action or decision made by the pilot was the cause of, or contributing factor which led to an accident or incident. This definition also includes failure of the pilot to make a decision or take action.

POOR JUDGMENT CHAIN—A series of mistakes that may lead to an accident or incident. Two basic principles generally associated with the creation of a poor judgement chain are: (1) one bad decision often leads to another; and (2) as a string of bad decisions grows, it reduces the number of subsequent alternatives for continued safe flight. Aeronautical decision making is intended to break the poor judgement chain before it can cause an accident or incident.

PRACTICAL TEST STANDARDS (PTS)—An FAA published list of standards which must be met for the issuance of a particular pilot certificate or rating. FAA inspectors and designated pilot examiners use these standards when conducting pilot practical tests and flight instructors should use the PTS while preparing applicants for practical tests.

PREPARATION—The first step of the teaching process, which consists of determining the scope of the lesson, the objectives, and the goals to be attained. This portion also includes making certain all necessary supplies are on hand. When using the telling-and-doing technique of flight instruction, this step is accomplished prior to the flight lesson.

PRESENTATION—The second step of the teaching process, which consists of delivering information or demonstrating the skills which make up the lesson. The delivery could be by either the lecture method or demonstration-performance method. In the telling-and-doing technique of flight instruction, this is where the instructor both talks about and performs the procedure.

PRETEST—A test used to determine whether a student has the necessary qualifications to begin a course of study. Also used to determine the level of knowledge a student has in relation to the material that will be presented in the course.

PRIMACY—A principle of learning where the first experience of something often creates a strong, almost unshakable impression. The importance to an instructor is that the first time something is demonstrated, it must be shown correctly since that experience is the one most likely to be remembered by the student.

PSYCHOMOTOR DOMAIN—A grouping of levels of learning associated with physical skill levels which range from perception through set, guided response, mechanism, complex overt response, and adaptation to origination.

READINESS—A principle of learning where the eagerness and single-mindedness of a person toward learning affect the outcome of the learning experience.

RECEIVER—In communication, the listener, reader, or student who takes in a message containing information from a source, processes it, reacts with understanding, and changes behavior in accordance with the message.

RECENCY—A principle of learning that things learned today are remembered better than things that were learned some time ago. The longer time passes, the less will be remembered. Instructors use this principle when summarizing the important points at the end of a lecture in order for students to better remember them.

RELAY QUESTION—Used in response to a student's question, the question is redirected to the group in order to stimulate discussion.

RELIABILITY—Is the degree to which test results are consistent with repeated measurements.

REPRESSION—Theory of forgetting where a person is more likely to forget information which is unpleasant or produces anxiety.

RESPONSES—Possible answers to a multiple-choice test item. The correct response is often called the keyed response, and incorrect responses are called distractors.

REVERSE QUESTION—Used in response to a student's question. Rather than give a direct answer to the student's query, the instructor can redirect the question to another student to provide the answer.

REVIEW AND EVALUATION—The fourth and last step in the teaching process, which consists of a review of all material and an evaluation of the students. In the telling-and-doing technique of flight instruction, this step consists of the instruc-

tor evaluating the student's performance while the student performs the required procedure.

RHETORICAL QUESTION—A question asked to stimulate group thought. Normally answered by the instructor, it is more commonly used in lecturing rather than in guided discussions.

RISK ELEMENTS IN ADM—Take into consideration the four fundamental risk elements: the pilot, the aircraft, the environment, and the type of operation that comprise any given aviation situation.

RISK MANAGEMENT—The part of the decision making process which relies on situational awareness, problem recognition, and good judgment to reduce risks associated with each flight.

ROTE LEARNING—A basic level of learning where the student has the ability to repeat back something learned, with no understanding or ability to apply what was learned.

SAFETY PROGRAM MANAGER—Designs, implements, and evaluates the Aviation Safety Program within the FAA Flight Standards District Office (FSDO) area of responsibility.

SELECTION-TYPE TEST ITEMS—Questions where the student chooses from two or more alternatives provided. True-false, matching, and multiple-choice type questions are examples of selection-type test items.

SELF-CONCEPT—A perception factor that ties together how people feel about themselves with how well they will receive further experiences.

SENSORY REGISTER—That portion of the brain which receives input from the five senses. The individual's preconceived concept of what is important will determine how much priority the register will give in passing the information on to the rest of the brain for action.

SITES—Internet addresses which provide information and often are linked to other similar sites.

SITUATIONAL AWARENESS—The accurate perception and understanding of all the factors and conditions within the four fundamental risk elements that affect safety before, during, and after the flight.

SKILLS AND PROCEDURES—The procedural, psychomotor, and perceptual skills used to control a specific aircraft or its systems. They are the stick and rudder or airmanship abilities that are gained through conventional training, are perfected, and become almost automatic through experience.

SOURCE—In communication, the sender, speaker, transmitter, or instructor who composes and transmits a message made up of symbols which are meaningful to listeners and readers.

STEM—The part of a multiple-choice test item consisting of the question, statement, or problem.

STRESS MANAGEMENT—The personal analysis of the kinds of stress experienced while flying, the application of appropriate stress assessment tools, and other coping mechanisms.

SUPPLY-TYPE TEST ITEMS—Questions where the student supplies answers as opposed to selecting from choices provided. Essay or fill-in-the-blank type questions are examples of supply-type test items.

SYMBOLS—In communication, simple oral and visual codes such as words, gestures, and facial expressions which are formed into sentences, paragraphs, lectures, or chapters to compose and transmit a message that means something to the receiver of the information.

TASKS—Knowledge areas, flight procedures, or maneuvers within an area of operation in a practical test standard.

TAXONOMY OF EDUCATIONAL OBJECTIVES—A systematic classification scheme for sorting learning outcomes into three broad categories (cognitive, affective, and psychomotor) and ranking the desired outcomes in a developmental hierarchy from least complex to most complex.

TEACHING LECTURE—An oral presentation that is directed toward desired learning outcomes. Some student participation is allowed.

TELLING-AND-DOING TECHNIQUE—A technique of flight instruction that consists of the instructor first telling the student about a new procedure and then demonstrating it. This is followed by the student telling and the instructor doing. Third, the student explains the new procedure while doing it. Last, the instructor evaluates while the student performs the procedure.

TEST—A set of questions, problems, or exercises for determining whether a person has a particular knowledge or skill.

TEST ITEM—A question, problem, or exercise that measures a single objective and calls for a single response.

TIME AND OPPORTUNITY—A perception factor where learning something is dependent on the student having the time to sense and relate current experiences in context with previous events.

TRAINING COURSE OUTLINE—Within a curriculum, describes the content of a particular course by statement of objectives, descriptions of teaching aids, definition of evaluation criteria, and indication of desired outcome.

TRAINING MEDIA—Any physical means that communicates an instructional message to students.

TRAINING SYLLABUS—A step-by-step, building block progression of learning with provisions for regular review and evaluations at prescribed stages of learning. The syllabus defines the unit of training, states by objective what the student is expected to accomplish during the unit of training, shows an organized plan for instruction, and dictates the evaluation process for either the unit or stages of learning.

TRANSITION TRAINING—An instructional program designed to familiarize and qualify a pilot to fly types of aircraft not previously flown such as tailwheel aircraft, high performance aircraft, and aircraft capable of flying at high altitudes.

TRUE-FALSE TEST ITEMS—Consist of a statement followed by an opportunity for the student to determine whether the statement is true or false.

UNDERSTANDING—A basic level of learning where a student comprehends or grasps the nature or meaning of something.

USABILITY—Refers to the functionality of tests.

VALIDITY—Is the extent to which a test measures what it is supposed to measure.

VIRTUAL REALITY (VR)—A form of computer-based technology that creates a sensory experience that allows a participant to believe and barely distinguish a virtual experience from a real one. VR uses graphics with animation systems, sounds, and images to reproduce electronic versions of real life experience.

WEB BROWSER—Any software program that provides access to sites on the World Wide Web (WWW).

WORKING OR SHORT-TERM MEMORY—The portion of the brain that receives information from the sensory register. This portion of the brain can store information in memory for only a short period of time. If the information is determined by an individual to be important enough to remember, it must be coded in some way for transmittal to long-term memory.

INDEX